FEMALE PSYCHOLOGY:

A PARTIALLY ANNOTATED BIBLIOGRAPHY

Edited by

Carole Dilling, Ph.D.
Barbara L. Claster, Ph.D.

Project sponsored by the
New York City Coalition for Women's Mental Health

1985

Printed in the United States of America

COPIES MAY BE ORDERED FROM:
New York City Coalition for Women's Mental Health
c/o Dr. Joan Einwohner
320 West 86 Street
New York, NY 10024

Library of Congress Cataloging in Publication Data
Main entry under title:

Female Psychology: A Partially Annotated Bibliography.

Includes bibliography and index.

    1. Women--Mental Health

I. Dilling, Carole, 1940-1984 II. Claster, Barbara L.,
1931-
ISBN 0-9616028-0-5

TABLE OF CONTENTS

Foreword   7

The Bibliography Committee   11

Preface   12

Acknowledgments   15

   I.   THE HISTORICAL PERSPECTIVE

        A.   Freud's Original Thesis   17

        B.   Elaboration of Freud's Concepts   20

        C.   Biographical Look at Freud's
            Relationships with Women   22

        D.   Early Critiques and Additions to
            Freud's Theory   23

        E.   Current Reexamination of Freudian Theory .   27

        F.   Other Theoretical Perspectives   34

            1.   French Influences - Lacan
               Levi-Strauss and French Feminists . .   34

            2.   Behavior Modification Therapy and
               Assertiveness Training with Women . .   37

            3.   Jung   38

            4.   Existential Analysis   40

continued

II. GENDER DIFFERENCES IN THE LIFE CYCLE AND
     CURRENT RESEARCH ON FEMALE DEVELOPMENT

        A. Infancy (0 to 1 year) 41

        B. Toddler Phase (1-3 years) 50

        C. Early Childhood (3-6 years) 55

            1. Precursors of Oedipal Situation . . . 55

            2. Penis Envy and Castration Anxiety . . 59

            3. Oedipal Situation 62

            4. Superego Development 64

            5. The Role of the Father 66

        D. Latency (7-12 years) 71

            1. Psychosexual Development 71

            2. Intellectual Functioning 73

        E. Adolescence 75

        F. Adulthood 80

III. SPECIAL ISSUES

        A. Abortion 90

        B. Achievement 92

        C. Adoption 99

        D. Aggression 100

        E. Day Care and Maternal Employment 102

continued

F. Dependency-autonomy . . . . `104

G. Depression 106

H. Drugs and Alcohol 112

I. Dual Careers 117

J. Eating Disorders 119

K. Family Violence 138

L. Health 145

M. Hysteria 149

N. Lesbianism 154

O. Marriage and Divorce 161

P. Masculinity-Femininity, Sex-roles, and
    Androgyny 164

Q. Masochism and Passivity 172

R. Mothering 179

S. Narcissism 189

T. The Older Woman 190

U. Phobias 193

V. Rape and Incest 194

W. Reproductive Issues 203

X. Sexuality 210

Y. Women Alone 218

Z. Women and Work 219

continued

IV. MENTAL HEALTH ISSUES 227

V. SEX ROLE ISSUES IN PSYCHOTHERAPY AND SUPERVISION

    A. Psychotherapeutic Issues 240

    B. Sex Role Issues in Supervision 274

    C. Psychotherapy Research 278

VI. FEMALE PSYCHOLOGY IN A BIOLOGICAL, POLITICAL AND
SOCIOLOGICAL CONTEXT

    A. Anthropology and Sociobiology. 282

    B. Ethnicity and Women 291

    C. Feminist Theory 295

APPENDIX: Sources and Other Bibliographies 301

INDEX 304

Foreword

The New York City Psychotherapy Training Institute's
Task Force on Gender Issues was convened in October 1982 by
Dr. Barbara L. Claster. In addition to our monthly
meetings, we divided into three working sub-committees that
focused us on specific goals. The Administrative Sub-
committee, under the leadership of Dr. Carolida Steiner of
The Gordon F. Derner Institute of Advanced Psychological
Studies of Adelphi University, conducted a survey of the
forty-one New York City training institutes by reviewing
current bulletins and catalogues. Their findings indicated
a lack of systematic programming of women's issues in the
curricula and, further, regardless of theoretical
orientation, a lack of representation by women in the
institutes' leadership even though the majority of the
institutes' candidates and graduates were women.

The Clinical Sub-committee, under the leadership of
Dr. Ann Schwanke of the School of Medicine, State University
of Milan, Italy and Ms. Lee Zevy C.S.W. of the New York
Institute for Gestalt Therapy began to explore psychotherapeutic issues relevant to the woman's experience, to
identify psychotherapeutic techniques and issues relevant to
women as patients/clients, and to explore differences in
theoretical orientations that enhance and/or misdirect the
therapeutic process (i.e., transference; gender of patient/
client, therapist, supervisor; socio-cultural influences;
developmental lifespan theory).

The Curriculum and Training Sub-committee, under the
leadership of Dr. Carole Dilling of the Training Institute
for Mental Health Practitioners, decided that if women's
issues were to be integrated into curricula and training
programs that their first goal would be the compilation of a
bibliography which could be utilized for curriculum
development, clinical training, and research as well as for
individual exploration leading to personal and professional
development.

By the spring of 1984 we recognized that our
experiences were similar to those reported by other mental
health professionals: the delivery of human services for
women was failing to recognize and therefore failing to
incorporate women's personal and socio-cultural experiences.

As a Task Force we endorsed the Curriculum Sub-committee's goal and undertook a unified effort under Dr. Dilling's leadership to compile a bibliography.

It was Dr. Carole Dilling's devotion to this project which kept her hard at work on it in spite of her illness. Only after she had edited the first phase, eighty-eight pages of theoretical annotations, that she turned the project over to us. Carole died on November 6, 1984, leaving us a sensitive, scholarly beginning. Upon undertaking the continuation of the project, we asked six recognized interdisciplinary leaders for their opinion as to what we needed to do to complete it. Unanimously they suggested we expand it, keeping with our original goal.

Thus, we have left the bibliography conceptually the same, adding only additional citations. Dr. Dilling's Preface, Acknowledgments and annotations have been left clearly recognizable. The only revision was organizational --combining all Special Issues into Section III. The only additional substantive comments have been the introductory remarks to several sections by Nancy Auster, C.S.W., of the Training Institute for Mental Health Practitioners and by Dr. Laura S. Brown, the author of the Committee for Women in Psychology of the American Psychological Association's position paper on the proposed revision to DSM-III. Their initials appear after their respective entries in order to distinguish their work from Dr. Dilling's. The selection of citations beyond Dr. Dilling's eighty-eight pages has been based on frequency of use as a reference and for topical relevance. The last entries were made in March 1985.

In the appendix we have listed other bibliographies. We know that Dr. Dilling utilized some of these; when possible we have identified the source of her annotations. It is very likely that we have not identified all the quoatations; these oversights were not intentional.

We were unsuccessful in obtaining extra-mural funding. This project is supported by individual and institute donations, advance sales, and a private loan. In our financial search, we discovered that women's mental health per se is also a neglected topic among many feminists who have concentrated their efforts in challenging social, cultural and economic situations. We felt the need for increasing consumer awareness of mental health issues and turned for support to another task force, also initiated by Dr. Claster. The New York City Interdisciplinary Task Force on Women's Issues was a network and caucus of psychiatrists, psychiatric nurses, psychoanalysts, psychologists, and social workers, including clinical social workers. Through informal dialogues they were undertaking to localize the national agenda for women's mental health proposed by the National Coalition for Women's Mental Health. As we, the Task Force on Gender Issues, proceeded to incorporate as a Not-For-Profit corporation we sought a more permanent organization and approached the other task force to join us in forming the New York City Coalition for Women's Mental Health. Thus, our overlapping efforts would be eliminated and we could focus more directly on professional issues in the public and private sector and extend our membership to consumers. The bibliography would provide us with "seed money" after we have fulfilled our financial obligations.

All work on this project has been volunteer with the exception of two people. Dr. Gita Voivodas undertook the job of preparing the manuscript for publication with Dr. Dilling. She has been tireless and caring in her word processing, formatting and stylistic editing responsibilities and of steady support to us as we carried forth the project. In the last few months, Ms. Robyn Cirillo has masterfully handled administrative details allowing us to concentrate more fully on the last details of our work. Their steady, guiding efforts are greatly appreciated.

The bibliography is our way of substantiating the women's experience and helping to effect a change in the delivery of mental health services for women and indirectly, for all people. It asks that consideration be given to women's needs. It challenges the traditional intrapsychic and biomedical approaches to mental disorder and asks that we recognize the impact of the social-cultural context on women and on mental health. Further, it raises consciousness about issues of access and appropriateness of service. We accept and incorporate the recommendations of the four national documents that will guide women's mental health into the 21st. century.[1] We hope these bibliographic references will facilitate the development of mental health policy that is responsible to women's needs in training, service, research, and prevention.

Barbara L. Claster
Chair, Task Force on Gender Issues of the
New York City Psychotherapy Training Institutes
November 1985

[1]Subpanel on the Mental Health of Women. (1978). _Report to the President_ (Vol. III) (pp. 1022-1116). Washington, DC: U.S. Government Printing Office.

Report to the Public Health Service Task Force on Women's Health Issues. (1985). _Public Health Reports_, _100_(1), 73-106.

Russo, N. F. (Ed.). (1985). _Developing a national agenda to address women's mental health needs_. Washington, DC: American Psychological Association.

The Association for Women in Psychology. (1985). _An international feminist mental health agenda_. Washington, DC: Author.

The Bibliography Committee

Nancy Auster, C.S.W., Training Institute for Mental Health Practitioners

Carol Butler, Ph.D., Washington Square Institute for Psychotherapy and Mental Health

Barbara L. Claster, Ph.D., (Chair), Postgraduate Center for Mental Health

Mimi Crowell, M.S.W., Center for Modern Psychoanalytic Studies

Joan Einwohner, Ph.D., Postgraduate Center for Mental Health

Judy Ann Kaplan, C.S.W., National Psychological Association of Psychoanalysis

Anne Schwanke, Ph.D., School of Medicine, State University of Milan, Italy

Florence Williams, R.N., M.A., Institute for Psychoanalytic Training and Research

Mary Morris Williams, M.S.W., Training Institute for Mental Health Practitioners

Lee Zevy, C.S.W., New York Institute for Gestalt Therapy

<u>Preface</u>

Up until a decade ago developmental theory, psychoanalytic theory, and psychopathology had been presented from
a general, universalistic and largely masculine perspective.
This picture has dramatically changed in the last few years
as researchers, clinicians and theorists began to explore
female development and gender differences in an energetic
and fruitful manner. However, we believe there is still a
tremendous gap between this emerging research and its
integration into the curriculum of psychotherapy/psycho-
analytic institutes where it would enhance practitioners'
understanding of their male and female patients.

To address this gap the Curriculum Subcommittee of the
New York City Psychotherapy Training Institutes' Task Force
on Gender Issues has compiled this selectively annotated
bibliography. We feel that this compilation of the recent
research can be helpful to faculty in integrating this
evolving new perspective of female development into their
courses on personality development, psychopathology, psychotherapeutic techniques and process. This is an initial
report which, in spite of its broad perspective and numerous
notations, offers only a beginning summary of the vast
amount of work that has been done in this area.

Section I of the bibliography begins by examining
concepts of female development from a historical perspective
with Freud's seminal theses. Early critiques and additions
to Freud's theory from writers such as Jones, Horney and
Thompson then follow. The current reexamination of female
development within psychoanalytic theory , including Lacan's
works, is then given with new theoretical formulations
emerging. Finally, work from theoretical orientations other
than psychoanalytic--Behavior Modification and Jungian
thinking--add other dimensions.

Section II of the bibliography documents writings on
current research in female development and gender differences in the life cycle. Gender differences noted by
researchers from birth through early developmental phases
are noted in various papers although questions such as what
gender specific developmental theories can be postulated
from this research have yet to be answered. A range of

13

writings on the adult woman has been assembled. It provides
a look at female seriality, marriage, parenting and reproductive issues as well as conflicts for the older woman.
Thus in this section studies of psychodynamic development
and changes in the female from birth to death are examined.

In Section III work is compiled that has focused on
the personality correlates that have evolved in women as
they have confronted their fast changing role in society.
These include conflicts in areas of achievement, work life,
dependency-autonomy, masochism, aggression and sex role
definition. Several papers dealing with issues of
lesbianism are references in this section.

Current work on the reevaluation of the diagnostic
categories that most involve women, namely hysteria,
phobias, depression, eating disorders and narcissism is the
focus of Section IV. These disorders are traced from their
historical definitions to more current understandings of the
psychopathology and social issues involved. In addition, a
range of references is provided on issues that mental health
practitioners often confront with women patients today: the
psychodynamic interplay in family violence; the inter- and
intra-psychic effects of rape and specific genetic issues
leading to drug and alcohol abuse in women.

In Section V, a number of papers looking at sex-role
issues in the psychotherapeutic process has been complied.
Of note are some seminal papers on the interacting effect of
sex of therapist and sex of patient on cross-sex treatment
dyads. Other papers focusing on these same sex role issues
in the supervisory process are also included. Of special
import are a group of papers looking at sexual contact
between patient and therapist particularly in terms of its
effect on the patient and the countertransference problem of
the therapist.

Section VI puts female psychology in a sociological-
political context and brings together a few papers
discussing issues of maternal employment, day care, and dual
careers.

The bibliography does not exhaust all the work being
done, but we hope it raises the consciousness of the mental
health practitioner to the issues emerging in the area of
the comparative perspective on the psychological development
of men and women. Our focus has been on women but that work
can only lead to a new understanding of male development.

If this bibliography leads to further professional exploration and opens up new areas of thinking that emerge in the
teaching, supervision, and clinical practice of mental
health practitioners, we will feel we have accomplished our
purpose.

Carole Dilling
The Training Institute for Mental Health Practitioners
September 1984

Acknowledgments

   This work was accomplished by many people who gave generously of their time in a variety of ways; reviewing the literature, annotating and editing were only a few of many tasks.

   Here is a listing of the main contributors:

Judith Alpert, Ph.D., New York University, Postdoctoral Program in Psychoanalysis & Psychotherapy

Nancy Auster, C.S.W., Training Institute for Mental Health Practitioners

Gerry Barist, Ph.D., National Institute for Psychotherapies

Doris Bernstein, M.A., Institute for Psychoanalytic Training and Research

Judy Butt, Ph.D., Society for Psychoanalytic Study and Research

Barbara L. Claster, Ph.D., Postgraduate Center for Mental Health

Mimi Crowell, M.S.W., Center for Modern Psychoanalytic Studies

Betsy Distler, M.P.S., Institute for Psychoanalytic Training and Research

Judy Ann Kaplan, C.S.W., National Psychological Association of Psychoanalysis

Anne Pretzel

Carol Schultz, M.A., New York Center for Psychoanalytic Training

Ann Schwanke, Ph.D., School of Medicine, State University of Milan, Italy

Susan Spieler, Ph.D., American Institute for Psychotherapy and Psychoanalysis

Carolida Steiner, Ph.D., The Gordon F. Derner Institute of
    Advanced Psychological Studies of Adelphi University

Florence Williams, R.N., M.A., Institute for Psychoanalytic
    Training andResearch

Mary Morris Williams, M.S.W., Training Institute for Mental
    Health Practitioners

Heather Wilson, M.S.W., National Psychological Association
    of Psychoanalysis

A special acknowledgement needs to be given to Barbara
L. Claster, Ph.D., who was the convener of the New York City
Psychotherapy Training Institutes' Task Force on Gender
Issues Her special energy and long-term work in the area of
female psychology provided a crucial impetus for the
project.

Elizabeth Kendall served as an assistant to the project.

We have also cited some annotated references from the
following annotated bibliographies. We thank them for the
contribution their work provided in our endeavors.

Walstedt, J. J. (1972). The psychology of women. Know,
    Inc., P. O. Box 86031, Pittsburgh, Pa. 15221.

Midlarsky, E. (1977). Women, psychopathology and psycho-
    therapy: A partially annotated bibliography. Journal
    Supplement Abstract Service of the American Psychological
    Association (JSAS).

Carole Dilling
The Training Institute for Mental Health Practitioners
September 1984

PART I

THE HISTORICAL PERSPECTIVE

Freud's early statements on female sexuality have stirred much reflection and controversy. As such they have served as a reflection of the times and as a catalyst for reconsideration and change. (N.A.)

A. Freud's Original Thesis

Freud, S. (1933). Femininity. In J. Strachey (Ed. and Trans.), The standard edition of the complete psychological works of Sigmund Freud (Vol. 22, pp. 112-135). London: Hogarth Press.

Freud traces the psychosexual development of the little girl as she learns of her anatomical destiny. "Her self-love is mortified by the comparison with the boy's superior equipment" and she repudiates her mother for causing her "castration." The wish for a penis finds fulfillment later on through having a baby, particularly a boy baby. The masculinity complex and the weaker super-ego are also discussed. If you can read only one essay on women by Freud, this should be the one to read. (Walstedt)

Freud, S. (1924). The dissolution of the oedipus complex. In J. Strachey (Ed. and Trans.), The standard edition of the complete psychological works of Sigmund Freud (Vol. 19, pp. 172-179). London: Hogarth Press.

Here Freud explains why it is more difficult for the little girl to resolve her complex than it is for the boy. Her penis envy and sense of incompleteness are reiterated. (Walstedt)

Other essays of interest:

Freud, S. (1893-1895). Studies in hysteria. In J.
     Strachey (Ed. and Trans.), The standard edition of
     the complete psychological works of Sigmund Freud
     (Vol. 2). London: Hogarth Press.

Freud, S. (1905). Three essays on the theory of sexuality.
     In J. Strachey (Ed. and Trans.), The standard edition
     of the complete psychological works of Sigmund Freud
     (Vol. 7, pp. 125-243). London: Hogarth Press.

Freud, S. (1908). On the sexual theories of children.
     In J. Strachey (Ed. and Trans.), The standard edition
     of the complete psychological works of Sigmund Freud
     (Vol. 9, pp. 209-226). London: Hogarth Press.

Freud, S. (1914). On narcissism: An introduction.
     In J. Strachey (Ed. and Trans.), The standard edition
     of the complete psychological works of Sigmund Freud
     (Vol. 14, pp. 67-102). London: Hogarth Press.

Freud, S. (1919). A child is being beaten: A contribution
     to the study of the origin of sexual perversions. In
     J. Strachey (Ed. and Trans.), The standard edition of
     the complete psychological works of Sigmund Freud
     (Vol. 17, pp. 177-204). London: Hogarth Press.

Freud, S. (1920). The psychogenesis of a case of
     homosexuality in a woman. In J. Strachey (Ed. and
     Trans.), The standard edition of the complete psycho-
     logical works of Sigmund Freud (Vol. 18, pp. 145-174).
     London: Hogarth Press.

Freud, S. (1924). The economic problem of masochism.
     In J. Strachey (Ed. and Trans.), The standard edition
     of the complete psychological works of Sigmund Freud
     (Vol. 19, pp. 157-170). London: Hogarth Press.

Freud, S. (1925). Some psychological consequences of the
     anatomical distinction between sexes. In J. Strachey
     (Ed. and Trans.), The standard edition of the
     complete psychological works of Sigmund Freud
     (Vol. 19, pp. 243-258). London: Hogarth Press.

Freud, S. (1931). Female sexuality. In J. Strachey
     (Ed. and Trans.), <u>The standard edition of the complete</u>
     <u>psychological works of Sigmund Freud</u> (Vol. 21,
     pp. 223-243). London: Hogarth Press.

"Female Sexuality" is a restatement of the findings
first announced by Freud six years earlier in "Some
Psychical Consequences of the Anatomical Distinction
Between the Sexes." Freud discusses his views (1)
that the girl has the task of giving up what was
originally her leading genital zone, the clitoris, in
favor of the new zone, the vagina; (2) that the female
acknowledges the fact of her castration, the superiority of the male, and her own inferiority, but she
rebels against this resulting in three possible out-
comes: (a) a general revulsion from sexuality, (b)
clinging with defiant self-assertion to her threatened
masculinity, or (c) to the final normal female attitude, in which she takes her father as her object and
finds her way to the feminine form of the Oedipal
Complex. Freud lays further emphasis on the intensity
and long duration of the little girl's pre-oedipus
attachment to her mother and discusses the active
element in the little girl's attitude towards her
mother.

Freud, S. (1933). New introductory lectures on
     psycho-analysis. In J. Strachey (Ed. and Trans.),
     <u>The standard edition of the complete psychological</u>
     <u>works of Sigmund Freud</u> (Vol. 22, pp. 3-182). London:
     Hogarth Press.

Freud, S. (1937). Analysis terminable and interminable--
     Sections VI - VIII. In J. Strachey (Ed. and Trans.),
     <u>The standard edition of the complete psychological</u>
     <u>works of Sigmund Freud</u> (Vol. 23, pp. 240-253). London:
     Hogarth Press.

B. Elaboration of Freud's Concepts

Bonaparte, M. (1935). Passivity, masochism, and
    femininity. International Journal of Psycho-Analysis,
    16, 325-333.

Bonaparte, M. (1950). Notes on excision. The
    Psychoanalytic Study of the Child, 2, 67-84.

Bonaparte, M. (1953). Female sexuality. New York:
    International Universities Press.

    A highly Freudian book, along the lines of Deutsch.
    The view that women are essentially masochistic and
    passive is presented.

Brunswick, R. M. (1940). The preoedipal phase of the
    libidinal development. In R. Fliess (Ed.), The
    psychoanalytic reader (pp. 231-254). New York:
    International Universities Press.

    Brunswick, with Freud as collaborator, contends that
    phallic masturbation is repressed because the true
    object of clitoral activity is the mother, who has
    denied the girl a penis and has forbidden masturba-
    tion. She further contends that the wish for a baby
    is based on the primitive identification with the
    active mother as well as the discovery of her lack of
    a penis. While this work acknowledges the girl's pre-
    phallic attachment to the mother, it still neglects
    noting its importance in establishing a developmental
    continuity from which further feminine growth evolves.

Deutsch, H. (1944). The psychology of women: A
    psychoanalytic interpretation (Vols. 1 and 2).
    New York: Grune and Stratton.

    See especially Vol. 1, pages 219-324. The author, a
    student of Freud's, expanded upon his theories of
    women and went beyond him in describing the passive,
    masochistic nature of women. To her the most mature
    women were those who lived through men and did not
    aggressively attempt a separate career or existence.

The second volume is devoted almost entirely to
motherhood. Her books are highly speculative and are
based on very few cases, but she writes in an autho-
ritative manner. These volumes had a tremendous impact on teachers, theorists, and guidance counselors
for about 20 years after they were written. They
constitute, however, a brief for women's biological
inferiority. (Walstedt)

C. Biographical Look at Freud's Relationships with Women

Freeman, L. & Strean, H. S. (1981). Freud and women. New
     York: Frederick Ungar.

     An interesting look at Freud's relationships with
     women--mother, five sisters, nurse, wife, sister-in-
     law, three daughters, friends, women patients, and
     colleagues.   Showing him as a human with his biases
     and ambivalences, the authors look at Freud's atti-
     tudes toward women as they affected his theories about
     the emotional conflicts and psychosexual development
     of the female.   A book for both feminists and psycho-
     analysts.

Spiegel, R. (1977). Freud and the women in his world.
     Journal of American Academy of Psychoanalysis, 5,
     377-402.

     This article examines Freud's dicta about female sex-
     uality in two special aspects: the disparity between
     Freud's actual relationships with the women who became
     prominent in the psychoanalytic movement and his theo-
     ries about women; and the richness of his relation-
     ships with the women in his family with whom he played
     many different roles.

Wickert, G. (1984). Freud's heritage: Fathers and daugh-
     ters in German literature (1750-1850). In M. Lewin
     (Ed.), The shadow of the past: Psychology portrays
     the sexes (pp. 26-38). New York: Columbia University
     Press.

D. Early Critiques and Additions to Freud's Theory

Garrison, D. (1981). Karen Horney and feminism. Signs,
     6(4), 672-691.

Greenacre, P. (1948). Anatomical structure and superego
     development. In Trauma, growth, and personality
     (pp. 149-164). New York: Norton.

Greenacre, P. (1950). Special problems of early female
     sexual development. In Trauma, growth, and
     personality (pp. 237-258). New York: Norton.

     Greenacre points to several aspects of female sexual
     development which deviate from the original Freudian
     thesis. She suggests that there is an early awareness
     of the vagina which is not adequately differentiated
     from the rectum. She feels that both oral and anal
     stimulation influence vaginal awareness. She sees the
     clitoris and vagina as having a relationship to each
     other and patterning sexual response, as well as char-
     acter development.

Horney, K. (1924). On the genesis of the castration com-
     plex in women. International Journal of
     Psycho-analysis, 5, 50-65.

Horney, K. (1932). The dread of women. International
     Journal of Psycho-analysis, 13, 348-360.

Horney, K. (1933). The denial of the vagina.
     International Journal of Psycho-analysis, 14, 55-70.

     In these essays Horney gives anecdotal and observa-
     tional data to support her thesis that the girl is
     female from the start. She contends that the girl is
     interested in her vaginal orifice from an early age
     and that the clitoris is an integral part of the
     female apparatus. The phallic phase for her is a
     secondary neurotic structure which arises out of her
     fear that the father's large penis will destroy her

small genital.   Thus, penis envy for Horney is neurotic and related to hostile fantasies toward the parent
which arose from conflict-laden experiences and inter-
fered with later identification with the parents.

Horney, K. (1973). The flight from womanhood. In
     J. B. Miller (Ed.), Psychoanalysis and women (pp.
     3-16). New York: Brunner/Mazel. (Reprinted from
     International Journal of Psycho-analysis, 1926,
     7, 324-339)

Jones, E. (1933). The phallic phase. International
     Journal of Psycho-analysis, 14, 1-33.

In this historical, theoretical paper, the phallic
phase of development for the male and the female is
discussed from a phallocentric point of view.   At the
beginning of this phase, human beings are divided into
a penis-possessing class and a castrated (mutilated,
second) class. Fears of mutilation, disappointment in
the (masculine) clitoris, penis envy, and dread of the
female genital are discussed.   The author does state
that more knowledge about early sexuality is needed
before some questions, such as the masculine primacy
of the female infant and the feminine primacy of the
male infant are settled.

Jones, E. (1935). Early female sexuality. International
     Journal of Psycho-analysis, 16, 263-273.

In   this   paper Jones arrives at a position   that de-
viated from the original Freudian position.   His view
is in agreement with Karen Horney. Penis envy does
not result from the girl's fear of castration or fear
of something being taken away.   Instead it is related
to hostile fantasies toward the parents which derived
from conflict-laden experiences.   Jones says in conclusion: "In short, I do not see a woman... as 'un
homme manque'...a permanently disappointed creature
struggling to console herself with secondary substi-
tutes alien to her nature."

Miller, J. B. (Ed.). (1973). Psychoanalysis and women.
     New York: Brunner/Mazel.

     An anthology of the early psychoanalytic papers
     written on women.

Moulton, R. (1975). Early papers on women: Horney to
     Thompson. American Journal of Psychoanalysis, 35,
     207-223.

     Moulton discusses Horney's early papers (1922-1932)
     which criticize Freud's phallus-centered point of view
     and his theory of female sexuality. Among other
     points, these papers emphasize the social disadvan-
     tages of women, stress the positive satisfactions of
     motherhood, assert that the vagina plays an important
     role in female sexuality from early childhood, and
     attribute to male narcissism the assumption that penis
     envy occurs in all females. The views of other promi-
     nent psychoanalysts of this period who tended to agree
     with Horney are summarized briefly. The beginnings of
     new studies of women in the 1940's dealing with pre-
     viously neglected cultural factors are also described.

Rubin, J. (1978). Karen Horney, the gentle rebel of
     psychoanalysis. New York: Dial Press.

Strouse, J. (Ed.). (1974). Women and analysis. New York:
     Grossman.

     Key writings by major psychoanalytic figures from
     Freud to Erikson presented in counterpoint with
     specially commissioned responses to the original
     classics.

Thompson, C. (1973). Cultural pressures in the psychology
     of women. In J. B. Miller (Ed.), Psychoanalysis and
     women (pp. 49-64). New York: Brunner/Mazel.
     (Reprinted from Psychiatry, 1942, 5, 331-339)

     Thompson discusses the context within which Freud's
     culturally bound ideas of women took place. She con-
     cludes that what Freud took to be a biologically
     induced feeling of inferiority in women due to the

lack of a penis, might be better explained as due to developments arising in and growing out of Western woman's "historic situation of underprivilege, restriction of development . . . and social and economic dependency. The basic nature of woman is still unknown. (Walstedt)

Thompson, C. (1973). Penis envy in women. In J. B. Miller (Ed.), Psychoanalysis and women (pp. 43-48). New York: Brunner/Mazel. (Reprinted from Psychiatry, 1943, 6, 123-125)

Thompson is one of the first to invoke the black analogy equating white skin and penises as means used by the group in power to put down visibly different others. The author considers penis envy as a picturesque way of referring to a type of warfare which often goes on between men and women, due to their unequal positions. Her comments, though stemming from a psychoanalytic view, sound like political ones at times. It's a pity that this brilliant woman psychoanalyst did not get the exposure in the mass media that her male counterparts did. She was one of the giants of her time. (Walstedt)

Thompson, C. (1973). Some effects of the derogatory attitude towards female seriality. In J. B. Miller (Ed.), Psychoanalysis and women (pp. 65-74). New York: Brunner/Mazel. (Reprinted from Psychiatry, 1950, 13, 349-354)

Thompson, C. (1974). The role of women in this culture. In J. Strouse (Ed.), Women and analysis (pp. 265-277). New York: Grossman. (Reprinted from Psychiatry, 1941, 4, 1-8)

In these two articles the author refers to women's learned denial of their sexuality; that denial has incorrectly been interpreted by others as evidence of women's "natural masochism."

E. Current Reexamination of Freudian Theory

Chasseguet-Smirgel, J. (Ed.). (1970). Female sexuality.
    Ann Arbor, MI: University of Michigan Press.

This volume amplifies theories formulated by Melanie
Klein and stresses the early mother-child relation
during the first year as the determinant of all future
sexual development. Kleinian metapsychology places
much greater emphasis on oral and early phallic
aggression than on the vicissitudes of the oedipus
complex. The contributors to this volume point to the
early life experience of girls as more characterized
by aggression and sadism than that of boys.   For the
girl, the mother is seen as an "inadequate" sexual
object and is thus perceived as more frustrating and
rejecting by her than by the boy.

Chasseguet-Smirgel, J. (1976). Freud and female sexuality:
    The consideration of some blind spots in the
    exploration of the "dark continent." International
    Journal of Psychoanalysis, 57, 275-286.

The author presents a paper given as part of a
dialogue on Freud and female sexuality held during the
29th International Psychoanalytic Congress (London,
July 1975).   In Freudian theory female sexuality is a
series of lacks: of a penis, of the awareness of a
vagina, of specific sexuality, and of an adequate
erotic object. In contrast, the primal maternal imago
is omnipotent.   It is suggested that the theory of
sexual phallic monism eradicates the narcissistic
wound common to all humanity which springs from the
child's helpless and complete dependency on the
mother. The lasting impression of primary helplessness on the psyche is discussed as it bears upon (1)
renunciation of the oedipal object, (2) recognition of
the difference between generations, and (3) homosexuality and other issues.

Cohen, M. B. (1973). Personal identity and sexual
     identity. In J. B. Miller (Ed.), <u>Psychoanalysis and
     women</u> (pp. 131-155). New York: Brunner/Mazel.
     (Reprinted from <u>Psychiatry</u>, 1966, <u>29</u>, 1-14)

de Beauvoir, S. (1952). <u>The second sex</u>. New York: Knopf.

Fast, I. (1984). <u>Gender identity: A differential model</u>.
     Hillsdale, N. J.: Lawrence Erlbaum Associates.

     A reformulation of Freud's theories of gender identity
     and its disturbances. The differentiation model pre-
     sented is congruent with developmental perspectives in
     academic psychology, specifically with the theories of
     Piaget. It suggests that the central importance of
     the mother for both boys and girls in early develop-
     ment, typical in American family organization, can be
     considered a major factor in sex differences in gender
     identity. The book aims throughout to demonstrate
     that this particular model of gender differentiation
     can organize and illuminate Freud's observations more
     fully than the framework he himself utilized.

Fliegel, Z. O. (1973). Feminine psychosexual development
     in Freudian theory. <u>Psychoanalytic Quarterly</u>, <u>42</u>,
     385-409.

     Fliegel contends that a gap exists in the psychoanaly-
     tic literature on the subject of feminine development
     because of the Horney-Jones-Freud debate in the 1920's
     and 1930's. Freud, feeling threatened in the survival
     of his ideas, reacted with the most dogmatic stand of
     his career to the thinking coming from Jones and
     Horney in this area. This paper gives an interesting
     historical perspective.

Fliegel, Z. O. (1982). Half a century later: Current
     status of Freud's controversial views on women.
     <u>Psychoanalytic Review</u>, <u>69</u>, 7-28.

     In this paper, a follow-up on his earlier work,
     Fliegel briefly reviews Freud's views on female devel-
     opment, presents current observational and clinical
     research findings, and critically reviews the wide

range of conjectures and conclusions drawn from these
findings by the voices of "contemporary psychoanalysis." Fliegel points out that many of these views are
quite similar to the views voiced by Horney and Jones,
early dissenters from Freud in the 20's, and notes
that credit is rarely given to them as having originated these ideas. Fliegel critically reviews conclusions drawn by Galenson and Roiphe, Stoller, Kleeman,
Edgcumbe and Burgner, Barglow and Schaefer and Lacan.
She notes that the evidence opposing Freud's theories
leads to two contradictory paths: one directly confronting Freud's views and the other attempting to
salvage his formulations even at the "expense of its
internal logic."

Gillespie, W. H. (1975). Woman and her discontents: A
    reassessment of Freud's views on female sexuality.
    International Review of Psychoanalysis, 75, 1-9.

Gillespie discusses Freud's views on female sexuality
in relation to the work of W. Masters and V. Johnson,
K. Horney and M. Klein. The topics discussed include
the oedipus complex in women, comparisons with animal
sexual development, socially imposed requirements on
females, the importance of the clitoris in childhood
sexuality, and the impact of parental expectations on
a child's behavior. The anatomical differences between the sexes are considered important as an outward
sign of the extensive differences in the reproductive
roles assigned by evolution.

Gilligan, C. (1982). In a different voice: Psychological
    theory and women's development. Cambridge, MA:
    Harvard University Press.

Gilligan speaks in terms of psychology rather than
psychoanalysis and reviews the main theorists who have
proposed criteria for standards of morality. She
finds that each has based his schema on a male model
of development. In the systems of Kohlberg, Piaget,
Freud, Erikson, the female never attains the highest
levels of mature morality. She reexamines some of the
data on which their conclusions are based and demonstrates the misinterpretation of the conclusion of

"deficient" and reinterprets the data as "different." Her basic conclusions suggest that men see danger in intimacy while women see danger in separation. Women are preoccupied with preserving connection while men want to preserve autonomy. Men perceive justice as the preservation of their rights; women, on the other hand, see moral choices as focusing on their responsibility to others. Men are in danger of protected isolation and find their way to connectedness through the need to extend their rights to others. They must bring into focus the rights of others as well as the needs and feelings of others. Women, who are concerned with preserving connection, must learn to take the risk of hurting in the assertion of their own rights. Ideally each arrives at maturity capable of both respect for separation and connectedness--for a morality of justice (male) and context (female).

Gilligan, C. (1984). The conquistador and the dark cont inent: Reflections on the psychology of love. Daedalus, 113(3), 75-95.

Kaplan, A. G., & Yasinki, L. (1980). Psychodynamic perspectives. In A. M. Brodsky & R. T. Hare-Mustin (Eds.), Women and psychotherapy: An assessment of research and practice (pp. 191-215). New York: Guilford Press.

This is a good critique of a number of psychodynamic theorists in addition to Freud.

Kleeman, J. (1976). Freud's views on early female sexuality in the light of direct child observation. Journal of American Psychoanalytic Association, 24(5), 3-27.

Lang, J. A. (1984). Notes toward a psychology of the feminine self. In P. Stepansky & A. Goldberg (Eds.), Kohut's legacy: Contributions to self psychology (pp. 51-69). Hillsdale, NJ: The Analytic Press.

Lerner, L. (Ed.). (1982). Women and individuation: Emerging issues [Special issue]. Psychoanalytic Review, 69.

Lewis, H. B. (1976). Is Freud an enemy of women's
     liberation. In <u>Psychic war in men and women</u>
     (pp. 163-181). New York: New York University Press.

     Lewis contends that psychoanalysis was developed in a
     male dominated, exploitative atmosphere and that some
     of its propositions contribute to women's subjugation
     and to the maintenance of an exploitative status quo.
     However, she also points optimistically to our being
     able to use the conceptual tool developed by Freud to
     analyze the distortions to which our own acculturation
     makes us prey.

Masson, J. M. (1984). <u>The assault on truth: Freud's
     suppression of the seduction theory</u>. New York:
     Farrar, Straus & Giroux.

McDougall, J. (1980). <u>Plea for a measure of abnormality</u>.
     New York: International Universities Press.

Mendell, D. (Ed.). (1982). <u>Early female development:
     Current psychoanalytic views</u>. New York: SP Medical &
     Scientific Books.

Miller, A. (1984). <u>Thou shalt not be aware: Society's
     betrayal of the child</u>. New York: Farrar, Straus &
     Giroux.

Miller, J. B. (Ed.). (1973). <u>Psychoanalysis and women</u>.
     New York: Brunner/Mazel.

     This volume includes a collection of essays by various
     analysts critical of Freud's original theories of
     penis envy, masochism, and innate passivity.

Miller, J. B. (1976). <u>Toward a new psychology of women</u>.
     Boston: Beacon Press.

     Among the first books to lay out a framework for the
     psychology of women, this book is an important part of
     the tranistory process in our understanding of the
     women's experience. The spirit of both sharing with
     one another and a search for truths about all women is

the underlying theme that has subsequently been
expanded into Miller's later work. Women are viewed
in a positive manner and as normal, with special
emphasis on "women in relationships." (B.L.C.)

Millett, K. (1970). Freud and the influence of psycho-
    analytic thought. In Sexual politics (pp. 176-233).
    New York: Doubleday.

A comprehensive discussion of women and psychoanalytic
thought. Freud and his disciples come under enlight-
ened attack. However, as a non-psychologist, Millett
doesn't always know how much weight to give recent
historical trends. She gives an excellent bibliography. The volume is good to read along with Horney,
Thompson, and Klein for the counter arguments to
Freud's feminine psychology. (Walstedt)

Nagera, H. (1975). Female sexuality and the Oedipus
    complex. New York: Jason Aronson.

Person, E. S. (1974). Some new observations on the origins
    of femininity. In J. Strouse (Ed.), Women and
    analysis (pp. 250-261). New York: Grossman.

Person, E. S. (1980). Sexuality as the mainstay of
    identity: Psychoanalytic perspectives. Signs, 5(4),
    605-630.

Person, E. S. (1983). The influence of values in
    psychoanalysis: The case of female psychology.
    Psychiatry Update, 2, 36-50.

Rosenbaum, M., & Muroff, M. (Eds.). (1984). Anna O:
    Fourteen contemporary reinterpretations. New York:
    The Free Press.

Schafer, R. (1974). Problems in Freud's psychology of
    women. Journal of The American Psychoanalytic
    Association, 22, 459-485.

It is proposed that Freud's generalizations concerning
girls and women do injustice to both his psychoanalytic method and his clinical findings. Areas discussed

include: ego and superego development in boys and
girls; penis envy; biologically predestined procreati-
vity; the role of the mother in the neglected prephallic development; the fateful linkages of male with
masculine-active-aggressive-dominant and female with
feminine-passive-masochistic-submissive.

Sherman, J. A. (1975). <u>On the psychology of women</u>.
Springfield, IL: Charles C. Thomas.

Stoller, R. (1973). The bedrock of masculinity and
femininity: Bisexuality. In J. B. Miller (Ed.),
<u>Psychoanalysis and women</u> (pp. 245-258). New York:
Brunner/ Mazel. (Reprinted from <u>Archives of General
Psychiatry</u>, 1972, <u>26</u>, 207-212)

Van Herck, J. (1984). <u>Freud on femininity and faith</u>.
Berkeley, CA: University of California Press.

Wimpfheimer, M., & Schafer, R. (1977). Psychoanalytic
methodology in Helene Deutsch's "The psychology of
women." <u>Psychoanalytic Quarterly</u>, <u>46</u>(2), 287-318.

The authors criticize Deutsch's focus on biology and
her negation of social factors and learning in the
development of the female. Her theories are described
as value-laden, and she is criticized for making no
attempt to submit them to study either by observation
or by experimentation.

F.   Other Theoretical Perspectives

1. French Influences - Lacan, Levi-Strauss and French Feminists.

Burke, C. (1981). Irigaray through the looking glass.
    Feminist Studies, 7, 288-306.

    A discussion of the work of Irigaray, a dissident
    Lacanian psychoanalyst and feminist.

Gallop, J. (1982). The daughter's seduction: Feminism and
    psychoanalysis. Ithaca, N.Y.: Cornell University
    Press.

    Gallop examines the relationship between contemporary
    feminism and the psychoanalytic theories of Jacques
    Lacan. Standing at the intersection of French psycho-
    analysis and feminism, she confronts topics of sexual
    difference, desire, reading, writing, power, family,
    phallocentrism, and language.   Her approach is to
    create hypothetical dialogues between two or more
    authors such as Lacan and Ernest Jones, Irigaray and
    Lacan, Irigaray and Freud and others.   In her final
    chapter, she focuses on Freud's Dora through a reading
    of Cixous and Clement's book, La jeunne nee. She does
    not endorse either psychoanalysis or feminism but
    feels an "encounter of the two can bring both to its
    most radical potential."

Irigaray, L. (1985). Speculum of the other woman. Ithaca:
    Cornell University Press.

Jones, A. R. (1981). Writing the body: Toward an
    understanding of L'ecriture feminine. Feminist
    Studies, 7, 247-263.

    A discussion of the writings of French feminists
    Cixous, Irigaray, Kristeva and Wittig. (Kristeva has
    recently become a psychoanalyst).

Kolbenschlag, M. (1979). <u>Kiss sleeping beauty goodbye</u>.
    New York: Doubleday.

Lacan, J. (1983). <u>Feminine sexuality: Jacque Lacan and
    the ecole Freudienne</u> (J. Mitchell, Ed., and J. Rose,
    Trans.). London and New York: Norton.

    This volume includes translations of eight texts of
    Lacan's (the discussion of Dora in "Intervention on
    Transference" among them) along with two lengthy and
    helpful introductory essays by the translator, Jacque-
    line Rose, and her co-editor, Juliet Mitchell.

Leonard, L. S. (1983). <u>The wounded woman</u>. Berkeley, CA:
    Shambahla Publishers.

Mitchell, J. (1974). <u>Psychoanalysis and feminism</u>. New
    York: Random House.

    Mitchell dismisses Jones and Horney as too biologistic
    and criticizes many current feminist writers as
    "denying the unconscious." She then sets about to
    make Freud more acceptable to the feminist movement by
    reinterpreting his work in terms of Claude Levi-
    Strauss, Jacques Lacan, and Frederick Engels. The
    oedipus complex for her is seen as an inborn memory of
    conflict over the economic barter of women. The
    structure of the unconscious will be modified and
    oppression of women will end when the nuclear family
    (seen as economic system) is destroyed.

Montgrain, N. (1983). On the vicissitudes of female
    sexuality: The difficult path from "anatomical
    destiny" to psychic representation. <u>International
    Journal of Psychoanalysis</u>, <u>64</u>(2), 169-186.

    Drawing particularly from the French psychoanalytic
    frame of Chasseguet-Smirgel, Montgrain points to seve-
    ral important issues on female sexuality: (1) feminine
    orgastic pleasure has a spreading out quality which
    lends to genital psychic representation that lacks
    precise limits; (2) vaginal erotism includes oral and
    anal fantasy elements; (3) lacking a clearly visible
    organ, the girl can experience sexual excitation as

dangerous to the whole body; (4) for the girl, the
sensual attachment to the primitive mother-body is
less readily given up than for the boy. Such attachment can block adult female sexuality; (5) penis envy
is seen as multidimensional and is linked to both
parents.

Ortner, S. B. Oedipal father, mother's brother and the
     penis [Review of Juliet Mitchell's Psychoanalysis
     and feminism]. Feminist Studies, 167-182.

     Mitchell's complex and difficult work is reviewed by a
     feminist anthropologist.

Rubin, G. (1975). The traffic in women: Notes on the
     "political economy" of sex. In R. R. Reiter (Ed.),
     Toward an anthropology of women. New York: Monthly
     Review Press.

     A very original anthropological article defining what
     the author calls the sex/gender system. It also con-
     nects with Levi-Strauss, Lacan and Mitchell.

Wenzel, H. W. (1981). The text as body/politics: An
     appreciation of Monique Wittig's writings in context.
     Feminist Studies, 7, 264-287.

2. Behavior Modification Therapy and Assertiveness Training with Women.

Blechman, E. A. (Ed.). (1984). Behavior modification with women. New York: Guilford Press.

Fodor, I. G. (1980). The treatment of communication problems with assertiveness training. In A. Goldstein & E. Foa (Eds.), Handbook of behavioral interventions: A clinical guide (pp. 501-603). New York: Wiley.

Fodor, I. G., & Epstein, R. (1983). Assertiveness training for women: Where are we failing. In P. Emmelkamp & E. Foa (Eds.), Failures in behavior therapy. New York: Wiley.

Fodor, I. G., & Wolfe, J. (1977). Assertiveness training for mothers and daughters: Learning new ways of communicating and relating. In R. Alberti (Ed.), Assertiveness: Innovations, applications, issues. San Luis Obispo, CA: Impact.

Jakubowski-Spector, P. (1973). Facilitating the growth of women through assertive training. The Counseling Psychologist, 4(1), 75-86.

Phelps, S., & Austin, N. (1975). The assertive woman. San Luis Obispo, CA: Impact.

Wolfe, J., & Fodor, I. (1975). A cognitive behavioral approach to assertiveness training in women. The Counseling Psychologist, 5(4), 45-52.

3. Jung

Bolen, J. S. (1984). <u>Goddesses in everywoman: A new psychology of women</u>. San Francisco: Harper & Row.

De Castillejo, I. C. (1974). <u>Knowing women: A feminine psychology</u>. New York: Harper & Row.

Friedrich, P. (1978). <u>The meaning of Aphrodite</u>. Chicago: University of Chicago Press.

Gelpi, B. C. (1974). The androgyne. In J. Strouse (Ed.), <u>Women and analysis</u> (pp. 227-238). New York: Grossman.

Johnson, R. (1977). <u>She: Understanding feminine psychology</u>. New York: Harper & Row.

Neumann, E. (1973). <u>Amor and Psyche: The psychic development of the feminine</u>. Princeton, NJ: Princeton University Press.

Otto, W. F. (1979). Aphrodite. In <u>The Homeric Gods</u> (M. Hadas, Trans.) (pp. 91-103). New York: Thames & Hudson/Pantheon Books.

Perera, S. B. (1981). <u>Descent to the Goddess: A way of initiation for women</u>. Toronto, Ontario, Canada: Inner City Books.

Shuttle, P., & Redgrove, P. (1980). <u>The wise wound: Menstruation and everywoman</u>. Harmondsworth: Penguin Books.

Singer, J. (1976). <u>Androgyny: Toward a new theory of sexuality</u>. New York: Anchor Press.

Ulanov, A. B. (1981). <u>Receiving women</u>. Philadelphia: Westminster Press.

Von Franz, M. (1972). <u>The feminine in fairy tales</u>. Zurich, Switzerland: Spring Publication.

Woodman, M. (1982). <u>Addiction to perfection: The still unravished bride</u>. Toronto, Ontario, Canada: Inner City Books.

Woodman explores the psychology of modern women and finds a witchlike complex, "a Medusa or Lady Macbeth," which functions in an autonomous, archetypal way and prevents women from integrating body, mind and spirit. This is seen as stemming from a cultural bias that favors patriarchal values, and the author describes what she sees as the budding constellation of a new archetypal pattern, a feminine one, which is compensating "the specious masculine ideals and the loss of numinous spiritual values in our culture."

4. Existential Analysis

Binswanger, L. (1958). The case of Ellen West (W. M.
     Mendel & J. Lyons, Trans.). In R. May, E. Angel, &
     H. F. Ellenburger (Eds.), Existence: A new dimension
     in psychiatry and psychology. New York: Basic Books.
     (Original work published in 1944)

     Binswanger is the father of existential analysis and
     the only dissident who remained friendly with Freud.
     This is his famous existential analysis of a despair-
     ing woman (not actually his case) who committed sui-
     cide.

Burstow, B. (1980-81). A critique of Binswanger's
     existential analysis. Review of Existential Psychology
     and Psychiatry, 17, 245-252.

     A critique of the reductiveness of Binswanger's analy-
     sis with the addition of a feminist viewpoint.

French feminist theory [Special section]. (1981). Signs,
     7(1), 5-86.

PART II

GENDER DIFFERENCES IN THE LIFE CYCLE AND

CURRENT RESEARCH ON FEMALE DEVELOPMENT

Gender differentiation begins in infancy and continues over the life span. This developmental process occurs physiologically, psychologically and socially. (N.A.)

A. Infancy (0 to 1 year)

Current research substantiates that gender differences and differentiation begins at birth.

Baker, S. W. (1980). Biological influences on human sex and gender. Signs, 6(1), 80-96.

Barnett, M. (1966). Vaginal awareness in the infancy and childhood of girls. Journal of The American Psycho-analytic Association, 14(1), 129-140.

Barnett theorizes that girls are anatomically capable of having vaginal sexual activity from birth and unlike boys are capable of orgastic release. However, she does not give the basis of her assumption.

Bell, R. Q., & Darling, J. F. (1965). The prone head reaction in the neonate: Relation with sex and tactile sensitivity. Child Development, 36(4), 943-949.

Birns, B. (1976). The emergence and socialization of sex differences in the earliest years. Merrill-Palmer Quarterly, 22(3), 229-254.

Chodorow, N. (1971). Being and doing: A cross-cultural
        examination of the socialization of males and females.
        In V. Gornick & B. Moran (Eds.), Woman in Sexist
        Society: Studies in Power and Powerlessness
        (pp. 173-197). New York: Basic Books.

        Using cross-cultural studies as her base Chodorow
        refutes the claim of universal and necessary sex dif-
        ferences, pointing to socialization practices as
        accounting for these differences. Western society, in
        particular, perpetuates a cycle of polarized sexual
        identities. The male must reject all that is feminine
        in women and in himself; female children and adults
        must accept a devalued position in this sociological
        context.

Chodorow, N. (1978). Mothering, object-relations, and the
        female oedipal configuration. Feminist Studies, 4(1),
        137-158.

Chodorow, N. (1979). Feminism and difference: Gender,
        relation and difference in psychoanalytic perspective.
        Socialist Review, 46, 51-69.

Culp, R. E., Cook, A. S., & Housley, P. C. (1983). A
        comparison of observed and reported adult-infant
        interactions: Effects of gender stability and age.
        Sex Roles, 9(4), 475-480.

Dinnerstein, D. (1976). The mermaid and the minotaur:
        Sexual arrangements and human malaise. New York:
        Harper & Row.

        Dinnerstein looks to the ambivalence inherent in the
        infant experience to explain later gender arrangement
        and the larger human predicament. Dinnerstein
        suggests that we have short circuited integration and
        projected onto women all that we fear and wish to
        control.

Eichenbaum, L., & Orbach, S. (1983). Understanding women:
     A feminist psychoanalytic approach. New York: Basic
     Books.

     These authors have blended work on gender identity,
     object relations and feminist theory to derive a new
     developmental model of female development. Their main
     focus is the mother-daughter relationship and the
     process by which women are raised. Women are raised
     to look after the needs of others and restrain their
     own desire for autonomy and independence.

Formanek, R. (1982). On the origins of gender identity.
     In D. Mendell (Ed.), Early female development:
     Current psychoanalytic views (pp. 1-24). New York:
     SP Medical and Scientific Books.

Galenson, E., & Roiphe, H. (1977). Some suggested
     revisions concerning early female development. In H.
     Blum (Ed.), Female psychology: Contemporary
     psychoanalytic views (pp. 29-57). New York:
     International Universities Press.

     During their research at Albert Einstein College of
     Medicine, 70 children were studied from age 10-12
     months through the end of their second year, in natu-
     ralistic informal nursery settings. Findings support
     in part Freud's original position that penis envy and
     feminine castration complex exert crucial influence on
     feminine development. However, the authors suggest
     several revisions: the discovery of sexual differ-
     ences occurs earlier (15-17 months) than Freud pro-
     posed; the impact of such a discovery is closely
     interwoven with fears of object and anal loss. This
     developmental phase strongly interacts with an already
     developing sense of femininity stemming from early
     bodily and affective experiences with both parents.

Kleeman, J. (1977). Freud's views on early female sexuality in the light of direct child observation. In H. Blum (Ed.), _Female psychology: Contemporary psychoanalytic views_ (pp. 3-27). New York: International Universities Press.

Freud's writings on early female sexuality are reviewed in order to assess which of his central assumptions are supported and which show need for modification from data provided by observation of young children. General conclusions include: (1) Cognitive functions, learning experience, and language are believed to be more important than Freud stressed while penis envy and feelings of inferiority are relegated to a less universal place in the onset of femininity. (2) The role of the father is given different emphasis. (3) The clarification of masturbation in the young female tends to refute Freud's contention that masturbation is further removed from the nature of women than men.

Kohlberg, L. (1966). A cognitive-developmental analysis of children's sex-role concept and attitudes. In E. E. Maccoby (Ed.), _The development of sex differences_ (pp. 82-172). Stanford, CA: Stanford University Press.

Korner, A. F. (1973). Sex differences in newborns with specific reference to differences in the organization of oral behavior. _Journal of Child Psychology and Psychiatry and Allied Disciplines_, _14_(1), 19-29.

Lang, J. A. (1984). Notes toward a psychology of the feminine self. In P. E. Stepansky & A. Goldberg (Eds.), _Kohut's legacy: Contributions to self psychology_ (pp. 51-69). Hillsdale, NJ: The Analytic Press.

One of the few elaborations of gender difference in self psychology.

Lewis, H. B. (1976). What are little girls made of. In
     Psychic war in men and women (pp. 61-89). New York:
     New York University Press.

     In this chapter Lewis details the early differences
     between male and female infants. She summarizes and
     draws conclusions from infant research. Her conclu-
     sions suggest that the girl baby brings to the inter-
     action with mother more and earlier attachment. The
     female infant's responsive, affectionate qualities
     interact with mothers' responsiveness. The result is
     the girl's earlier preference for and stronger tie to
     mother and a smoother more peaceful relationship.
     Lewis hypothesizes that this might be a factor in the
     girl's earlier language and cognitive development and
     also in the finding that nursery school girls are more
     person-oriented, nurturant and helpful as compared to
     their more object-oriented boy peers.

Lewis, M. (1972). State as an infant-environment
     interaction: An analysis of mother infant interaction
     as a function of sex. Merrill-Palmer Quarterly,
     18(2), 95-121.

Lichtenberg, J. (1983). Psychoanalysis and infant research.
     Hillsdale, NY: The Analytic Press.

     The findings of infant research are reviewed for the
     first two years of life. Several gender differences
     are noted. A female newborn has greater responsive-
     ness to taste, greater mouth activity, more tongue
     involvement during feeding and a greater overall tac-
     tile sensitivity. A mother may respond differently to
     the above empathically sensing the girl baby's
     affinity for oral comforting and conversely a mother
     may respond to a boy baby's greater need for proximal
     tactile stimulation. Mothers tend to maintain greater
     physical contact with a 6 month old girl. By the
     first year mothers respond more quickly to girls'
     rescue appeals. Boys range further and make more
     problem solving efforts to return when artificially
     separated.

Maccoby, E. E. (Ed.). (1966). <u>The development of sex differences</u>. Stanford, CA: Stanford University Press.

This old, yet seminal, book presents several major theories on the development of sex differences. The following theories are considered in the book: sex hormones and the development of sex differences; sex differences in intellectual functioning; social-learning view of sex differences; cognitive-developmental view of sex differences; and a cultural view of sex differences.

Maccoby, E. E., & Jacklin, C. N. (1974). <u>The psychology of sex differences</u>. Stanford, CA: Stanford University Press.

This book offers a systematic analysis and interpretation of a massive body of reported research. Findings are included that show no sex differences in such areas as perception, cognition, self-concept, activity level, sociability, aggression, competition, dominance, modeling and socialization; hormonal levels and genetic factors. The book also presents an exhaustive annotated bibliography of over 1400 research studies published since 1965 and assesses the validity of the most widely held beliefs about sex differences. While this book is quoted widely, there are methodological problems with their study. See reviews of this book by C. Dwyer [<u>American Educational Research Journal</u>, 1975, <u>12</u>(4), 513-530]; J. Bloch [<u>Contemporary Psychology</u>, 1976, <u>21</u>(8), 517-522]; W. Emmerich [<u>Science</u>, 1975, <u>19</u>, 140-141]; and Brooks [<u>Library Journal</u>, 1974, <u>99</u>, 3204].

Mischel, W. (1966). A social-learning view of sex differences in behavior. In E. E. Maccoby (Ed.), <u>The development of sex differences</u> (pp. 56-81). Stanford, CA: Stanford University Press.

Money, J. (1956). Sexual incongruities and psychopathology:
    Evidence of human hermaphroditism. <u>Bulletin of Johns
    Hopkins Hospital, 98</u>, 43-57.

    Money concludes that sexual behavior and orientation
    as male or female does not have an innate instinctive
    basis. He rejects psychoanalytic arguments, stating
    that sexual orientation is learned or imprinted.
    (Walstedt)

Money, J., & Ehrhardt, A. (1973). <u>Man and woman, boy and
    girl: Differentiation and dimorphism of gender
    identity from conception to maturity</u>. Baltimore, MD:
    The Johns Hopkins University Press.

    Money and Ehrhardt, who have studied people with mixed
    sexual characteristics, conclude that concepts of
    femininity and masculinity relate to cultural prac-
    tices and not to biological imperatives. They found
    that hermaphrodites who are brought up as females
    despite the lack of ovaries and even with male
    secondary characteristics, continue to see themselves
    as females. Hermaphrodites raised as males were
    equally determined to remain male.

Moss, H. A. (1967). Sex, age and state as determinants of
    mother-infant interaction. <u>Merrill-Palmer Quarterly,
    13</u>(1), 19-36.

Moss, H. A., & Robson, K. S. (1968). Maternal influences
    in early social-visual behavior. <u>Child Development,
    39</u>(2), 401-408.

Parsons, J. E. (1980). Psychosexual neutrality: Is anatomy
    destiny? In J. E. Parsons (Ed.), <u>The psychobiology of
    sex differences and sex roles</u>. New York: McGraw-Hill.

Person, E. S., & Ovesey, L. (1983). Psychological theories
    of gender identity. <u>Journal of the American Academy
    of Psychoanalysis, 11</u>(2), 203-226.

Rothbart, M. K., & Jaccoby, E. E. (1966). Parents
    differential to sons and daughters. <u>Journal of
    Personality and Social Psychology, 4</u>(3), 237-243.

Silverman, D. K. (1984). Some proposed modifications of
    psychoanalytic theories of early childhood
    development. In J. Masling (Ed.), Empirical studies
    of psychoanalytic theories (Vol. 2). Hillsdale, NJ:
    Lawrence Erlbaum Associates.

Stoller, R. (1968). Sex and gender: The development of
    masculinity and feminity. New York: Science House.

    Stoller and his group at the UCLA Gender Identity
    Research Clinic emphasize the decisive influence of
    early parental rearing for the determination of "core
    gender identity," and they establish a critical period
    for the formation of gender identity at 18 months.
    They describe the importance of prephallic feminine
    identification in a group of transsexual males whose
    mothers share a particular type of psychosexual con-
    stellation. Their findings dispute Freud's emphasis
    on the phallic phase as the beginning of gender devel-
    opment of the girl.

Stoller, R. (1977). Primary femininity. In H. Blum (Ed.),
    Female psychology: Contemporary psychoanalytic views
    (pp. 59-78). New York: International Universities
    Press.

    Stoller proposes an early nonconflictual phase in the
    origin of femininity. He reviews factors that make up
    this stage: (a) a biological force--fetal sex hormones
    on the brain of the fetus; (b) sex assignment; (c)
    effect of sex assignment on parents, then reflected
    back onto the infant; (d) conditioning or other forms
    of learning; and (e) developing body ego, especially
    from genitals. The later oedipal phase then adds and
    enriches this primary femininity or core gender iden-
    tity but is secondary to it.

Thomas, E. B., Laiderman, P. H., & Olson, J. P. (1972).
    Neonate-mother Interaction during breast feeding.
    Developmental Psychology, 6(1), 110-118.

Watson, J. S. (1969). Operant conditioning of visual fixa-
    tion in infants under visual and auditory reinforce-
    ment. <u>Developmental Psychology</u>, <u>1</u>(5), 508-516.

Weller, G. M., & Bell, R. Q. (1965). Basal skin
    conductance and neonatal state. <u>Child Development</u>,
    <u>36</u>(3), 647-657.

Zuger, B. (1970). Gender role determination: A critical
    review of the evidence from hermaphroditism (and the
    reply by Dr. Money). <u>Psychosomatic Medicine</u>, <u>32</u>(5),
    449-468.

    Zuger attempts to refute the evidence that individuals
    with ambiguous sex at birth will accept the sex role
    of rearing over that indicated by chromosomes, gonads,
    hormones, internal and external genitalia. He does
    not accept the conclusions of Money and the Hampsons
    and uses cases in the literature to try to prove that
    biology overrides sex rearing. He attempts to show
    that sex change was successful at much later ages than
    previously claimed. Money replies to Dr. Zuger saying
    doctors always report their successful cases, and
    suggests that Zuger may have also looked for cases to
    prove his point.
    <u>Comments</u>: Parents sometimes raise their children in an
    ambivalent manner if they are unsure of their sex,
    which could account for the Zuger results. (Walstedt)

B. Toddler Phase (1-3 years)

Gender differentiation and sex role identity are further refined and elaborated during this phase. (N.A.)

Abelin, E. L. (1971a). The role of the father in the
    separation-individuation process. In J. B. McDevitt &
    C. F. Settlage (Eds.), Separation-individuation:
    Essays in honor of Margaret S. Mahler (pp. 229-252).
    New York: International Universities Press.

This article stresses the positive preoedipal role of the father in ego organization and development. Particular attention is given to natural observations that suggest that the father plays an important role in separation-individuation as early as the symbiotic phase and that his role is of equal significance in the practicing and rapprochment subphases. The role of the father as significant exciting other and early rival is noted as are sex differences in toddler behavior toward male adults. This paper strongly suggests that (mental) triangulation is a significant preoedipal factor in ego organization and development and that infants may have an inner readiness to respond to certain primordial differences—men against women and adults against children. Abelin also suggests the qualitative character of this readiness may be different in girls than in boys.

Abelin, E. L. (1971b). Triangulation, the role of the
    father, and the origin of core gender identity during
    the rapprochment phase. In J. B. McDevitt & C. F.
    Settlage (Eds.), Separation-individuation: Essays in
    honor of Margaret S. Mahler. New York: International
    Universities Press.

This study focuses on the role of the father in the child's development of symbolic language. Central to symbolic development are specific genetic analogs which are awakened and recognized through mirroring; recapitulation, recognition and identification with the rivals for mother's attention. The attainment of selfhood is the bridge between sensory and symbolic functioning. The father plays a significant role in the development of the toddler's early concept of self. He is the pre-rapproachment infant's second attachment object. During the rapproachment period, he becomes a significant exciting unambivalent other. Abelin emphasizes that during rapproachment the identificatory process in boys is different than that in girls, as is the development of the core gender identity in both sexes. The oedipal phase behavior is seen as a recapitulation at a higher symbolic level of earlier triangulation experiences.

Bergman, A. (1982). Considerations about the development of the girl during separation-individuation process. In D. Mendell (Ed.), <u>Early female development: Current psychoanalytic views</u> (pp. 61-80). New York: SP Medical and Scientific Books.

Bergman presents her understanding of the influence of the separation-individuation process and psychosexual development on female sexual identity. She uses direct child observation and parent reports during the first three years of life plus a follow-up study during elementary school. She points to the following factors which influence the girl's experiences of her feminine identity: the girl's identification with her mother, her resolution of the rapproachment crisis and the mother's reaction to her own and her daughter's femininity.

Brooks-Gunn, J., & Mathews, W. S. (1979). <u>He and she: How children develop their sex-role identity</u>. Englewood Cliffs, NJ: Spectrum.

Distler, B., Kaplan, J., & Williams, F. (1984, April). <u>The impact of gender on the separation-individuation process: Clinical implications for interpretation</u>. Paper presented at the meeting of the New York State Psychological Association, New York, NY.

The separation-individuation process is reexamined from the perspective of gender specificity. Traditional Freudian concepts are discussed in the light of current research and thinking. Such issues as the wish for a baby and penis envy are examined through psychoanalytic case material and the meanings of these developmental issues are expanded to reflect the en- riching perspectives offered by differentiation, nar- cissistic, and object relations theories. The early roots and meanings of these developmental issues are stressed, especially through the introduction of ob- servations from infant research which point to gender difference.

Fast, I. (1979). Development of gender identity: Gender differentiation in girls. International Journal of Psychoanalysis, 60, 443-453.

Fast places the problem of sexual differentiation within a more general framework of ongoing self-other differentiation as a clarification of gender issues. The model proposed included: an initial narcissistic, undifferentiated period followed by a recognition of limits with response of protest, sense of loss, denial; then a recategorization of experience in which one differentiation product is integrated as part of self, the other independent of self, the two in productive relationship. Within this frame, penis envy is seen as a wish to hold onto undifferentiated state where narcissistic gratification can be ful- filled.

Fleishman, E. G. (1983). Sex-role acquisition, parental behavior, and sexual orientation: Some tentative hypotheses. Sex Roles, 9(10), 1051-1059.

It is hypothesized that sexual orientation is not an aspect of sex-role socialization but is acquired during a sensitive period from birth to 3 years through physical contact with adults. Research is reviewed that tentatively supports this hypothesis by suggesting that (a) sexual orientation is highly resistant to change after adolescence; (b) infants respond to sexual stimulation and discriminate between the sexes; (c) gender identity is fixed between birth and 3 years of age; (d) during their infancy, homo- sexuals were psychosocially and presumably physically

responded to as children of the opposite sex; and (e)
parents touch boys and girls differently. Collective-
ly, studies of infant-parent interaction suggest that
mothers and fathers establish different and perhaps
stronger physical bonds with their same- rather than
their opposite-sex offspring. Stronger support for
the hypothesis must be gained from longitudinal observation of parent-infant physical and social interaction and the infant's eventual sexual orientation.

Lerner, L. (Ed.) (1982). Women and individuation:
    Emerging views [Special issue]. The Psychoanalytic
    Review, 69(1), 5-6.

In this special issue on women, clinicians, social
scientists, and humanists focus on the changing perspectives on narcissism, preoedipal years, and gender
identity formation. In particular, vicissitudes of
the girl's struggle to free herself from a primary
identification with mother and to establish an autonomous self is viewed in various essays as the root of
Lesbian attachments, of envy and idealization of men
and as a source of work inhibition and failure of
creativity. An important focus is presented but some
essays lack theoretical and empirical vigor. Special
book review on Chodorow's Reproduction of mothering is
noteworthy. Career and motherhood by A. Roland and B.
Harris is also reviewed.

Oliner, M. (1982). The anal phase. In D. Mendell (Ed.),
    Early female development: Current psycho-analytic views
    (pp. 25-60). New York: SP Medical & Scientific Books.

Oliner, in this theoretical paper, contends that on
this side of the Atlantic psychoanalysts telescope the
oral and phallic phases. Therefore, she turns to the
French school of psychoanalysis (influenced by Melanie
Klein and Ernest Jones) which considers the anal
struggle between mother and daughter the most important determinant of psychosexual development. She
arrives at a new and integrated view of female development during the anal phase based on drive theory,
ego psychology, and the contributions of the French
school.

Parens, H.   (1971).   A contribution of separation-
    individuation to the development of psychic structure.
    In J. B. McDevitt & C. F. Settlage (Eds.), <u>Separation-
    Individuation: Essays in honor of Margaret S. Mahler</u>
    (pp. 100-112).   New York: International Universities
    Press.

Sarlin, C.   (1963).   Feminine identity.   <u>Journal of American
    Psychoanalytic Association</u>, <u>11</u>, 790-816.

    Sarlin attempts to link a libidinal drive organization
    issue, the renunciation of clitoral sexuality, with
    the girls' need to relinquish her maternal attachment.
    This allows the clear differentiation of the self and
    the object in the ego.

C. Early Childhood (3-6 years)

1. Precursors of Oedipal Situation

Bergmann, M. (1982). The female oedipal complex: Its
     antecedents and evolution. In D. Mendell (Ed.), Early
     female development: Current psychoanalytic views
     (pp. 175-201). New York: SP Medical & Scientific
     Books.

     Bergmann focuses upon the development of pregenital
     and genital psychic precursors--maternal identifica-
     tion, the resolution of the rapproachment crisis,
     object relations and ego experience--which influence
     and distort the oedipal situation. The preoedipal
     mother and her psychic representation are stressed in
     her reassessment of traditional thinking about maso-
     chism and superego development, presenting a profile
     of a female patient whose unresolved preoedipal
     problems result in an inability to deal with oedipal
     problems.

Dervin, D. (1978). Over the rainbow and under the twister:
     A drama of the girl's passage through the phallic
     phase. Bulletin of the Menninger Clinic, 42(1),
     51-57.

Edgucumbe, R., & Burgner, M. (1975). The phallic
     narcissistic phase. The Psychoanalytic Study of the
     Child, 30, 161-180.

     In this paper, the phallic phase is divided into the
     preoedipal phallic-narcissistic stage and phallic
     oedipal stage. Both stages are examined through data
     taken from observations of and treatment of children
     in this age group. Different manifestations of
     developing body self-representation processes of iden-
     tification and the acquisition of a sexual identity in
     boys and girls are shown. Case material demonstrates
     both the normal processes of phallic phase development

and cases where development is held up in the phallic
phase because of prephallic conflicts which contribute
to the difficulties in the phallic phase.

Frankel, S., & Sherick, I. (1979). Observations of the
emerging sexual identity of three and four year old
children: With emphasis on female sexual identity.
International Review of Psychoanalysis, 6, 297-309.

Glover, L., & Mendell, D. (1982). A suggested
developmental sequence for a preoedipal genital phase.
In D. Mendell (Ed.), Early female development: Current
psychoanalytic views (pp. 127-174). New York:
SP Medical and Scientific Books.

Concurring with current theorists who emphasize the
very early root of femininity, these psychoanalysts
study the unconscious derivatives of dream material in
six of their female adult patients and conclude the
existence of a "discreet phase in female psychosexual
development, which occurs between the anal and oedipal
periods and in which the dominant zone is the genital
and the dominant task is that of defining oneself as
female" (p. 128). They substitute the term "preoedipal genital" for the traditional term "phallic,"
differentiating this phase into four stages.
Misinterpreted traditional terms such as "penis envy,"
"castration anxiety," "narcissistic development" and
"development of a consolidated female sense of self"
are elaborated and explicated.

Kestenberg, J. S. (1956a). Vicissitudes of female
sexuality. Journal of The American Psychoanalytic
Association, 4, 453-476.

Kestenberg, J. S. (1956b). On the development of maternal
feelings in early childhood. The Psychoanalytic Study
of the Child, 11, 275-291.

Kestenberg, using both case studies of children and
adults and direct observational studies of children,
stresses the early vaginal sensations for the psychology of the girl. She postulates that anatomical
differences between the boy and girl have an important

impact on the maturation of certain ego functions and on the development of sexual identity. Remaining within the Freudian psychosexual frame, she introduces an inner-genital phase that follows the pregenital and precedes the phallic phase.

Kestenberg, J. S. (1968). Outside and inside, male and female. Journal of The American Psychoanalytic Association, 16(3), 457-520.

The premise of this paper is that the universal repudiation of femininity is based on the anxiety-provoking nature of inner genital sensations. Within this frame she postulates that feminine integration can only be completed through the help of a man who unifies her inside and outside genitality.

Kestenberg, J. S. (1980). The three faces of femininity. Psychoanalytic Review, 67(3), 313-335.

Kestenberg proposes three specific phases in the development of the female: inner-genital preoedipal-maternal; phallic-negative-oedipal-rivalrous; phallic-positive-oedipal-heterosexual; The integration of all these facets of femininity allows a woman to be mother, achiever, wife.

Kestenberg, J. S. (1982). Inner-genital phase--prephallic and pre-oedipal. In D. Mendell (Ed.), Early female development: Current psychoanalytic views (pp. 81-125). New York: SP Medical and Scientific Books.

Kestenberg summarizes her scheme of the female life cycle emphasizing the role of the inner-genital modality during each developmental phase. In addition, she presents the pre-genital phallic phases from a feminine viewpoint rooted in female anatomy and physiology.

Sherif, C. W. (1982). Needed concepts in the study of gender identity. Psychology of Women, 6(4), 375-398.

Silverman, D. K. (1984). Some proposed modifications of
     psychoanalytic theories of early childhood
     development. In J. Masling (Ed.), <u>Empirical studies
     of psychoanalytic theories</u> (Vol. 2.). Hillsdale, NJ:
     Lawrence Erlbaum Associates.

Torok, M. (1970). The significance of penis envy in women.
     In J. Chasseguet-Smirgel (Ed.), <u>Female sexuality</u>
     (pp. 135-176). Ann Arbor, MI: University of Michigan
     Press.

Torok, using a Kleinian frame, suggests that penis
envy is the girl's unconscious pledge to a jealous-
possessive maternal image that she will not achieve
genital fulfillment and will deny herself pleasure
with the penis for mother's sake. Therefore, penis
envy does not have its primary roots in objective
anatomical realities but is a symptom reflecting the
girl's difficulties in identifying with and differentiating from a mother who is experienced as jealous or
intrusive. According to Torok, the mother who forbids
masturbation communicates that she would lapse into
envy if the child achieves satisfaction without her.

Tyson, P. (1982). A developmental line of gender identity,
     gender role, and choice of love object. <u>Journal of
     the American Psychoanalytic Association</u>, <u>30</u>(1), 61-86.

A theoretical schema of the development of male and
female gender identity is presented from the oral
phase through late adolescence. To negotiate the
phallic phase successfully, the girl must give up her
fantasy of one day having a penis, finding a way of
coping with her penis envy and finding narcissistic
pleasure and value in her female body. The authors
state that lowered self-esteem associated with penis
envy in some girls, reflects prephallic disturbances
in object relations. Penis envy can no longer be
regarded as the major organizer of femininity. Core
gender identity and a female gender role are established prior to the phallic phase.

2. Penis Envy and Castration Anxiety

The classical Freudian concepts of penis envy and castration anxiety are reexamined with attempts to remove these concepts from their phalocentric bias. (N.A.)

Bassin, D. (1982). Woman's images of inner space: Data towards expanded interpretive categories. International Review of Psycho-analysis, 9(2), 191-203.

> Bassin criticizes the limited interpretive categories for woman's affective/cognitive experiences, such as "castration anxiety" and "penis envy." She suggests that a proactive manifestation of women's psychobiological development is needed rather than only the reactive orthodox view of female development as a series of compensations for being not-male. She believes that analysts need to be more sensitive to images of inner space in their female patients' productions which will encourage the development of a more detailed schematization of the representations of women's interiority and not her inferiority.

Grossman, W., & Stewart, W. (1977). Penis envy: From childhood wish to developmental metaphor. In H. Blum (Ed.), Female psychology: Contemporary psychoanalytic views (pp. 193-212). New York: International Universities Press. (Reprinted from Journal of American Psychoanalytic Association, 1976, 24)

> The authors consider two phases of penis envy: (1) an early phase where awareness of genital differences become meaningful in terms of a girl's attempts to differentiate herself from her mother; during this phase narcissistic needs and self-object differentiation are critical developmental issues; (2) a later phase where relationship to both parents as a function of sexual difference is an important issue and leads to phallic and oedipal fantasies. They stress the importance in differentiation between these two phases and feel such clarification will help resolve some

current criticism of the penis envy concept. They offer two clinical examples in which envy of men was only part of a tendency to envy in a narcissistic character disorder and stress in such cases the necessity to consider penis envy as the manifest content of a symptom that needs analysis rather than as "bedrock" or ultimate conflict.

Lerner, H. E. (1977). Parental mislabeling of female genitals as a determinant of penis envy and learning inhibitions in women. In H. Blum (Ed.), Female psychology: Contemporary psychoanalytic views (pp. 269-283). New York: International Universities Press.

Lerner contends that when the visible and sensitive aspects of the girl's genitals are not labeled for her she may feel that she does not have permission to develop into a sexually responsive woman. A case is presented in which the failure to label the girl's external genitals was a contributing factor to penis envy as well as to conflicts about looking which led to symptomatic learning inhibitions. This paper's main contribution is its clear statement that the clitoris is a valid and important organ of female sexuality and needs to be directly confronted in our parenting and in our therapeutic work.

Lerner, H. E. (1980). Penis envy: Alternatives in conceptualization. Bulletin of the Menninger Clinic, 44(1), 39-48.

Lerner suggests that interpretation of penis envy may be counter-therapeutic unless the analyst explores the unique and complex meaning that the symptom may have for particular women.

Moulton, R. (1973). A survey and re-evaluation of the concept of penis envy. In J. B. Miller (Ed.), Psychoanalysis and women (pp. 207-230). New York: Brunner/Mazel. (Reprinted from Contemporary Psychoanalysis, 1970, 7, 84-104)

Siegel, B. (1982). Penis envy. The Bulletin of the Menninger Clinic, 46(4), 363-376.

Thompson, C. (1973). Penis envy in women. In J. B. Miller
     (Ed.), <u>Psychoanalysis and women</u> (pp. 43-48). New
     York: Brunner/Mazel. (Reprinted from <u>Psychiatry</u>,
     1943, <u>6</u>, 123-125)

3. Oedipal Situation

The classical Freudian concept of the female oedipal situation is researched and reviewed in an attempt to make it a
more accurate reflection of the female child's biological,
psychological, and social development. (N.A.)

Chasseguet-Smirgel, J. (1970). Feminine guilt and the
    oedipus complex. In J. Chassequet-Smirgel (Ed.),
    Female Sexuality. Ann Arbor, MI: University of
    Michigan Press.

    Chasseguet-Smirgel stresses issues around identifica-
    tion and differentiation as essential in understanding
    sex differences. Using a Kleinian frame, she sees the
    girl's struggle to emancipate herself from the omnipo-
    tent preoedipal mother as crucial. This struggle is
    seen as the source of penis envy since the girl re-
    gards the boy's distinguishing physical attributes as
    helpful to him in separating from mother.

Edgucumbe, R. (1976). Some comments on the concept of the
    negative oedipal phase in girls. Psychoanalytic Study
    of the Child, 31, 35-61.

    Edgucumbe and her colleagues, using clinical data from
    the analysis of girls, dispute the concept of the
    negative oedipal phase (as described by Lampl-de
    Groot). From their data they arrive at an alternate
    conceptualization: the impact of the phallic drive
    development creates an awareness of physical differ-
    ences between boys and girls and helps consolidate
    sexual identity.

Fu, V. R., Hinkle, D. E., & Korslund, M. K. (1983). A
    developmental study of ethnic self-concept among
    preadolescent girls. Journal of Genetic Psychology,
    142(1), 67-73.

Glover, L., & Mendell, D. (1982). A suggested
      developmental sequence for a preoedipal genital phase.
      In D. Mendell (Ed.), Early female development: Current
      psychoanalytic views (pp. 127-174). New York:
      Spectrum.

Lampl-de Groot, J. (1948). The evolution of the oedipus
      complex in women. In R. Fleiss (Ed.), The Psycho-
      analytic reader. New York: International Universities
      Press.

Lester, E. (1975). On the psychosexual development of the
      female child. Journal of the American Academy of
      Psychoanalysis, 4(4), 515-527.

      The psychoanalytic concepts of femaleness and the
      oedipal complex in young females are explored. The
      theory that female children view themselves as
      castrated males is contraindicated by data pointing to
      the emergence of sexual identity in children at a very
      early age. Moreover, the concept of the female
      oedipus complex is theoretically ambiguous and is "not
      consistent with current objective data on child
      development."

Parens, H., Stern, J., & Kramer, S. (1977). On the girl's
      entry into the oedipus complex. In H. Blum (Ed.),
      Female Psychology: Contemporary psychoanalytic views
      (pp. 79-107). New York: International Universities
      Press.

      A detailed child observational study does not support
      the generalizability of Freud's 1925 postulate that
      the girl enters her oedipus complex by way of her
      castration complex. Instead, it is proposed that a
      biological and constitutional disposition to hetero-
      sexuality is expressed in a somatopsychic continuum
      and differentiation of the libido. They particularly
      noted an explicit wish for a baby prior to indications
      of castration anxiety.

4. Superego Development

These authors accent the differences between male and female
superego development and take issue with the phalocentric
formulation of female superego development. (N.A.) More
recently, the intrapsychic view has been expanded into a
social-cultural context with current discussions focusing on
moral development issues. (B.L.C.)

Bernstein, D. (1983). The female superego: A different
     perspective. _International Journal of Psychoanalysis_,
     _64_(2), 187-201.

     Bernstein, within a Freudian frame, examines superego
     development in girls and boys by using 3 axes:
     strength, structure, and contents. She find no
     support for the original analytic position that women
     have defective superegos, and points to the core of
     the superego as emerging out of oral and anal issues.
     The child's actual experiences of its own body and the
     child-parent interactions in the areas of separation-
     individuation and identifications are important deter-
     minants in superego development.

Gilligan, C. (1982). _In a different voice: Psychological
     theory and women's development_. Cambridge, MA:
     Harvard University Press.

Jacobson, E. (1937). Ways of female superego formation
     and the female castration complex. _Psychoanalytic
     Quarterly_, _45_, 525-538.

Lewis, H. B. (1976a). The superego experience: Shame and
     guilt. In _Psychic war in men and women_ (pp. 182-187).
     New York: New York University Press.

Lewis, H. B.   (1976b).   The superego by sexes: Shame and
     guilt in character formation.   In <u>Psychic war in men
     and women</u> (pp. 198-215).   New York: New York
     University Press.

     In these two chapters Lewis clarifies the differences
     in the superego experience for men and women by dif-
     ferentiating   between   the   superego's   internalized
     threat of punishment operating to the signal of guilt
     and its ego-ideal which signals shame.   Women operate
     more in the shame mode where loss of love and sensiti-
     vity to others are important issues.   For the male the
     guilt mode with its internalizations of moral stan-
     dards and the ideal of goodness becomes the prevalent
     aspect.   She correlates her findings with Witkins'
     conceptualization of field dependence and field inde-
     pendence.

Sachs, H.   (1979).   One of the motive factors in the forma-
     tion of the superego in women.   <u>International Journal
     of Psycho-analysis</u>, <u>60</u>, 39-50.

5. The Role of the Father

The father's role in the emotional and characerological development of female as well as male children is being examined as a significant compliment to the original bond with the mother. (N.A.)

Abelin, E. L. (1971). The role of the father in the separation-individuation process. In J. B. McDevitt & C. F. Settlage (Eds.), Separation-Individuation: Essays in honor of Margaret S. Mahler (pp. 229-252). New York: International Universities Press.

Abelin, E. L. (1980). Triangulation, the role of the father and the origin of core gender identity during the rapprochement subphase. In R. Lax, S. Bach, & A. Burland (Eds.), Rapprochement: The critical subphase of separation-individuation. New York: Jason Aronson.

Bannon, J. A., & Southern, M. L. (1980). Father-absent women: Self-concept and modes of relating to men. Sex Roles, 6(1), 75-84.

Barnett, R. C., & Baruch, G. K. (1984). Determinants of fathers' participation in family work (Working Paper No. 136). Wellesley, MA: Wellesley College Center for Research on Women.

Baruch, G. K., & Barnett, R. C. (1984). Fathers' participation in family work: Effects on children's sex role attitudes (Working Paper No. 126). Wellesley, MA: Wellesley College Center for Research on Women.

Benedek, T. (1970). Fatherhood and providing. In E. J. Anthony & T. Benedek (Eds.), Parenthood: Its psychology and psychopathology. Boston: Little Brown.

Biller, H. B., & Weiss, S. D. (1970). The father-daughter relationship and the personality development of the female. The Journal of Genetic Psychology, 116(1), 79-93.

> This review of theories and empirical data indicates that problems in father-child relationships are related to disorders in both male and female children. The personality adjustment and feminine identification of the daughter are influenced both by her interaction with her father, and by his relationship with his wife and other family members. The authors indicate that numerous studies exist concerning the relationship between fathers and daughters. However, the need remains to expand the scope of studies to include the examination of sociocultural, cognitive and temperamental factors, to introduce more precise definitions of the research variables, and to achieve more representative selections of subject and control groups. (JSAS)

Biller, H. B. (1971). Fathering and female sexual development. Medical Aspects of Sexuality, 5(11), 129-131, 136-138.

> Adult female sexuality is enhanced by having had a relationship with a masculine father who reinforced his daughter's femininity, was accepting of her, and had a good marital relationship with her mother. (JSAS)

David, D., & Brannon, R. (Eds.) (1976). The forty-nine percent majority: The male sex role. Boston: Addison-Wesley.

Doyle, J. A. (1983). The male experience. W. C. Brown.

Forrest, T. (1966). Paternal roots of female character of development. Contemporary Psychoanalysis, 3(1), 21-28.

Forrest, T. (1967). The paternal roots of male character development. Psychoanalytic Review, 54(1), 51-68.

Grady, K. E., Brannon, R., & Pleck, J. H. (1979). The male sex role: A selected and annotated bibliography. Rockville, MD: U.S. Department of Health, Education & Welfare, Public Health Service.

Hammer, S. (1982). Passionate attachments: Fathers and daughters in America today. Fairfield, PA: Chappel.

Heilbrun, A. B., Jr. (1968). Sex-role identity in adolescent females: A theoretical paradox. Adolescence, 3(9), 79-88.

Henderson, J. (1982). The role of the father in separa tion-individuation. The Bulletin of the Menninger Clinic, 46(3), 231-254.

Kestenbaum, C. J. (1983). Fathers and daughters: The father's contribution to feminine identification in girls depicted in fairy tales and myths. The American Journal of Psychoanalysis, 43(2), 119-127.

Lamb, M. E. (1980). The father's role in the facilitation of infant mental health. Infant Mental Health Journal, 1(3), 140-149.

Lamb, M. E., & Bronson, S. K. (1980). Father in the context of family influences: Past, present, and future. School Psychology Review, 9(4), 336-353.

Leonard, M. (1966). Fathers and daughters: The significance of "fathering" in the psychosexual development of the girl. International Journal of Psychoanalysis, 47(2-3), 325-334.

Lewis, R. A. (1984). Emotional intimacy among men. In P. P. Rieker & E. Carmen (Eds.), The gender gap in psychotherapy: Social realities and psychological processes (pp. 181-193). New York: Plenum Press. (Reprinted from Journal of Social Issues, 1978, 34[1], 108-121)

Male roles and the male experience [Special issue]. (1978). Journal of Social Issues, 34(1).

Man's role in the family [Special issue]. (1979). The
     Family Coordinator: Journal of Education, Counseling
     and Services, 28(4).

Oakland, T. (1983). Divorced fathers: Reconstructing a
     viable life. New York: Human Sciences Press.

Pleck, J. H. (1978). Men's traditional perceptions and
     attitudes about women: Correlates of adjustment or
     maladjustment. Psychological Reports, 42(3, P.1),
     975-983.

Pleck, J. H. (1981). The myth of masculinity. Cambridge,
     MA: MIT Press.

Pleck, J. H., & Brannon, R. (1978). Male roles and male
     experience [Special issue]. Journal of Social Issues,
     34(1), 1-4.

Pleck, J. H., & Sawyer, J. (Eds.) (1974). Men and
     masculinity. Englewood Cliffs, NJ: Prentice-Hall.

Ross, J. M. (1979). Fathering: A review of some
     psychoanalytic contributions of paternity.
     International Journal of Psychoanalysis, 60, 317-327.

     Ross traces psychoanalysis' gradual appreciation of
     the father's facilitative impact on children's growth.
     Using a developmental ego psychology frame, he points
     to issues of the difference between the father's rela-
     tionship with sons and with daughters and the impact
     the father's character and fantasies have on his
     children.

Spender, D. (Ed.). (1981). Men's studies modified: The
     impact of feminism on the academic disciplines. New
     York: Pergamon.

Spieler, S. (1984). Preoedipal girls need fathers.
     Psychoanalytic Review, 71(1), 63-68.

     Spieler suggests that the father is critically
     important to preoedipal female development and

discusses the likely impact on adult female development of a father's lack of involvement in the early
care of his daughter. She cites clinical material and
findings of observational research.

Tessman, L. H. (1982). A note on the father's contribution
to the daughter's way of loving and working. In S. H.
Cath, A. R. Gurwitt, & J. M. Ross (Eds), Father and
child. Boston: Little, Brown & Co.

Tessman suggests that the father helps the daughter
transform excitement into initiative and vitality in
work and "into tolerance for experiencing her passions
profoundly in love." Some clinical material is cited.

D. Latency (7-12 years)

Sex role differentiation continues in latency years. At
this developmental stage the environmental influences of the
socialization process dominate over biology.   This period
is currently receiving acknowledgement as an active developmental stage.   (N.A.)

1. Psychosexual Development

Best, R.   (1983).   We've all got scars: What boys and girls
      learn in elementary school. Bloomington, IN: Indiana
      University Press.

Clower, V. L. (1977).   Theoretical implications in current
      views of masturbation in latency girls. In H. Blum
      (Ed.), Female psychology: Contemporary-psychoanalytic
      views (pp. 109-125). New York: International
      Universities Press.

      Current views of masturbation in latency girls are
      evolved from direct observation and clinical work with
      children and from recollections of adult women. The
      classical Freudian theory--the girl's discovery of her
      lack of a penis causes her to turn away from self-
      stimulation--is not supported. When such a repression
      of satisfying masturbatory activity and fantasy does
      occur, it is seriously pathological.

Erikson, E. (1968). Womanhood and the inner and outer
      space. In Identity, youth and crisis (pp. 261-294).
      New York: W. W. Norton.

      Erikson attempts to combine his neo-Freudian social
      views of personality with the anatomical view of sex
      differences postulated by Freud. Based on some
      studies of eleven and twelve year old boys and girls
      who were asked to construct an exciting movie scene,
      Erikson concludes that women, by virtue of having
      wombs, are more concerned with inner space, i.e., home

and family.   As an artist, Erikson sees the field, or
arena, of creative production as an extension of the
body self.

Fraiberg, S. (1972). Some characteristics of genital
    arousal and discharge in latency girls. The
    Psychoanalytic Study of the Child, 27, 439-475.

    Fraiberg reports on genital sensations in two latency
    girls in analysis. She does not find in these cases a
    flight   from masturbation and genital excitement
    because of disgust or disappointment in the clitoris.
    Furthermore, where a latency girl has abandoned mas-
    turbation, there is evidence of a hysterical (genital)
    anesthesia.

Silverman, M. (1982). The latency period. In D. Mendell
    (Ed.), Early female development: Current
    psychoanalytic views (pp. 203-226). New York:
    SP Medical and Scientific Books.

    Silverman portrays the intense fantasy and inter-
    personal life of the latency girl and points to ways
    she used her evolving ego apparatus, independence and
    reality testing to correct early distortions about
    deprivation and damage and to compensate for oedipal
    loss.

2. Intellectual Functioning

Durden-Smith, J., & Desimone, D. (1983). Sex and the brain. New York: Arbor House.

Maccoby, E. E. (1966). Sex differences in intellectual functioning. In E. Maccoby (Ed.), The development of sex differences (pp. 25-55). Stanford, CA: Stanford University Press.

This review of studies of sex differences in intellectual functioning concentrates on verbal, numerical, spatial, and analytic ability; general intelligence; creativity; and achievement. Correlations are presented for intellectual performance and personality and socialization variables; explanations of performance differences between boys and girls are evaluated.

Maccoby, E. E., & Jacklin, C. N. (1973). Sex differences in intellectual functioning. In Assessment in a Pluralistic Society: Proceedings of the Educational Testing Service Invitational Conference on Testing Problems (pp. 37-51). Princeton, NJ: Educational Testing Service.

This selective review of the literature published since 1966 on sex differences in intellectual functioning emphasizes areas needing reconsideration and further research. To dispel misconceptions about intellectual sex differences, recent studies are compared. In the large, unselected samples of children very few sex differences in verbal skills appear between ages 3 to 11, but girls gain an advantage at adolescence. The majority of studies of math ability show no sex differences up to adolescence, but when differences are found in the age range 9 to 13, they tend to favor boys. In spatial ability sex differences remain minimal and inconsistent until approximately age 10 or 11, when boys score consistently higher on a wide range of tests. Examination of

social-emotional   factors has not yielded explanations
adequately tying either girls' verbal superiority or
boys' spatial and mathematical superiority to dif-
fering elements in their socialization or childhood
activities.

Wittig, M. A., & Petersen, A. C.   (1979).   Sex-related
     differences in cognitive functioning: Developmental
     issues.   New York: Academic Press.

E. Adolescence

Biological gender differentiation and socialization place
the adolescent girl in a conflict-laden experiential world
quite distinct from that of her male counterpart and quite
different from that of previous generations. (N.A.)

Brooks-Gunn, J., & Petersen, A. C. (Eds). (1983). Girls
    at puberty: Biological and psychological perspectives.
    New York: Plenum.

Brooks-Gunn, J., & Ruble, D. N. (1982). The experience of
    menarche from a developmental perspective. In J.
    Brooks-Gunn & Peterson (Eds.), Girls at puberty:
    Biological and psychosocial perspectives (pp.
    155-177). New York: Plenum Press.

Canter, R. J., & Ageton, S. S. (1984). The epidemiology of
    adolescent sex-role attitudes. Sex Roles, 11(7/8),
    657-676.

Connell, D. M., & Johnson, J. E. (1970). Relationships
    between sex-role identification and self-esteem in
    early adolescents. Developmental Psychology, 3(2),
    268.

Douvan, E. (1970). New sources of conflict in females at
    adolescence and early adulthood. In J. M. Bardwick,
    E. Donovan, M. S. Horner, & D. Gutmann (Eds.),
    Feminine personality and conflict (pp. 31-43).
    Belmont, CA: Brooks/Cole.

    In discussing the conflicts faced by girls at adoles-
    cence, she notes that there are "some that seem inti-
    mately related to the course of female development at
    this stage; other conflicts, and even the outcome of
    some of the biologically induced conflicts, seem to
    stem from a somewhat overspecialized, narrowly
    conceived set of sex-role expectations that are strin-
    gently imposed on adolescents in our culture." (from
    the authors' summary) (JSAS)

Englander, S. W. (1984). Some self-reported correlates of runaway behavior in adolescent females. <u>Journal of Consulting and Clinical Psychology</u>, <u>52</u>(3), 484-485.

Fu, V. R., Hinkle, D. E., & Korslund, M. K. (1983). A developmental study of ethnic self-concept among preadolescent girls. <u>Journal of Genetic Psychology</u>, <u>142</u>(1), 67-73.

Golub, S. (Ed.). (1984). Health care of the female adolescent [Special issue]. <u>Women and Health</u>, <u>9</u>(2/3).

Hawkey, L. (1970). Case study of an adolescent girl. <u>Journal of Analytic Psychology</u>, <u>15</u>(2), 138-147.

Heilbrun, A. B., Jr. (1964). Perceived maternal attitudes, masculinity-femininity of the maternal model and identification as related to incipient pathology in adolescent girls. <u>Journal of General Psychology</u>, <u>70</u>(1), 33-40.

Heilbrun, A. B., Jr. (1968). Sex-role identity in adolescent females: A theoretical paradox. <u>Adolescence</u>, <u>3</u>(9), 79-88.

Many studies on female identification are reviewed and the father's role in identity formation is considered. Dual identification with both expressive and instrumental role facilitates adjustment in the college environment. (Walstedt)

Homeless Youth Steering Committee. (1984). <u>Meeting the needs of homeless youth</u>. Albany, NY: New York State Council on Children and Families.

Kestenberg, J. S. (1961). Menarche. In S. Lorand & H. Schneer (Eds.), <u>Adolescents</u> (pp. 19-50). New York: Hoeber Press.

Konopka, G. (1966). <u>The adolescent girl in conflict</u>. Englewood Cliffs, NJ: Prentice-Hall.

Konopka, G. (1983). *Young girls: A portrait of adolescence*. New York: Haworth Press.

Leonard, M. (1966). Fathers and daughters: The significance of "fathering" in the psychosexual development of the girl. *International Journal of Psychoanalysis*, *47*(2-3), 325-334.

> Through clinical vignettes, this psychoanalytic paper examines the impact on female adolescents of absent, non-participating, possessive and seductive fathers.

Lerner, R. M., & Sorell, G. T., & Brackney, B. E. (1981). Sex differences in self-concept and self-esteem of late adolescents: A time-lag analysis. *Sex Roles*, *7*(7), 709-722.

Lieberman, F. (1973). Sex and the adolescent girl: Liberation or exploitation. *Clinical Social Work Journal*, *1*, 224-243.

Milner, E. (1949). Effects of sex role and social status on the early adolescent personality. *Genetic Psychology Monographs*, *40*, 231-325.

> This ambitious study demonstrated that major sex differences in personality had been established by adolescence. By this age girls often felt inferior and discouraged because they had to be concerned with social conformity to roles which were often in conflict with their inner desires. They had already suppressed overt impulse expression whereas boys of the same age were concerned with impulse control. There are also many other findings and descriptions of adolescents in the study.

Petersen, A. C. (1976). Physical androgyny and cognitive functioning in adolescence. *Developmental Psychology*, *12*, 524-533.

Petersen, A. C. (1979) Female pubertal development. In M. Sugar (Ed.), *Female adolescent development* (pp. 47-59). New York: Brunner/Mazel.

Petersen, A. C.   (1982).   A biopsychosocial perspective on
        sex differences in the human brain. The Behavioral
        and Brain Sciences, 2, 312.

Petersen, A. C.   (in press).   Pubertal development as a
        cause of disturbance: Myths, realities and unanswered
        questions. Journal of Genetic Psychology.

Rosenberg, F. R., & Simmons, R. G.   (1975).   Sex differences
        in the self-concept in adolescence. Sex Roles, 1,
        147-160.

Steinhorn, A.   (1979).   Lesbian adolescents in residential
        treatment. Social Casework Family Service of America,
        60(8), 494-498.

Sugar, M.   (1979).   Female adolescent development. New
        York: Brunner/Mazel.

        This volume provides a comprehensive view of normative
        female development. Complimentary views are presented
        from experts using different perspectives: biological
        issues; social issues; intrapsychic issues (including:
        the use of menstrual tampons and the rediscovery of
        the vagina, the changing body image, the development
        of autonomy, the superego, alterations in the ego-
        ideal). The important contribution of this book is
        its examining female adolescent development on its own
        terms rather than as a derivative of male development,
        thus allowing both male and female development to be
        explored and compared.

Tacts-Van Amerongen, S.   (1971).   The psychoanalysis of a
        young adolescent girl. Journal of the American
        Academy of Child Psychiatry, 10(1), 23-53.

Teenage parenting: Social determinants and consequences
        [Special issue]. (1980). Journal of Social Issues,
        36(1).

Warren, M. P.   (1983).   Physical and biological aspects of
        puberty. In J. Brooks-Gunn & A. C. Peteresen (Eds.),
        Girls at puberty: Biological and psychosocial perspectives
        (pp. 3-28). New York: Plenum Press.

Webb, A. P. (1963). Sex-role preferences and adjustment in
     early adolescents. Child Development, 34(3), 609-618.

Weber, D. P. (1976). Sex differences in cognition: A
     function of maturational rate? Science, 192, 572-574.

Weber, D. P. (1977). Sex difference in mental abilities,
     hemisphere lateralization, and rate of physical growth
     at adolescence. Developmental Psychology, 13, 29-33.

Weber, D. P. (in press). Physical maturation rate and
     cognitive performance in early adolescence: A
     longitudinal examination. Developmental Psychology.

Williams, J. H. (1973). Sex-role identification and
     personality functioning in girls: A theory revisited.
     Journal of Personality, 4(1), 1-8.

     Psychoanalytic theory posits that while psychologi-
     cally healthy females identify with passive, retiring
     traits, healthy males identify with dominant-ascen-
     dant traits. Williams' study of adolescent females
     provides no support for this theory. Two-thirds of
     the females identified with father, saw themselves as
     dominant-ascendant --and it was this group that was
     highest in personal adjustment. (JSAS)

F. Adulthood

The contemporary adult woman emerges from her biologically
innate gender identity and the socialization process with
qualitatively distinct characteristics which affect her
relationship to herself, significant others, her work and
society as a whole. (N.A.)

Al-Issa, I. (1980). The psychopathology of women.
     Englewood Cliffs, NJ: Prentice-Hall.

Al-Issa, I. (1983). Gender and psychopathology. New York:
     Academic Press.

American Psychiatric Association. (1984). Female
     friendships (Nonsexual relationships) 1979-84:
     Bibliography. Washington, DC: Author.

     (Can be ordered from the American Psychiatric Associa-
     tion, APA Library, 1400 K Street, N.W. Washington,
     D.C.)

Baker, S. W. (1980). Biological influences on human sex
     and gender. Signs, 6(1), 80-96.

Bardwick, J. M., Douvan, E., Horner, M. S., & Gutmann, D.
     (1970). Feminine personality and conflict. Belmont,
     CA: Brooks/Cole.

Bardwick, J. M. (1971). Psychology of women. New York:
     Harper & Row.

Barglow, P., & Schaefer, M. (1977). A new female
     psychology. In H. P. Blum (Ed.), Female psychology
     (pp. 393-438). New York: International Universities
     Press.

Barnett, R. C., & Baruch, G. K. (1978). Women in the
     middle years: A critique of research and theory.
     Psychology of Women Quarterly, 3(2), 187-197.

Baruch, G. K. (1984). The psychological well-being of women in the middle years. In G. Baruch & J. Brooks-Gunn (Eds.), Women in midlife (pp. 161-180). New York: Plenum Press.

Baruch, G. K., & Barnett, R. C. (1975). Implications and application of recent research on feminine development. Psychiatry, 38(4), 318-327.

Berman, P. W., & Ramey, E. R. (Eds.). (1982). Women: A developmental perspective. Washington, DC: National Institute of Health Publication No. 82-2298.

Bernard, J. (1981). The female world. New York: The Free Press.

Block, M. R., & Davidson, J. L., & Grambs, J. D. (1981). Women over forty: Visions and realities. New York: Springer.

Blum, H. P. (Ed.). (1977). Female psychology: Contemporary psychoanalytic views. New York: International Universities Press.

Brooks-Gunn, J., & Kirsh, B. (1984). Life events and the boundaries of midlife for women. In G. Baruch & J. Brooks-Gunn (Eds.), Women in midlife (pp. 11-30). New York: Plenum Press.

Carlson, R. (1971). Sex differences in ego functioning: Exploratory studies of agency and communion. Journal of Consulting and Clinical Psychology, 37(2), 267-277.

A series of two empirical studies and one literature review tested two related theoretical formulations of sex differences in personality: The first study tested D. Gutmann's formulation of ego functioning in the two sexes and D. Bakan's constructs of agency and communion. The second study tested the agency-communion formulation in conceptualizing sex differences in ego-functioning. The results supported the predicted sex differences. A review of the literature, which included abstracts relating to the development of sex differences, also supports the predicted sex difference in terms of the agency-communion formulation.

De Rosis, H. (1979). Women and anxiety. New York: Delacorte Press.

Dorr, D., & Friedenberg, L. (1984). Mothering and the young child. In A. U. Rickel, M. Gerrard, & I. Iscoe (Eds.), Social and psychological problems of women: Prevention and crisis intervention (pp. 45-60). New York: Hemisphere Publishing Co.

Eckenrode, J., & Gore, S. (1981). Stressful events and social supports: The significance of context. In B. Gottlieb (Ed.), Social networks and social support (pp. 43-68). Beverly Hills, CA: Sage.

Eichenbaum, L., & Orbach, S. (1983a). Understanding women: A feminist psychoanalytic approach. New York: Basic Books.

Eichenbaum, L., & Orbach, S. (1983b). What do women want: Exploring the myth of dependency. New York: Coward-McCann, Inc.

Erikson, E. H. (1964). The inner and outer self: Reflections on womanhood. Daedelus, 93, 582-606.

Fried, E. (1970). Active passive. New York: Grune & Stratton.

Frieze, I. H., Parsons, J. E., Johnson, P. B., Ruble, D. N., Zellman, G. L. (1978). Women and sex roles: A social psychological perspective. New York: W. W. Norton.

Giele, J. Z. (1982). Women in the middle years: Current knowledge and directions for research and policy. New York: John Wiley.

Gilbert, L. A., & Webster, P. (1982). <u>Bound by love: The sweet trap of daughterhood</u>. Boston: Beacon Press.

A critical look at the internal and external constraints which prevent women from developing self-realization.

Gilligan, C. (1979). Woman's place in man's life cycle. <u>Harvard Educational Review</u>, <u>49</u>(4), 431-446.

Gilligan, C. (1982). <u>In a different voice: Psychological theory and women's development</u>. Cambridge, MA: Harvard University Press.

Goldman, G. P., & Milman, D. S. (Eds.). (1969). <u>Modern woman: Her psychology and sexuality</u>. Springfield, IL: Charles C. Thomas.

This book is the product of a conference held at Adelphi University in which 31 mental health professionals, many of whom were female psychotherapists, spoke concerning female psychology. (JSAS)

Gorham, D. (1982). <u>The Victorian girl and the feminine ideal</u>. Bloomington, IN: University of Indiana Press.

Gullahorn, J. (Ed.). (1979). <u>Psychology and women: In transition</u>. Washington, DC: V. H. Winston.

A collection of eight scholarly articles, most of which are expanded versions of papers presented at the May 1977 conference on Perspectives on the Psychology of Women at Michigan State University. Focuses on three areas of psychology of women: (1) psychobiological research on sex differences, (2) socio-cultural influences on male-female relations and the family, (3) appraisals of the present state of the study of the psychology of women.

Haber, B. (1981). <u>The women's annual, 1980: The year in review</u>. Boston, MA: G. K. Hall.

Heckerman, C. L. (Ed.). (1980). The evolving female:
    Women in psychosocial context. New York: Human
    Sciences Press.

Heilbrun, C. G. (1979). Reinventing womanhood. New York:
    W. W. Norton.

Hendricks, M. C. (1984). Women, spirituality, and mental
    health. In L. E. Walker (Ed.), Women and mental
    health policy (pp. 95-116). Beverly Hills, CA: Sage
    Publications.

Henley, N. M. (1977). Body Politics: Sex and nonverbal
    communication. Englewood Cliffs, NJ: Prentice-Hall.

Hoffman, D. M., & Fidell, L. S. (1979). Characteristics of
    androgynous, undifferentiated, masculine, and feminine
    middle-class women. Sex Roles, 5(6), 765-781.

Kaplan, A. G., & Surrey, J. L. (1984). The relational self
    in women: Developmental theory and public policy. In
    L. E. Walker (Ed.), Women and mental health policy.
    Beverly Hills, CA: Sage Publications.

Lachman, M. E. (1984). Methods for a life-span
    developmental approach to women in the middle years.
    In G. Baruch & J. Brooks-Gunn (Eds.), Women in midlife
    (pp. 31-68). New York: Plenum Press.

Lerner, H. E. (1984). Early origins of envy and
    devaluation of women: Implications for sex-role
    stereotypes. In P. P. Rieker & E. Carmen (Eds.),
    The gender gap in psychotherapy: Social realities and
    psychological processes (pp. 111-124). New York:
    Plenum. (Reprinted from Bulletin of the Menninger
    Clinic, 1974, 38[6], 538-553)

Lerner, L. (Ed.). (1982). Women and individuation:
    Emerging views. New York: Human Sciences Press.

Lerner, L. (Ed.). (1982). Women and individuation [Special
    issue]. The Psychoanalytic Review, 69(1).

Lewin, M. (Ed.). (1984). In the shadow of the past: Psychology portrays the sexes. New York: Columbia University Press.

Long, J., & Porter, K. L. (1984). Multiple roles of midlife women: A case for new directions in theory, research and policy. In G. Baruch & J. Brooks-Gunn (Eds.), Women in midlife (pp. 109-159). New York: Plenum Press.

Lopata, H. A., & Barnewott, D. (1984). The middle years: Changes and variations in social-role commitments. In G. Baruch & J. Brooks-Gunn (Eds.), Women in midlife (pp. 83-108). New York: Plenum Press.

Lowe, M., & Hubbard, R. (Eds.). (1983). Woman's nature: Rationalizations of inequality. New York: Pergamon.

Mayo, C., & Henley, N. M. (Eds.). (1981). Gender and nonverbal behavior. New York: Springer.

McGuin, D. G. (Ed.). (1980). New research on women and sex roles. Ann Arbor: University of Michigan, Center for Continuing Education of Women.

McGuin, D. G. (Ed.). (1980). Women's lives: New theory, research and policy. Ann Arbor, MI: University of Michigan Press.

Mednick, M. T. S., Safir, M., Israel, D., & Bernard, J. (Eds.). (1984). Women's world: The new scholarship. New York: Praeger.

Miller, A. (1981). Prisoners of childhood: The drama of the gifted child and the search for the true self. New York: Basic Books.

Miller, A. (1984). Thou shalt not be aware. New York: Farrar, Strauss, and Giroux.

Miller, J. B. (1976). Toward a new psychology of women. Boston: Beacon Press.

Miller, J. B.   (1982).   Women and power: Some psychological dimensions (Work in Progress, Working Paper No. 1.). Wellesley, MA: The Stone Center for Developmental Studies at Wellesley College.

Moulton, R. (1977).   Some effects of the new feminism. American Journal of Psychiatry, 134(1), 1-6.

Notman, M. T. (1982). The psychology of women: A contemporary appraisal.   In A. Jacobson (Ed.), Psychoanalysis: Critical explorations in contemporary theory and practice. New York: Brunner/Mazel.

Notman, M. T., & Nadelson, C. C. (Series Editors). Women in context: Development and stresses. New York: Plenum.

Vol. 1.   Nadelson, C. C., & Notman, M. T. (Eds.). (1978). Sexual and reproductive aspects of women's health care.

Vol. 2.   Nadelson, C. C., & Notman, M. T. (Eds.). (1982a). Concepts of femininity and the life cycle.

Vol. 3.   Nadelson, C. C., & Notman, M. T. (Eds.). (1982b). Aggression, adaptations, and psychotherapy.

Vol. 4.   Kopp, C. B. (Ed.). (1979). Becoming female: Perspectives on development.

Vol. 5.   Kirkpatrick, M. (Ed.). (1980). Women's sexual development: Explorations of inner space.

Vol. 6.   Kirkpatrick, M. (Ed.). (1982). Women's sexual experience: Explorations of the dark continent.

Vol. 7.   Horner, M. S., Nadelson, C. C., & Notman, M. T. (Eds.). (1983). The challenge of change: Perspectives on family, work and education.

Vol. 8. Baruch, G. K., & Brooks-Gunn, J. (Eds.). (1984). Women in midlife.

O'Leary, V. E. (Ed.). (1981). Special section of feminist research. Psychology of Women Quarterly, 5(4), 595-653.

O'Leary, V. E., Unger, R. K., & Wallston, B. S. (Eds.). (1985). Women, gender, and social psychology. Hillsdale, NJ: Lawrence Erlbaum Associates.

Parsons, J. E. (Ed.). (1980). The psychobiology of sex differences and sex roles. New York: McGraw-Hill.

Porcino, J. (1983). Growing older, getting better: A handbook for women in the second half of life. Boston: Addison Wesley.

Reese, M. (1982). Growing up: The impact of loss and change. In D. Belle (Ed.), Lives in stress: Women and depression (pp. 65-80). Beverly Hills, CA: Sage.

Rossi, A. S. (1980). Life-span theories and women's lives. Signs, 6(1), 4-32.

Rubin, L. B. (1984). Intimate strangers: Men and women together. New York: Harper and Row.

Russell, M. S. (1983). The female veteran population. (RSM 70-84-1). Washington, DC: Office of Reports and Statistics, Veterans Administration.

Russianoff, P. (Ed.). (1981). Women in crisis. New York: Human Sciences Press.

Safilios-Rothschild, C. (Ed.). (1981). Relationships [Special issue]. Psychology of Women, 5(3).

Seiden, A. M. (1976). Overview: Research on the psychology of women II. Women in families, work and psychotherapy. American Journal of Psychiatry, 133(10), 1111-1123.

Sherif, C. W. (1982). Needed concepts in the study of gender identity. Psychology of Women Quarterly, 6(4), 375-398.

Sherman, J. A. (1971). On the psychology of women. Springfield, IL: C. C. Thomas.

Sherman, J. A., & Beck, E. (Eds.). (1979). The prism of sex. Madison, WI: University of Wisconsin Press.

Sherman, J. A., & Denmark, F. (Eds.). (1978). The psychology of women: Future directions of research. New York: Psychological Dimensions.

Smelser, N. J., & Erikson, E. H. (1980). Themes of work and love in adulthood. Cambridge, MA: Harvard University Press.

Stimpson, C. R., & Person, E. S. (Eds.). (1980). Women: Sex and sexuality. Chicago: University of Chicago Press.

Stueve, A., & O'Donnell, L. (1984). The daughter of aging parents. In G. Baruch & J. Brooks-Gunn (Eds.), Women in midlife (pp. 203-225). New York: Plenum Press.

Turkel, A. R. (1980). The power dilemma of women. The American Journal of Psychoanalysis, 40(4), 301-311.

Unger, R. K. (1979a). Female and male: Psychological perspectives. New York: Harper & Row.

Unger, R. K. (1979b). Toward a redefinition of sex and gender. American Psychologist, 34(11), 1085-1094.

Unger, R. K., & Denmark, F. L. (1975). Women: Dependent or independent variable. New York: Psychological Dimensions.

Verbrugge, L. (1983). Multiple roles and physical health of women and men. Journal of Health and Social Behavior, 24(1), 16-30.

Veterans Administration Advisory Committee on Women
     Veterans. (1984). <u>Report of the Veterans
     Administration Advisory Committee on Women Veterans</u>.
     Washington, DC: Author.

Whiting, B. B. (1984). Problems of American middle-class
     women in their middle years: A comparative approach.
     In G. Baruch & J. Brooks-Gunn (Eds.), <u>Women in midlife</u>
     (pp. 261-273). New York: Plenum Press.

Williams, J. H. (1983). <u>Psychology of women: Behavior in a
     biosocial context</u> (2nd ed.). New York: W. W. Norton.

Witkin-Lanoil, G. (1984). <u>The female stress syndrome: How
     to recognize and live with it</u>. Boston: Newmarket Press.

PART III

SPECIAL ISSUES

Social scientists and psychotherapists have noted these issues in their attempts to emphasize the difficulties, conflicts and identities that have crystalized as women go through the process of adapting to new roles and opportunities in contemporary society. (N.A.)

A. Abortion

Cohen, M. B., & Parry, J. (1981). Abortion on demand: Policy and implementation. Health and Social Work, 6(1).

The authors trace the roots and analyze the policy implications of recent Supreme Court decisions on abortion. They argue for a strong social work commitment to making abortion an accessible alternative for all women in the US. (CSWE)

Comstock, B. S. (1983). Abortion: Psychosexual issues. In W. Fann & I. Karacan (Eds.), Phenomenology treatment of psychosexual disorders (pp. 157-163). New York: SP Medical and Scientific Books.

Gould, K. H. (1979). Family planning and abortion policy in the United States. Social Service Review, 53(3), 452-463.

This article describes a special group of women from all levels of society who formed child welfare organizations, proposed legislation and lobbied for its passage. (CSWE)

Joffe, C. (1979). Abortion work: Strains, coping
    strategies, policy implications. _Social Work_, _24_(6),
    485-490.

    The author describes the strains involved in abortion
    counseling and offers suggestions about formulating
    policy on abortion that will take these factors into
    account. (CSWE)

Luker, K. (1975). _Taking chances_. Berkeley, CA:
    University of California Press.

Luker, K. (1984). _Abortion and the politics of motherhood_.
    Berkeley, CA: University of California Press.

Russo, N. F., & David, H. P. (1983). _When children are
    unwanted_. Washington, DC: American Psychological
    Association.

B. Achievement

Applegarth, A. (1977). Some observations on work
     inhibitions in women. In H. Blum (Ed.), Female
     psychology: Contemporary psychoanalytic views (pp.
     251-268). New York: International Universities Press.

     The author points to dynamic issues that lead to work
     inhibitions: narcissistic conflict which results in
     preoccupation with risk of failure; conflicts around
     aggression with paralyzing guilt; reluctance in giving
     up dependent gratifications.

Bayes, M., & Newton, P. (1978). Women in authority: A
     sociopsychological analysis. Journal of Applied
     Behavioral Science, 14(1), 7-20.

Berenbaum, S., & Resnick, S. (1982). Somatic androgyny and
     cognitive abilities. Developmental Psychology, 18(3),
     418-423.

Birnbaum, J. A. (1975). Life patterns and self-esteem in
     gifted family oriented and career committed women. In
     M. T. Mednick, S. S. Tangri, & L. W. Hoffman (Eds.),
     Women and achievement: Social and motivational
     analyses (pp. 396-419). Washington, DC: Hemisphere.

Bremer, T. H., & Wittig, M. A. (1980). Fear of success: A
     personality trait or a response to occupational
     deviance and role overload? Sex Roles, 6(1), 27-46.

Cano, L., Solomon, S., & Holmes, D. S. (1984). Fear of
     success: The influence of sex, sex-role identity, and
     components of masculinity. Sex Roles, 10(5/6),
     341-346.

Clance, P. R. (1978). The imposter phenomenon in high
     achieving women: Dynamics and therapeutic intervention.
     Psychotherapy: Theory, Research and Practice, 15(3),
     241-247.

Crockett, L. J., & Petersen, A. C. (1984). Biology: Its role in gender-related educational experiences. In E. Fennema & M. J. Ayer (Eds.), Women and education: Equity or equality? (pp. 85-116). Berkeley, CA: McCutchan.

Deitch, I. (1984). A feminist approach to math-anxiety reduction. In C. M. Brody (Ed.), Women therapists working with women: New theory and process of feminist therapy (pp.144-156). New York: Springer.

Dweck, C. S., & Gilliard, D. (1975). Expectancy statements as determinants of reactions of failure: Sex differences in persistence and expectancy change. Journal of Personality and Social Psychology, 32(6), 1077-1084.

Entwisle, D. R., & Baker, D. P. (1983). Gender and young children's expectations for performance in arithmetic. Developmental Psychology, 19(2), 200-209.

Etaugh, C., & Riley, S. (1983). Evaluating competence of women and men: Effects of marital and parental status and occupational sex-typing. Sex Roles, 9(9), 943-952.

Ferber, M. A. (1982). Women and work: Issues of the 1980s. Signs, 8(2), 273-295.

Fogel, R., & Paludi, M. A. (1984). Fear of success and failure, or norms for achievement? Sex Roles, 10(5/6), 431-434.

Fox, L. H., Brody, L., & Tabin, D. (Eds.). (1980). Women and the mathematical mystique. Baltimore, MD: Johns Hopkins Press.

Friedman, M. (1982). Overcoming the fear of success. New York: Warner Books.

Fyans, L. J. (1980). Achievement motivation: Recent trends in theory and research. New York: Plenum.

Gilbert, L. A. (1984). Female development and achievement.
In A. U. Rickel, M. Gerrard, & I. Iscoe, (Eds.),
Social and psychological problems of women: Prevention
and crisis intervention (pp. 5-17). New York:
Hemisphere Publishing.

Gilbert, L. A., Gallessich, J. M., & Evans, S. L. (1983).
Sex of faculty role model and students' self-
perceptions of competency. Sex Roles, 9(5), 597-607.

Heilbrun, A. (1963). Sex-role identity and achievement
motivation. Psychological Reports, 12(2), 483-490.

The hypothesis tested and confirmed was that the
social role demands of college and the feminine sex-
typed role were to some extent incompatible and that
this resulted in sex-role confusion among college
females and among males with a more feminine identification. (Walstedt)

Horner, M. S. (1969). Fail bright women. Psychology
Today, 3(6), 36-38, 62.

Anticipation of success provokes anxiety in women and
is feared because it may mean loss of femininity and
hence loss of self-esteem.

Horner, M. S. (1972). Towards an understanding of
achievement-related conflict in women. Journal of
Social Issues, 28(2), 157-175.

The motive to avoid success is conceptualized within
the framework of expectancy-value theory of motivation. It is identified as an internal psychological
representative of the dominant societal stereotype
which views competence, independence, competition, and
intellectual achievement as qualities basically inconsistent with femininity even though positively related
to masculinity and mental health. The expectancy that
success in achievement-related situations will be
followed by negative consequences arouses fear of
success in otherwise achievement-motivated women which
then inhibits their performance and level of aspira-
tion. The incidence of fear of success is considered

tion. The incidence of fear of success is considered as a function of age, sex, and educational and occupational levels of subjects tested between 1964 and 1971. Impairment of the educational and interpersonal functioning of those high in fear of success is noted and consequences for both the individual and society are discussed. (AUTHOR ABSTRACT)

Horner, M. S. (1981). Femininity and successful achievement: A basic inconsistency. In J. M. Bardwick, E. Douvan, M. S. Horner, & D. Gutman (Eds.), Feminine personality and conflict (pp. 45-74). Westport, CT: Greenwood Press.

Hustin-Stein, A. E., & Wiggins, A. (1978). Development of females from childhood through adulthood: Career and feminine role orientation. In P. S. Baltes (Ed.), Life-span development and behavior (pp. 258-297). New York: Academic Press.

Kaufman, D. R., & Richardson, B. L. (1982). Achievement and women: Challenging the assumptions. New York: Free Press.

Organized around the four main stages of the female life cycle, the structure of the book illustrates one of its principal tenets: achievement must be examined as part of a lifelong process. This important book examines the intrapsychic process of acquiring and maintaining the motive to achieve; the socialization literature that stresses the relationship of early gender learning to later success; the economic impact of industrialization on the sexual division of labor; the special problems faced by professional women; the way achievement is affected by longevity and mobility and by the gradual reduction of fertility; the current literature on women and the family, marriage, divorce, remarriage, and widowhood.

Kerson, T. S., & Alexander, L. B. (1979). Strategies for success: Women in social service administration. Administration in Social Work, 3(3), 313-326.

This article describes specific strategies through which administrators can bring women into social service management. (CSWE)

Krueger, D. W. (1984). Success and the fear of success in women. New York: The Free Press.

Lenney, E., Gold, J., & Browning, C. (1983). Sex differences in self-confidence: The influence of comparison to others' ability level. Sex Roles, 9(9), 925-942.

Linn, M., & Petersen, A. C. (in press). Meta-analyses of gender differences in spatial ability. In J. Hyde & M. Linn (Eds.), The psychology of gender: Advances through meta-analysis. Baltimore, MD: Johns Hopkins University Press.

Manley, R. O. (1977). Parental warmth and hostility as related to sex differences in children's achievement orientation. Psychology of Women Quarterly, 1(3), 229-246.

Mednick, M. T. S. (1976). Women and achievement. Washington, DC: Hemisphere Publishing Co.

Mednick, M. T. S., Tangri, S. S., & Hoffman, L. W. (Eds.). (1975). Women and achievement: Social and motivational analyses. New York: Halstead Press.

National Science Foundation. (1984). Women and minorities in science and engineering. Unpublished manuscript.

Newcombe, N. (1982). Sex-related differences in spatial ability: Problems and gaps in current approaches. In M. Potegal (Ed.), Spatial abilities: Development and physiological foundations (pp. 223-250). New York: Academic Press.

O'Connell, A. N., & Russo, N. F. (Eds.). (1980). Models
     of achievement: Eminent women in psychology [Special
     issue]. Psychology of Women Quarterly, 5(1).

O'Connell, A. N., & Russo, N. F. (Eds.). (1983). Models
     of achievement: Reflections of eminent women in
     psychology. New York: Columbia University Press.

Pasquella, M. J., Mednick, M. T. S., & Murray, S. R.
     (1981). Causal attributions for achievement outcomes:
     Sex-role identity, sex, and outcome comparisons.
     Psychology of Women Quarterly, 5(4), 586-590.

Parsons, J. E., Adler, T. F., & Kaczala, C. M. (1982).
     Socialization of achievement attitudes and beliefs:
     Classroom influences. Child Development, 53(2), 322-
     339.

Person, E. S. (1982). Women working: Fears of failure,
     deviance and success. Journal of the American Academy
     of Psychoanalysis, 10(1), 67-84.

     Looking at work inhibitions from intersecting frames
     of reference (role conflicts, ambition without clear-
     cut goals, fear of failure, fear of deviance, fear of
     success, special problems among successful women),
     Person concludes that contrary to Freud's view it is
     ambivalence toward the mother, not penis envy, that is
     the source of work inhibitions for women.

Reinharz, S. (1984). Women as competent community builders:
     The other side of the coin. In A. U. Rickel, M.
     Gerrard, & I. Iscoe, (Eds.), Social and psychological
     problems of women: Prevention and crisis intervention
     (pp. 19-43). New York: Hemisphere Publishing.

Romer, N. (1977). Sex-related differences in the
     development of the motive to avoid success, sex role
     identity, and performance in competitive and non-
     competitive conditions. Psychology of Women Quarterly,
     1(3), 260-272.

Schecter, D.   (1979).   Fear of success in women: A
       psychodynamic reconstruction.   <u>Journal of the American
       Academy of Psychoanalysis</u>, <u>7</u>, 33-43.

       Schecter uses clinical data to support her thesis that
       success is unconsciously perceived for many women as
       causing a breach on the primary dyadic bond with the
       pre-oedipal mother.

Schlossberg, N. K.   (1984).   The midlife woman as student.
       In G. Baruch & J. Brooks-Gunn (Eds.), <u>Women in midlife</u>
       (pp. 315-339).   New York: Plenum Press.

Schnitzer, P. K.   (1977).   The motive to avoid success:
       Exploring the nature of the fear.   <u>Psychology of Women
       Quarterly</u>, <u>1</u>(3), 273-282.

Sex differences in causal attributions for success and
       failure: A current assessment [Special issue]. (1982).
       <u>Sex Roles</u>, <u>8</u>(4).

Sherman, J. A.   (1976).   Social values, femininity and the
       development of female competence.   <u>Journal of Social
       Issues</u>, <u>32</u>(3), 181-195.

Stake, J. E.   (1979).   The ability/performance dimension of
       self-esteem: Implications for women's achievement
       behavior.   <u>Psychology of Women Quarterly</u>, <u>3</u>(4),
       365-377.

Tresemer, D.   (1976).   The cumulative record of research on
       "fear of success."   <u>Sex Roles</u>, <u>2</u>(3), 217-236.

Veroff, J.   (1977).   Process vs. impact in men's and women's
       achievement motivation.   <u>Psychology of Women Quarterly</u>,
       <u>1</u>(3), 283-293.

C. Adoption

Benet, M. K. (1976). _The politics of adoption_. New York: The Free Press.

Deykin, E. Y., Campbell, L., & Patti, P. (1984). The postadoption experience of surrendering parents. _American Journal of Orthopsychiatry_, 54(2), 271-280.

Lifton, B. J. (1973). _Lost and found: The adoption experience_. New York: Dial Press.

Pannor, R., Baran, A., & Sorosky, A. D. (1978). Birth parents who relinquished babies for adoption revisited. _Family Process_, 17(3), 329-337.

Rynearson, E. K. (1982). Relinquishment and its maternal complications: A preliminary study. _American Journal of Psychiatry_, 139(3), 338-340.

Silverman, P. R. (1981). _Helping women cope with grief_. Beverly Hills, CA: Sage Publications.

Sorosky, A. D. et al. (1978). _The adoption triangle: The effects of the sealed record on adoptees, birth parents, and adoptive parents_. Garden City, NY: Anchor/Doubleday.

D. Aggression

Bernardez, T. (1978). Women and anger: Conflicts with aggression in contemporary women. _Journal of the American Medical Women's Association_, _33_, 215-219.

Bloom, L., Coburn, K., & Pearlman, J. (1975). _The new assertive woman_. New York: Delacorte.

Frodi, A., Macaulay, J., & Thome, P. R. (1977). Are women always less aggressive than men? _Psychological Bulletin_, _84_(4), 634-660.

Green, A. (1972). Aggression, femininity, paranoia, and reality. _International Journal of Psychoanalysis_, _53_(2), 205-211.

This article is a paper read at the 27th International Psychoanalytic Congress. In it Green discusses the problem of the integration of aggressive drives in women in comparison to men. Sharing certain aggressive activities with men, the new role of women is noted, but attenuation of the differences between sexes is viewed as superficial. Psychological differences from childhood are analyzed in terms of the antagonism between erotic and destructive drives, and the disparity of identifications reflecting sexual difference. The role of the mother-fixation in female sexuality is discussed with emphasis on anatomical considerations. He concludes that the notions of sexual destiny and sexual reality are central to the problem.

Lerner, H. E. (1980). Internal prohibitions against female anger. _American Journal of Psychoanalysis_, _40_(2), 137-148.

Lerner, H. E. (1985). _The dance of anger_. New York: Harper and Row.

Lewittes, H. J., & Bem, S. L. (1983). Training women to be more assertive in mixed-sex task-oriented discussions. _Sex Roles_, _9_(5), 581-596.

Miller, J. B. (1983). <u>The construction of anger in women and men</u> (Working paper No. 1). Wellesley, MA: Stone Center Work in Progress, Wellesley College.

Nadelson, C. C., & Notman, M. T. (1982). <u>Aggression, adaptations, and psychotherapy</u>. New York: Plenum.

In the third volume of Notman and Nadelson's "Women in context: Development and stresses" series, there are papers providing a theoretical discussion of aggression, which provides a background for the presentation of patterns of aggression and violence affecting women, as well as papers showing the connection between physical and emotional symptoms and indirect expressions of aggression.

Rickles, N. K. (1971). The angry woman syndrome. <u>Archives of General Psychiatry</u>, <u>24</u>(1), 91-94.

Travis, C. (1982). <u>Anger</u>. New York: Simon & Schuster.

Zillman, D. (1984). <u>Connections between sex and aggression</u>. Hillsdale, NJ: Lawrence Erlbaum Associates.

E. Day Care and Maternal Employment

Belsky, J., Steinberg, L. D., & Walker, A. (1981). The ecology of day care. In M. Lamb (Ed.), Childrearing in nontraditional families. Hillsdale, NJ: Lawrence Erlbaum Associates.

Bronfenbrenner, U., & Crouter, A. C. (1982). Work and family through time and space. In S. B. Kamerman & C. D. Hayes (Eds.), Families that work: Children in a changing world. Washington, DC: National Academy Press.

Children's Defense Fund (1982). Employed parents and their children: A data book. Washington, DC: Author.

Dunlop, K. H. (Ed.). (1981). Maternal employment and child care [Special issue]. Professional Psychology, 12(1).

Hoffman, L. W. (1979). Maternal employment. American Psychologist, 34(10), 859-865.

Hoffman, L. W., & Nye, F. I. (1975). Working mothers. San Francisco: Jossey-Bass.

Hoffman, L. W. (1982). Maternal employment and the young child. Unpublished manuscript, Minnesota Symposium on Child Psychology.

Kamerman, S. B., & Hayes, C. D. (Eds.). (1982). Families that work: Children in a changing world. Washington, DC: National Academy Press.

Kamerman, S. B., & Kahn, A. J. (1981). Child care family benefits and working parents: A study in comparative policy. New York: Columbia University Press.

Kamerman, S. B., & Kingston, P. W. (1982). Employer responses to the family responsibilities of employees. In S. B. Kamerman & C. D. Hayes (Eds.), Families that work: Children in a changing world (pp. 144-208). Washington, DC: National Academy Press.

Piotrkowski, C. S. (1979). Work and the family system: A naturalistic study of working-class and lower middle-class families. New York: The Free press.

Piotrkowski, C. S., Rapoport, R., & Rapoport, R. (in press). Families and work: An evolving field. In M. Sussman & S. K. Steinmetz (Eds.), Handbook of marriage and the family (2nd ed.). New York: Plenum.

Zigler, E. F., & Gordon, E. W. (Eds.). (1982). Day care: Scientific and social policy issues. Boston: Auburn.

F. Dependency-Autonomy

Bernay, T. (1982). Separation and the sense of competence-loss in women. *American Journal of Psychoanalysis*, <u>42</u>(4), 293-305.

Dowling, C. (1981). <u>The Cinderella complex</u>. New York: Summit Books.

Dowling, through analysis of case studies, presents the thesis that equality of the sexes is hampered by a learned dependency that goes with growing up female. While her attention to the issue of dependency needs in the relationship between men and women is an important contribution, without a psychoanalytic base she often confuses economic dependence with emotional dependence and, therefore, limits the elucidation of the complexities of dependency needs in men and women.

Eichenbaum, L., & Orbach, S. (1983). <u>What do women want</u>: <u>Exploring the myth of dependency</u>. New York: Coward-McCann.

Drawing on object relations theory, the authors interweave theory with stories of men and women. They illustrate how men and women have been taught to deal with dependency in radically different ways. They see women as being schooled to be <u>depended</u> <u>upon</u> and as providing the basic support of others -- children, husbands. Emotional support is returned only symbolically through economic support or physical protection of a man. On the other hand, while men are taught to act independently, they learn there will always be a woman they can lean on emotionally. This book provides a new look at the issue of dependency with its complexities in men and women as they relate to each other.

Lerner, H. E. (1984). Female dependency in context: Some
    theoretical and technical considerations. In P. P.
    Rieker & E. Carmen (Eds.), The gender gap in
    psychotherapy: Social realities and psychological
    processes (pp. 125-134). New York: Plenum.
    (Reprinted from American Journal of Orthopsychiatry,
    1983, 53[4], 697-705)

Nadelson, C. C., & Polonsky, D. C. (Eds.). (1984).
    Marriage and divorce: A contemporary persepctive. New
    York: Guilford Press.

Post, R. D. (1982). Dependency conflicts in high achieving
    women: Towards an integration. Psychotherapy, Theory,
    Research, Practice, 19(1), 82-87.

Relationships [Special issue]. (1981). Psychology of Women
    Quarterly, 5(3).

Russianoff, P. (1982). Why do I think I am nothing without
    a man. New York: Bantam Books.

Shainess, N. (1982). Antigone: The neglected daughter of
    Oedipus: Freud's gender concepts in theory. Journal
    of the American Academy of Psychoanalysis, 10(3),
    443-455.

    The author refutes Freud's idea that women have weaker
    superegos than men because: (a) women as producers of
    life, nurturers, are more likely to value life and (b)
    gender differences, beyond the biological ones, are
    culturally rather than instinctually formed. Antigone
    is given as an example of autonomy and ethical pur-
    pose, not narcissistically self-involved. Shainess
    feels that Freud overlooked an important personality
    type in Antigone.

Stiver, I. (1984). The meaning of "dependency" in female-
    male relationships. (Work in Progress, Working Paper
    No. 11). Wellesley, MA: The Stone Center for
    Developmental Studies at Wellesley College.

G. Depression

Atkinson, A. K., & Rickel, A. U. (1984). Depression in women: The postpartum experience. In A. U. Rickel, M. Gerrard, & I. Iscoe (Eds.), Social and psychological problems of women: Prevention and crisis intervention (pp. 197-218). New York: Hemisphere Publishing.

Bart, P. B. (1971). Depression in middle-aged women. In V. Gornick & B. Moran (Eds.), Women in sexist society: Studies in power and powerlessness (pp. 163-186). New York: Basic Books.

Bart, a sociologist, describes interviews with 20 women hospitalized for depression. These were all middle-aged women whose children had grown up, married or left home. She posits that the loss of meaning when the mothering role is over is a prime cause of depression in middle-aged women.

Belle, D. (1982). Lives in stress: Women and depression. Beverly Hills, CA: Sage.

Belle, D. (1980). Fighting stress and depression: Exemplary programs for low-income mothers. Cambridge, MA: Stress and Families Project, Harvard University.

Bernard, J. (1976). Homosociality and female depression. Journal of Social Issues, 32(4), 213-238.

Berndt, D. J., & Berndt, S. M. (1984). Reply to "Comments on 'Attributional styles for helplessness and depression'." Sex Roles, 10(7/8), 559-562.

Brown, G. W., & Harris, T. (1978). The social origins of depression: A study of psychiatric disorder in women. New York: Free Press.

Costello, C. G. (1982). Social factors associated with depression: A retrospective community study. Psychological Medicine, 12(2), 329-339.

Deykin, E. Y., Jacobson, S., Klerman, G. L., & Solomon, M.
     (1966). The empty nest: Psychosocial aspects of
     conflict between depressed women and their grown
     children. American Journal of Psychiatry, 22(12),
     1422.

     The empty nest syndrome refers to a pattern of reac-
     tions occurring when the active maternal role termi-
     nates as the children move out of the home. As the
     active child-rearing phase ends, the formerly full-
     time mother must seek a new role, new interests and
     new gratifications. Until and unless this occurs,
     depression may result. In this study, 9 out of 15
     patients (60%) became depressed when the last child,
     or the youngest child left home. (JSAS)

Formanek, R. (1983, August). Depression and children.
     Paper presented at the meeting of the American
     Psychological Association, Anneheim, California.

     This paper contends that depression is more prevalent
     among women than men. Psychoanalytic views of penis
     envy suggest that girls tend toward depressive mood,
     but available statistics show that depressions are
     approximately equally distributed between boys and
     girls. Having thus disputed the psychoanalytic link-
     age between penis envy and depression in women,
     Formaneck suggests instead that the prevalence of
     women's depressions appears to be contributed to both
     socio-economic deficits (or precipitant factors) and
     intrapsychic and cognitive powerlessness and helpless-
     ness (susceptibility factors) which play a role in
     adulthood but not in childhood.

Hamilton, J. A., Lloyd, C., & Alagna, S. W. (1984).
     Gender, depressive subtypes and gender-age effects on
     antidepressant response: Hormonal hypotheses.
     Psychopharmacology Bulletin, 20(3), 475-480.

Hamilton, J. A., Alagna, S. W., & Sharpe, K. (In press).
     Cognitive approaches to the evaluation and treatment
     of premenstrual depression. In H. Osofsky (Ed.),
     Washington, DC: American Psychiatric Association
     Press.

Huesmann, L. R. (Ed.). (1978). Learned helplessness as a model of depression [Special issue]. _Journal of Abnormal Psychology, 87_(1).

Kleinke, C. L., Staneski, R. A., & Mason, J. K. (1982). Sex differences in coping with depression. _Sex Roles, 8_(8), 877-889.

Klerman, G. L., & Weissman, M. M. (1980). Depressions among women: Their nature and causes. In M. Guttentag, S. Salasin, & D. Belle (Eds.), _The mental health of women_ (pp. 57-92). New York: Academic Press.

Mathew, R. J., & Weinman, M. L. (1982). Sexual dysfunctions in depression. _Archives of Sexual Behavior, 11_(4), 323-328.

Mulvey, A., & Dohrenwend, B. (1983). The relationship of stressful life events to gender. _Issues in Mental Health Nursing, 5_(1-4), 219-237.

Pearlin, L. (1975). Sex roles and depression. In N. Datan, & L. Ginsberg (Eds.), _Life span developmental psychology: Normative life crises_. New York: Academic Press.

Peterson, C., & Villanova, P. (1984). Comments on "Attributional styles for helplessness and depression." _Sex Roles, 10_(7/8), 555-557.

Radloff, L. S. (1977) Sex differences in depression: The effects of occupation and marital status. _Sex Roles, 1_(3), 249-265.

Radloff, L. S. (1980a). Depression and the empty nest. _Sex Roles, 6_(6), 775-781.

Radloff, L. S. (1980b). Risk factors for depression: What do we learn from them? In M. Guttentag, S. Salasin, & D. Belle (Eds.), _The mental health of women_ (pp. 93-109). New York: Academic Press.

Radloff, L. S., & Cox, S. (1981). Sex differences in depression in relation to learned susceptibility. In S. Cox (Ed.), Female psychology: The emerging self (2nd ed.) (pp.334-363). New York: St. Martin's Press.

Robertson, J. (1980). A treatment mosdel for post-partum depression. Canada's Mental Health, 28(2), 16-17.

Savage, M. (1975). Addicted to suicide: A woman struggling to live. Santa Barbara, CA: Capra Press.

This book, written by the author of four novels, has an intensely personal and revealing confessional quality, similar to the tone of Plath's The Bell Jar. The book consists of 2 parts. In Part 1, Savage describes her continual attempts to end her life. Part 2 was written 7-8 months later when the confusion was ending and a new integration occurring. Fascinating. (JSAS)

Scarf, M. (1980). Unfinished business. New York: Doubleday.

Seligmann, M. E. (1974). Depression and learned helplessness. In Friedman & Katz (Eds.), The psychology of depression: Contemporary theory and research (pp. 83-113). Washington, DC: Winston.

Sobel, S. B., & Russo, N. F. (Eds.). (1981). Sex roles, equality, and mental health [Special issue]. Professional Psychology, 12(1).

Spiegel, R. (1969). Depressions and the feminine situation. In G. D. Goldman & D. S. Milman (Eds.), Modern woman: Her psychology and sexuality (pp.189-209). Springfield, IL: Charles C. Thomas.

Standish, C. (1956). Manic-depressive psychosis in a woman. In H. Weinberg & A. W. Hire (Eds.), Casebook in abnormal psychology (pp.305-320). New York: Knopf.

Stein, L., Del Gaudio, A. C., & Ansley, M. Y. (1976). A comparison of female and male neurotic depressives. Journal of Clinical Psychology, 32(1), 19-21.

Stewart, A., & Salt, P. (1981). Life stress, life-styles, depression and illness in adult women. _Journal of Personality and Social Psychology, 40_(6), 1063-1069.

Tinsley, E. G., Sullivan-Guest, S., & McGuire, J. M. (1984). Feminine sex role and depression in middle-aged women. _Sex Roles, 11_(1/2), 25-32.

Weissman, M. M. (1972). The depressed woman: Recent research. _Social Work, 17_(5), 19-35.

In comparison with a control group, depressed women showed diminished functioning in all of their roles -- sexual, marital, and parental; furthermore, these women felt resentment and guilt regarding their husbands and children and had difficulty in communicating with them, or sharing their feelings. While drug therapy was helpful on a short-term basis, psychological intervention was required in order to restore good social functioning. (JSAS)

Weissman, M. M., & Klerman, G. L. (1973). Psychotherapy with depressed women: An empirical study of content, themes and reflection. _The British Journal of Psychiatry, 123_(572), 55-61.

Weissman, M. M., & Klerman, G. L. (1977). Sex differences and the epidemiology of depression. _Archives of General Psychiatry, 34_(1), 98-111.

Weissman, M. M., & Klerman, G. L. (1977). Sex differences and the epidemiology of depression. In E. S. Gomberg, & V. Franks (Eds.), _Gender and disordered behavior_ (pp. 381- 425). New York: Brunner/Mazel. (Reprinted from _Archives of General Psychiatry,_ 1977, _34,_ 98-11)

Weissman, M. M., & Paykel, E. S. (1974). _The depressed woman: A study of social relationships._ Chicago: University of Chicago Press.

Over a period of 20 months, Weissman and Paykel studied the behavior of 40 depressed women during the acute phase, recovery and, in some cases, recurrence.

Systematic examination was made of the life experiences and social adjustment of the women, and the impact of depression on relations with others in their social milieu -- including spouse, neighbors, children, and work associates. A control group of nondepressed women was employed, in which the attempt was made to control for such factors as race, social class, religion, physical health and age. In comparison with the norms provided by the control group, the emerging picture was one of impairment in social relations which affected the woman's ability to communicate and have a satisfactory emotional life beyond the acute phase. (JSAS)

Weissman, M. M., Paykel, E. S., & Klerman, G. L. (1972). The depressed woman as a mother. Social Psychiatry, 7(2), 98-108.

Two studies were presented of mothering behavior among acutely depressed women. One study consisted of a longitudinal-clinical investigation of the degree of impairment in mothering by depressed women, and in the second, a comparison was made of the mothering behavior of the depressed women in comparison with a control group of nondepressed women. (JSAS)

Weissman, M. M., Pincus, C., Radding, N., Lawrence, R., & Siegel, R. (1973). The educated housewife: Mild depression and the search for work. American Journal of Orthopsychiatry, 43(4), 565-573.

One-third of the women who came to a career counseling center were depressed as the result of interrupted careers, role conflict, and/or geographical instability. It was suggested that emotional and social support be offered by such counseling centers. (JSAS)

H. Drugs and Alcohol

Anderson, S. C. (1984). Alcoholic women: Sex-role identification and perceptions of parental personality characteristics. Sex Roles, 11(3/4), 277-287.

Babcock, M. L., & Connor, B. (1981). Sexism and treatment of the female alcoholic: A review. Social Work, 26(3), 233-238.

This review of the literature documents how women are overlooked in the planning and evaluation of alcoholic treatment and are victims of sexist therapy. (CSWE)

Bateman, N., Peterson, I., & David, M. (1972). Factors related to outcome of treatment for hospitalized white males and female alcoholics. Journal of Drug Issues, 2(1), 66-74.

Beckman, L. J. (1978). Sex role conflict in alcoholic women: Myth or reality. Journal of Abnormal Psychology, 87(4), 408-417.

Belfer, M. L., Shader, R. I., Carroll, M., & Harmatz, J. S. (1971). Alcoholism in women. Archives of General Psychiatry, 25(6), 540.

Bry, B. H. (1984). Substance abuse in women: Etiology and prevention. In A. U. Rickel, M. Gerrard, & I. Iscoe, (Eds.), Social and psychological problems of women: Prevention and crisis intervention (pp. 253-272). New York: Hemisphere Publishing.

Burt, M. R., Glynn, T. S., & Sowder, B. J. (1979). Psychosocial characteristics of drug-abusing women. Washington, DC: U.S. Department of Health, Education and Welfare.

Burtle, V. (Ed.). (1979). Women who drink: Alcoholic experiences and psychotherapy. Springfield, IL: Charles C. Thomas.

Clarke, S. K. (1974). Self-esteem in men and women alcoholics. Quarterly Journal of Studies on Alcohol, 35(4), 1380-1381.

Cooperstock, R. (1971). Sex differences in the use of mood-modifying drugs: An explanatory model. Journal of Health and Social Behavior, 12(3), 238-244.

Corrigan, E. (1980). Alcoholic women in treatment. New York: Oxford University Press.

Curlee, J. (1969). Alcoholism and the "empty nest." Bulletin of the Menninger Clinic, 33(3), 165-171.

Curlee, J. (1970). A comparison of male and female patients at an alcoholic treatment center. The Journal of Psychology, 74(2), 239-247.

Cushey, W., Berger, J., & Densen-Gerber, J. (1981). Issues in the treatment of female addiction: A review and critique of the literature. In E. Howell, & M. Bayes (Eds.), Women and mental health (pp. 269-295). New York: Basic Books.

Durand, D. E. (1975). Effects of drinking on the power and affiliation needs of middle-aged females. Journal of Clinical Psychology, 31(3), 549-553.

Eldred, C. A., & Washington, M. N. (1975). Female heroin addicts in a city treatment program: The forgotten minority. Psychiatry, 38(1), 75-85.

This study was undertaken in response to the fact that there has existed an imbalance in our knowledge concerning male and female heroin addicts. Subjects were 79 male and 79 female clients of the District of Columbia methadone detoxification program. The females ranged in age from 20 to 29, whereas the males were primarily teenagers. The results of structured interviews indicated that males and females initiated drug abuse at similar ages, and both reported that the sex of their physician or counselor made no difference to them. Female addicts were typically unemployed, were receiving no financial assistance, were currently

unmarried, had children who might or might not be
living with them, wanted no more children in the
immediate future but typically were not using contra-
ception. In response to these results, Eldred and
Washington suggested that for female addicts, it may
be advisable to provide: (1) psychological support for
the mothers' parenting efforts, (2) assistance in
solving practical problems and securing services related to child rearing, and (3) provision of child
care services so that mothers may obtain adequate help
for themselves. (JSAS)

Ellinwood, E. H., Smith, W. G., & Vaillant, G. E. (1966).
Narcotics addiction in males and females: A
comparison. The International Journal of the
Addictions, 1(2), 33-45.

Fidell, L. S. (1977). Summary of psychotropic drug usage
among women (For President's Commission on Mental
Health). Northridge, CA: Psychology Department,
California State University.

Gomberg, E. S. (1974). Women and alcoholism. In V. Franks
& V. Burtle (Eds.), Women in therapy (pp. 169-190).
New York: Brunner/Mazel.

While alcoholism has been far more prevalent among men
than women, the gap appears to be narrowing. There
is virtually no information about women alcoholics who
are poor, black, lesbian, career women, and few on
older women. Most studies concern white, middle class
married females in their 30s and 40s. In regard to
these women, they appear to be individuals who have
strong needs for affection and support, and who "over
buy" into their marital and sexual roles in order to
obtain need satisfaction. When these needs aren't
met, they may turn to alcoholism, which may help them
achieve the goals of "oblivion, revenge, control,
self-destruction."

Gomberg, E. S. (1979). Problems with alcohol and other
drugs. In E. Gomberg & V. Franks (Eds.), Gender and
disordered behavior (pp. 204-240). New York: Brunner/
Mazel.

Gomberg, E. S. (1981). Women, sex roles and alcohol
     problems. _Professional Psychology, 12_(1), 146-155.

Gomberg, E. S. (1982). Historical and political perspec-
     tive: Women and drug use. _Journal of Social Issues,
     38_(2), 9-23.

Glynn, T. S., Pearson, H. W., & Sayers, M. (Eds.). (1983).
     Women and drugs. (Research Issues 31, ADM 83-1268).
     Washington, DC: U.S. Government Printing Office.

Hughes, R., & Brewin, R. (1979). _The tranquilizing of
     America: Pill popping and the American way of life_.
     New York: Harcourt Brace Jovanovich.

Kalant, O. (Ed.). (1980). _Alcohol and drug problems in
     women_. New York: Plenum.

Kinney, E. L., Trautmann, J., Gold, J. A., Vesell, E. S., &
     Zelis, R. (1981). Underrepresentation of women in
     new drug trials. _Annals of Internal Medicine, 95_(4),
     495-499.

Kinsey, B. A. (1966). _The female alcoholic: A social
     psychological study_. Springfield, IL: Charles C.
     Thomas.

Marsh, J. C., Colten, M. E., & Tucker, M. B. (Eds.).
     (1982). Women's use of drugs and alcohol: New
     perspectives [Special issue]. _Journal of Social
     Issues, 38_(2).

Morrissey, E., & Schuckit, M. (1977). Stressful life
     events and alcohol problems among women seen at a
     detoxification center. _Journal of Studies in
     alcoholism, 39_(9), 1559-1576.

National Institute on Alcohol Abuse and Alcoholism. (1980).
     Alcohol and women (DHEW Publication No. ADM 80-835).
     Washington, DC: U.S. Government Printing Office.

National Institute on Drug Abuse. (1983). <u>Women and drugs</u>
    (Research Issue No. 31). Washington, DC: U.S.
    Department of Health and Human Services.

Parker, F. B. (1972). Sex-role adjustment in women
    alcoholics. <u>Quarterly Journal of Studies on Alcohol</u>,
    <u>33</u>(3-A), 647-657.

Sandmaier, M. (1980). <u>The invisible alcoholics: Women and
    alcohol abuse in America</u>. New York: McGraw-Hill.

Schuckit, M. (1972). The woman alcoholic: A literature
    review. <u>Psychiatry in Medicine</u>, <u>3</u>(1), 37-43.

Stimmel, B. (1982). <u>Effects of maternal alcohol and drug
    abuse on the newborn</u>. New York: Haworth Press.

Swallow, J. (Ed.). (1984). <u>Out from under: Sober dykes
    and our friends</u>. San Francisco: Spinsters Ink.

Tamerin, J. (1978). Practical approaches to alcoholism
    psychotherapy. In <u>The psychotherapy of alcoholic women</u>
    (pp. 183-202). New York: Plenum Press.

Weiss, S., Buscher, M., Shannon, R., Sample, K., & Eidskess,
    P. (1984). <u>Alcohol, Drug Abuse and Mental Health
    Administration Women's Council Report to the
    Administrator: 1983-1984</u>. Washington, DC: U.S.
    Department of Health and Human Services.

Willack, S. C. (1973). Sex-role identity in female
    alcoholics. <u>Journal of Abnormal Psychology</u>, <u>82</u>,
    253-261.

I. Dual Careers

Bohen, H. H., & Viveros-Long, A. (1981). Balancing job and family life: Do flexible work schedules help? Philadelphia: Temple University Press.

Bryson, J. B., & Bryson, R. (Eds.). (1978). Dual-career couples [Special issue]. Psychology of Women Quarterly, 3(1).

Foster, M. A., Sallston, B. S., & Berger, M. (1980). Feminist orientation and job-seeking behavior among dual-career couples. Sex Roles, 6(1), 59-66.

Gilbert, L. A. (1985). Men in dual-career families: Current realities and future prospects. Hillsdale, NJ: Lawrence Erlbaum Associates.

Gray, J. D. (1983). The married professional woman: An examination of her role conflicts and coping strategies. Psychology of Women Quarterly, 7(3), 235-243.

McCartney, J. (1979). Dual-career families: A bibliography of relevant readings. Unpublished manuscript.

The bibliography is an annotated indexed listing developed for Catalyst (a national nonprofit organization that helps women choose, launch and advance their careers). It focuses on information that concerns the corporate world and the professional couple. Corporate practices and policies, sociological research, economic trends and forecasts, and child care are included.

Information can be obtained from the Career and Family Center at 14 East 60th Street, New York City.

Pepitone-Rockwell, F. (Ed.). (1980). Dual-career couples. Beverley Hills, CA: Sage.

Piotrkowski, C. S., & Crits-Cristoph, P. (1982). Women's jobs and family adjustment. In J. Aldous (Ed.), Two paychecks: Life in dual-career families. Beverly Hills, CA: Sage.

Rapoport, R., & Rapoport, R. (1971). Dual-career families. Baltimore, MD: Penguin.

Yogev, S. (1983). Judging the professional woman: Changing research, changing values. Psychology of Women Quarterly, 7(3), 219-234.

J. Eating Disorders

Eating Disorders are a predominantly female problem. The articles annotated and listed below were shared by the Center for the Study of Anorexia and Bulimia (1 West 91st. Street, New York, N.Y. 10024; [212] 595-3449). (N.A.)

a. Anorexia - Treatment Approaches

Psychotherapy

Bemis, K. M. (1974). Current approaches to the etiology and treatment of anorexia nervosa. American Psychological Association, 28, 593-617.

Benson, A., & Futterman, L. (1985). Psychotherapeutic partnering: An approach to the treatment of anorexia and bulimia. In Rev. S. W. Emmett (Ed.), Theory and treatment of anorexia nervosa and bulimia: Biomedical, sociocultural and psychological perspectives. New York: Brunner/Mazel.

Bruch, H. (1963). Effectiveness in psychotherapy, or the constructive use of ignorance. Psychiatric Quarterly, 37(2), 322-339.

Bruch, H. (1982). Anorexia nervosa: Therapy and theory. American Journal of Psychiatry, 139(12), 1531-1538.

Garner, D. M., Garfinkel, P. E., & Bemis, K. M. (1982). A multidimensional psychotherapy for anorexia nervosa. International Journal of Eating Disorders, 1(2), 3-46.

Geller, J. L. (1975). Treatment of anorexia nervosa by integration of behavior therapy and psychotherapy. Psychotherapy Psychosomatics, 26(3), 167-177.

Levenkron, S. A. (1982). Treating and overcoming anorexia nervosa. New York: Charles Scribner's Sons.

Parker, J., Blazer, D., & Wyrick, L. (1974). Anorexia
     nervosa: A combined therapeutic approach. Southern
     Medical Journal, 19, 449-452.

Piazza, E., Piazza, N., & Rollins, N. (1980). Anorexia
     nervosa: Controversial aspects of therapy.
     Comprehensive Psychiatry, 21(3), 177-189.

Pierloot, R., Wellens, W., & Houben, M. Elements of
     resistance to a combined medical and psychotherapeutic
     program in anorexia nervosa. Psychotherapy and
     Psychosomatics, 26, 317-324.

Thoma, H. (1977). On the psychotherapy of patients with
     anorexia nervosa. Bulletin of The Menninger Clinic,
     41(5), 437-452.

Tolstrup, K. (1975). The treatment of anorexia nervosa in
     childhood and adolescence. Journal of Child
     Psychology and Allied Disciplines, 16(1), 75-78.

Family Therapy

Aponte, H., & Hoffman, L. (1973). The open door: A
     structural approach to a family with an anorectic
     child. Family Process, 12(1), 1-44.

Barcai, A. (1971). Family therapy in the treatment of
     anorexia nervosa. American Journal of Psychiatry,
     128(3), 286-290.

Caille, P., Abrahamsen, P., Giholami, C., & Sorbye, B.
     (1977). A systems theory approach to a case of
     anorexia nervosa. Family Process, 16(4), 455-465.

Conrad, D. (1977). A starving family: An interactional
     view of anorexia nervosa. Bulletin of the Menninger
     Clinic, 41(5), 487-495.

Fishman, C. H. (1979). Family considerations in liaison
    psychiatry--a structural family approach to anorexia
    nervosa in adults. Psychiatric Clinic of North
    America, 2, 249-263.

Groen, J. J., & Feldman-Toledano, Z. (1966). Educative
    treatment of patients and parents in anorexia nervosa.
    British Journal of Psychiatry, 112(488), 671-681.

Palazzoli, M. S. (1970). The families of patients with
    anorexia nervosa. In E. J. Anthony & C. Kaupernik
    (Eds.), International yearbook of child psychiatry
    (Vol. 1). New York: Wiley-Interscience.

Behavior Modification

Agras, W. S., Barlow, D. H., Chapin, H., Abel, G., &
    Leitenberg, H. (1974). Behavioral modification of
    anorexia nervosa. Archives of General Psychiatry,
    30(3), 279-286.

Bhanji, S., & Thompson, T. (1974). Operant conditioning in
    the treatment of anorexia nervosa: A review and
    retrospective study of 11 cases. British Journal of
    Psychiatry, 124, 166-172.

Blinder, B. J., Freeman, D., & Stunkard, A. J. (1970).
    Behavior therapy of anorexia nervosa: Effectiveness of
    activity as a reinforcer of weight gain. American
    Journal of Psychiatry, 126(8), 1093-1098.

Bruch, H. (1974). Perils of behavior modification in
    treatment of anorexia nervosa. Journal of the
    American Medical Association, 230(10), 1419-1421.

Fodor, I. G., & Thal, J. (1984). Weight disorders:
    Overweight and anorexia. In E. Blechman (Ed.),
    Behavior modification with women (pp. 373-398). New
    York: Guilford Press.

Garner, D. M., & Bemis, K. M.   (1982).   A cognitive behavioral approach to anorexia nervosa. Cognitive Therapy and Research, 6(2), 123-150.

Halmi, K. A., Powers, P. A., & Cunningham, S.   (1975). Treatment of anorexia nervosa with behavior modification: Effectiveness of formula feeding and isolation. Archives of General Psychiatry, 32(1), 93-96.

Monti, P. M., McCrady, B. S., & Barlow, D. H.   (1977). Effect of positive reinforcement informational feedback and contingency contracting on a bulimic anorexic female. Behavior Research and Therapy, 8(2), 258-263.

Inpatient Hospitalization

Butler, B., Duke, M., & Stovel, T.   (1977).   Anorexia nervosa: A nursing approach. Canadian Nurse, 73, 22-24.

Crisp, A. H.   (1965).   A treatment regime for anorexia nervosa. British Journal of Psychiatry, 112(486), 505-512.

Galdston, R.   (1974).   Mind over matter--observations of 50 patients hospitalized with anorexia nervosa. Journal of American Academy of Child Psychiatry, 13(2), 246-263.

Maxmen, J. S., Silberfarb, P. M., & Ferrell, R. B.   (1974). Anorexia Nervosa: Practical initial management in a general hospital. Journal of the American Medical Association, 229, 801-803.

Talbot, E., Miller, S., & White, R.   (1964).   Some antitherapeutic side effects of hospitalization and psychotherapy. Psychiatry, 27(2), 170-176.

b. Anorexia Nervosa - Theory and Treatment

Psychodynamic Formulations

Crisp, A. H. (1980). Anorexia nervosa: Let me be. London: Academic Press.

Goodsit, A. (1977). Narcissistic disturbances in anorexia nervosa. Annals of Adolescent Psychiatry, 5, 304-312.

Goodsit, A. (1983). Self-regulatory disturbances in eating disorders. International Journal of Eating Disorders, 2(3), 51-60.

Herman, C. P., & Polivy, J. (1975). Anxiety restraint and eating behavior. Journal of Abnormal Psychology, 84(6), 666-672.

Katz, J., & Walsh, T. (1978). Depression in anorexia nervosa. American Journal of Psychiatry, 135(4), 507.

Palazzoli, M. S. (1974). Self-starvation: From individual to family therapy. New York: Jason Aronson.

Pillay, M., & Crisp, A. H. (1977). Some psychological characteristics of patients with anorexia nervosa whose weight has been newly restored. British Journal of Psychology, 50(4), 375-380.

Rizzuto, A., et al. (1981). The pathological sense of self in anorexia nervosa. Psychiatric Clinic of North America, 4(3), 471-487.

Smart, D. E., Beumont, P. J. V., & George, G. C. W. (1976). Some personality characteristics of patients with anorexia nervosa. British Journal of Psychiatry, 128, 57-60.

Sours, J. A. (1980). Starving to death in a sea of objects: The anorexia nervosa syndrome. New York: Jason Aronson.

Sours, J. A. (1981). Depression and the anorexia nervosa syndrome. Psychiatric Clinics of North America, 4(1), 145-158.

Swift, W. J., & Stern, S. (1982). The psychodynamic diversity of anorexia nervosa. International Journal of Eating Disorders, 2(1), 17-35.

Thoma, H. (1967). Anorexia nervosa. New York: International Universities Press.

Vigersky, R. H. (Ed.). (1977). Anorexia nervosa. New York: Raven Press.

Waller, J. V., Kaufman, M. R., & Deutsch, F. (1940). Anorexia nervosa: A psychosomatic entity. Psychosomatic Medicine, 2(1), 3-16.

c. Anorexia Nervosa-- Theory and Research

Sociocultural and Feminist Perspectives

Garner, D. M., Garfinkel, P. E., et al. (1980). Cultural
    expectations of thinness in women. Psychological
    Reports, 47(2), 483-491.

Boskind-Lodahl, M. (1976, Winter). Cinderella's
    stepsisters: A feminist perspective on anorexia
    nervosa and bulimia. Signs, 2(2), 342-356.

Orbach, S. (1981, March). Compulsive eating in women.
    British Journal of Sexual Medicine, 44-45.

Orbach, S. (1980). Fat is a feminist issue: The anti-diet
    guide to permanent weight loss. New York: Berkely
    Books.

Orbach, S. (1982). Fat is a feminist issue - II: A program
    to conquer compulsive eating. New York: Berkely
    Books.

The Family

Beumont, P. J. V., & Abraham, S. (1978). The onset of
    anorexia nervosa. Australian and New Zealand Journal
    of Psychiatry, 12(3), 145-149.

Crisp, A. H., Harding, B., & McGuinness, B. (1974).
    Anorexia nervosa: Psychoneurotic characteristics of
    parents: Relationship to prognosis--a quantitative
    study. Journal of Psychosomatic Research, 18(3),
    167-173.

Halmi, K. A., & Loney, J. Familial alcoholism in anorexia
    nervosa. British Journal of Psychiatry, 123, 53-54.

Hudson, J. I., Pope, H. G., Jonas, J. M., et al. (1983). Family history study of anorexia nervosa and bulimia. British Journal of Psychiatry, 142, 133-138.

Kalucy, R. S., Crisp, A. H., Harding, B. (1977). A study of 56 families with anorexia nervosa. British Journal of Medical Psychology, 50(4), 381-395.

Rampling, D. (1980). Abnormal mothering in the genesis of anorexia nervosa. Journal of Nervous and Mental Disease, 168(8), 501-504.

Winokur, A., March, V., & Mendels, J. (1980). Primary affective disorder in relatives of patients with anorexia nervosa. American Journal of Psychiatry, 137(6), 695-698.

Body Image and Personality Characteristics

Ben-Tovim, D. I., Marilov, V., & Crisp, A. H. (1979). Personality and mental states (P.S.E.) within anorexia nervosa. Journal of Psychosomatic Research, 23(5), 321-325.

Feighner, J. P., Robbins, E., Guze, S. B., Woodruff, R. A., Winokur, G., & Munoz, R. (1972). Diagnostic criteria for use in psychiatric research. Archives of General Psychiatry, 26(1), 57-63.

Garner, D. M., & Garfinkel, P. E. (1981-82). Body image in anorexia nervosa: Measurement, theory and clinical implications. International Journal of Psychiatry in Medicine, 11(3), 263-284.

Smart, D. E., Beumont, P. J. V., & George, G. C. W. (1976). Some personality characteristics of patients with anorexia nervosa. British Journal of Psychiatry, 128 (January), 57-60.

Strober, M., Goldenberg, I., Green, J., & Saxon, J. (1979).
    Body image disturbance in anorexia nervosa during
    acute and recuperative phase. Psychological Medicine,
    9(4), 695-701.

Prevalence Studies

Crisp, A. H., Palmer, R. L., Kalucy, R. S. (1976). How
    common is anorexia nervosa? A prevalence study.
    British Journal of Psychiatry, 128, 549-554.

Duddle, M. (1973). An increase of anorexia nervosa in a
    university population. British Journal of Psychiatry,
    123(577), 711-712.

Jones, D., et al. (1980). Epidemiology on anorexia nervosa
    in Monroe County, New York: 1960-1976. Psychosomatic
    Medicine, 42(6), 551-558.

Outcome Studies

Crisp, A. H., Hsu, L. K. G., & Stonehill, E. (1979,
    August). Personality, body weight and ultimate
    outcome in anorexia nervosa. Journal of Clinical
    Psychiatry, 40(8), 332-335.

Garfinkel, P. E., Moldofsky, H., & Garner, D. M. (1977).
    Prognosis in anorexia nervosa as influenced by
    clinical features, treatment and self-perception.
    Canadian Medical Association Journal, 117(9),
    1041-1045.

Halmi, K. A., Goldenberg, S. G., Casper, R. C., Eckert, E.
    D., Davis, J. M. (1979). Pretreatment predictors of
    outcome in anorexia nervosa. British Journal of
    Psychiatry, 134, 71-78.

Objective Instruments

Derogatis, L., Lipman, R., Rickles, N. K., Uhlenhuth, E. H.,
    & Covi, L. (1974). The Hopkins Checklist (HSCL): A
    self-report symptom inventory. <u>Behavioral Science</u>,
    <u>19</u>(1), 1-15.

Gerner, D. M., & Garfinkel, P. E. (1979). The Eating
    Attitudes Test: An index of the symptoms of anorexia
    nervosa. <u>Psychological Medicine</u>, <u>9</u>, 273-279.

Norman, D. K., & Herzog, D. B. (1983). Bulimia, anorexia
    nervosa and anorexia nervosa with bulimia: A
    comparative analysis of MMPI profiles. <u>International
    Journal of Eating Disorders</u>, <u>2</u>(2), 43-52.

Williams, P., Hand, D., & Tarnopolsky, A. (1982). The
    problem of screening for uncommon disorders - A comment
    on the Eating Attitudes Test. <u>Psychological Medicine</u>,
    <u>12</u>(2), 431-434.

d. Anorexia in the Male

Beumont, P. J. V. (1970). Anorexia nervosa in male
    subjects. Psychotherapy and Psychosomatics, 18(1-6),
    365-371.

Bruch, H. (1971). Anorexia nervosa in the male.
    Psycho-somatic Medicine, 33(1), 31-47.

Crisp, A. H., & Toms, D. (1972). Primary anorexia nervosa
    or weight phobia in the male: Report on 13 cases.
    British Medical Journal, 1, 334-338.

Falstein, E., Sherman, D., Feinstein, S., & Judas, I.
    (1956). Anorexia nervosa in the male child.
    American Journal of Orthopsychiatry, 26, 751-772.

e. Bulimia

Boskind-White, M., & White, W. C. (1983). Bulimarexia:
    The binge/purge cycle. New York: W. W. Norton.

Brenner, D. (1984). Self-regulatory functions of bulimia.
    Contemporary Psychotherapy Review, 1(1), 79-96.

Fairburn, C. G., & Cooper, P. J. (1982). Self-induced
    vomiting and bulimia nervosa--an undetected problem.
    British Journal of Medicine, 284, 1153-1155.

Green, R. S., & Rau, J. H. (1974). Treatment of compulsive
    eating disturbances with anti-convulsant medicine.
    American Journal of Psychiatry, 131(4), 428-432.

Center for the Study of Anorexia and Bulimia. (1984).
    Group Psychotherapy with Bulimics. New York: Author.

Herman, C. P., & Polivy, J. (1975). Anxiety restraint and
    eating behavior. Journal of Abnormal Psychology,
    84(6), 666-672.

Herzog, D. B. (1982). The secretive syndrome.
    Psychosomatics, 23(5), 481-487.

House, R. C., Grisius, R., et al. (1981). Perimolysis:
    Unveiling the surreptitious vomiter. Oral Surgery,
    51, 152-155.

Johnson, C., Connors, M. & Stuckey, M. (1983). Short term
    group treatment of bulimia: A preliminary report.
    International Journal of Eating Disorders, 2(4),
    199-208.

Johnson, C., & Larson, R. (1982). Bulimia: An analysis of
    moods and behavior. Psychosomatic Medicine, 44(4),
    341-351.

Johnson, C., Lewis, C. et al. (1982). Bulimia: A
    descriptive survey of 316 cases. International
    Journal of Eating Disorders, 2(1), 3-16.

Kornhaber, A. (1970). The stuffing syndrome. Psychosomatics, 1(6), 580-584.

Pope, H. G., Hudson, J. I., Honas, J. M., & Yurgelun-Todd, D. (1983). Bulimia treated with imipramine: A placebo-controlled double-blind study. American Journal of Psychiatry, 140(5), 554-558.

Pyle, R. L., Eckert, E. D., Mitchell, J., Halversen, P. A., Neuman, P. A., & Goff, G. (1983). The incidence of bulimia in freshmen college students. International Journal of Eating Disorders, 2(3), 75-85.

Rost, W., Neuhaus, M., & Florin, I. (1982). Bulimia nervosa: sex role attitudes, sex role behavior and sex role related locus of control in bulimarexic women. Journal of Psychosomatic Research, 26(4), 403-408.

Spencer, J. A., & Fremouw, W. J. (1979). Binge eating as a function of restraint and weight classification. Journal of Abnormal Psychology, 88(3), 262-267.

Sugarman, A., & Kurash, C. (1982). The body as a transitional object in bulimia. International Journal of Eating Disorders, 1(4), 57-67.

Wardle, J., & Beinart, H. (1981). Binge eating: A theoretical review. British Journal of Clinical Psychology, 20(2), 97-109.

Wermuth, B. M., Davis, K. L., Hollister, L. E., & Stunhard, A. J. (1977). Phenytoin treatment of the binge eating syndrome. American Journal of Psychiatry, 134(11), 1249-1253.

White, W. C., & Boskind-White, M. (1981). An experiential-behavioral approach to the treatment of bulimarexia. Journal of Psychotherapy Theory, Research and Practice, 18(4), 501-507.

Wilson, C. P., Philip, & Mintz, I. (1982). Abstaining and bulimic anorexics. Primary Care, 517-530.

f. General

Alderaran, (1975). The psychology of fat. RT: A Journal of Radical Therapy, 4(8).

American Psychiatric Association. (1984). Comparative studies on appetite disorders 1974-84: Bibliography. Washington, DC: Author.

(Can be ordered from the American Psychiatric Association, APA Library, 1400 K Street, N. W., Washington, D. C.)

Boskind-Lodahl, M. (1984). Cinderella's stepsisters: A feminist perspective on anorexia nervosa and bulimia. In P. P. Rieker & E. Carmen (Eds.), The gender gap in psychotherapy: Social realities and psychological processes (pp. 167-180). New York: Plenum. (Reprinted from Signs, 1976, 2, 342-356)

Boskind-Lodahl, M., & White, W. C. (1983). Bulimarexia: The binge/purge cycle. New York: W. W. Norton.

Bruch, H. (1962). Perceptual and conceptual disturbances in anorexia nervosa. Pychosomatic Medicine, 24(2), 187-194.

In this classic article, Bruch simplifies the concept of anorexia nervosa by focusing on the anorexic's gross disturbance in self-perception (body image) as an important diagnostic and prognostic tool. The degree to which a patient is unable to perceive his own body cues, such as hunger and his paradoxical need for hyperactivity are underscored as pathonomonic. Also, patients have a pervasive sense of themselves as ineffective, the result of a developmental deficit in mother-child interaction, that is, the child's self-initiated behaviors, particularly basic physiological functions such as hunger and feeding, have lacked confirmations from the mother. Bruch emphasizes the need for therapy which stimulates the patient's awareness of his impulses as originating from within himself, in order for treatment to be successful.

Bruch, H. (1978). <u>The golden cage: The enigma of anorexia nervosa</u>. Cambridge, MA: Harvard University Press.

Bruch, H. (1979). <u>Eating disorders: Obesity, anorexia, and the person within</u>. New York: Basic Books.

Bruch, H. (1981). Developmental considerations of anorexia nervosa and obesity. <u>Canadian Journal of Psychiatry</u>, <u>26</u>(4), 212-217.

Bruch highlights the major similarities and differences in obesity and anorexia nervosa. She emphasizes the quality of the maternal attunement, particularly the lack of appropriate maternal response to cues originating in the child as well as gross mislabeling of the child's physiological and feeling states. Such parental behavior then extends itself into the family system.

The child learns to mistrust the legitimacy of feelings and experiences. Bruch focuses primarily on perceptual and conceptual disturbance of bodily states (hunger) and body image, as well as the sense of helplessness and low self-esteem. Treatment focus is on stimulating the patient's ego activity toward the discovery of her own emotions, bodily cues and abilities.

Casper, R. C., Eckert, E. D., Halmi, K. A., Goldberg, S. C., & Davis, J. M. (1980). Bulimia: Its incidence and clinical importance in patients with anorexia nervosa. <u>Archives of General Psychiatry</u>, <u>37</u>(9), 1030-1035.

Cauwels, J. (1983). <u>Bulimia: The binge-purge compulsion</u>. New York: Doubleday.

Ceaser, M. (1977). The role of maternal identification in four cases of anorexia nervosa. <u>Bulletin of the Menninger Clinic</u>, <u>41</u>(5), 475-486.

Ceaser, M. (1979). Hunger in primary anorexia nervosa. <u>American Journal of Psychiatry</u>, <u>136</u>(7), 979-980.

Chernin, K. (1981). _Obsession: Reflections on the tyranny of slenderness_. New York: Harper & Row.

Good, well-written discussion of weight and weight control from an historical and cultural perspective.

Chernin, K. (1985). _The hungry self_. New York: NY Times Publishing Co.

Conrad, D. (1977). A starving family: An interactional view of anorexia. _Bulletin of the Menninger Clinic_, _41_(5), 487-495.

Crisp, A. H. (1980). _Anorexia nervosa: Let me be_. New York: Grune & Stratton.

Cullari, S., & Redmon, W. K. (1983). Bulimarexia, bulimia, and binge eating: A bibliography. _Professional Psychology: Research and Practice_, _14_(3), 400-405.

Fairburn, C. G. (1980). Self-induced vomiting. _Journal of Psychosomatic Research_, _24_(3/4), 193-197.

Fairburn, C. G. (1981). A cognitive behavioral approach to the treatment of bulimia. _Psychological Medicine_, _11_(4), 707-711.

Fodor, I. G. (1982). Behavior therapy for the overweight woman: A time for reappraisal. In M. Rosenbaum & C. Franks (Eds.), _Perspectives on behavior therapy in the eighties: Selected and updated proceedings from the First World Congress of Behavior Therapy_. New York: Springer.

Fodor, I. G. (1984). Weight disorders: Overweight and anorexia. In E. Blechman (Ed.), _Behavior modification with women_ (pp. 373-394). New York: Guilford Press.

Garfinkel, P. E., & Garner, D. M. (1982). _Anorexia nervosa: A multidimensional perspective_. New York: Brunner/Mazel.

Garfinkel, P. E., Moldofsky, H., & Garner, D. M. (1980). The heterogeneity of anorexia nervosa: Bulimia as a distinct subgroup. Archives of General Psychiatry, 37(9), 1036-1040.

Garner, D. M., Garfinkel, P. E., Schwartz, D., & Thompson, M. (1980). Cultural expectations of thinness in women. Psychological Reports, 47(2), 483-491.

Hall, S. M., & Havassy, B. (1981). The obese woman: Causes, correlates, and treatment. Professional Psychology, 12(1), 163-170.

Halmi, K. A., Falk, J. R., & Schwartz, E. (1981). Binge-eating and vomiting: A survey of a college population. Psychological Medicine, 11(4), 697-706.

Hawkins, R., II, Fremouw, W. J., & Clement, P. (Eds.). (1984). The binge-purge syndrome: Diagnosis, treatment and research. New York: Springer.

Lasagna, L. (Ed.). (1974). Obesity: Causes, consequences and treatment. New York: Medcom.

Lindner, R. (1973). The girl who couldn't stop eating. In H. Greenwald (Ed.), Great cases in psychoanalysis (rev. ed.) (pp. 107-151). New York: Ballantine.

Lodahl, M. R. (1984). Cinderella's stepsister: A feminist perspective on anorexia nervosa and bulimia. In P. P. Rieker & E. Carmen (Eds.), The gender gap in psychotherapy: Social realities and psychological processes (pp. 167-180). New York: Plenum Press. (Also in E. Howell & M. Bayles [Eds.], [1981], Women and mental health [pp. 248-262]. New York: Basic Books)

Maloney, M. J. & Klykylo. (1983). An overview of anorexia nervosa, bulimia and obesity in children and adolescents. Journal of the American Academy of Child Psychiatry, 22(2), 99-107.

Mazur, D. (1981). A starving family: An international view
    of anorexia nervosa. In E. Howell & M. Bayles (Eds.),
    Women and mental health (pp. 240-247). New York:
    Basic Books.

Millman, M. (1980). Such a pretty face: Being fat in
    America. New York: W. W. Norton.

Minuchin, S., Rosman, B. L., & Baker, L. (1978).
    Psycho-somatic families: Anorexia nervosa in context.
    Cambridge, MA: Harvard University Press.

Mowbray, C. T., Lanir, S., & Hulce, M. (Eds.). (1984).
    Section 3: Diagnoses applied to women: The evidence
    --Example Anorexia nervosa. Women and Therapy,
    3(3/4), 79-86.

Orbach, S. (1980). Fat is a feminist issue: The anti-diet
    guide to permanent weight loss. New York: Berkely
    Books.

Orbach, S. (1982). Fat is a feminist issue--II: A program
    to conquer compulsive eating. New York: Berkely
    Books.

Roth, G. (1982). Feeding the hungry heart. New York:
    Bobbs-Merrill.

Roth, G. (1985). Breaking free from compulsive eating.
    New York: Bobbs-Merrill.

Schlesier-Stropp, B. (1984). Bulimia: A review of the
    literature. Psychological Bulletin, 95(2), 247-257.

Sugarman, A., Quinlan, P., & Devinis, L. (1981). Anorexia
    nervosa as a defense against anaclitic depression.
    International Journal of Eating Disorders, 1(1),
    44-61.

Surrey, J. L. (1984). Eating patterns as a reflection of
    women's development (Work in Progress, Working Paper
    No. 9). Wellesley, MA: The Stone Center for
    Developmental Studies at Wellesley College.

Wilson, C. P. (Ed.). (1983). Fear of being fat: The treatment of anorexia nervosa and bulimia. New York: Jason Aronson.

Wooley, S. C., & Wooley, O. W. (1980). Eating disorders: Obesity and anorexia. In A. M. Brodsky & R. T. Hare-Mustin (Eds.), Women and psychotherapy: An assessment of research and practice (pp. 135-158). New York: Guilford Press.

K. Family Violence

Bass, E., & Thornton, L. (1983). I never told anyone: Writings by women survivors of child sexual abuse. New York: Harper & Row.

Bass, D., & Rice, J. (1979). Agency responses to the abused wife. Social Casework, 60(6), 338-342.

This study examines several issues that potentially affect a social service agency's response to the abused wife. (CSWE)

Blum, H. P. (1982). Psychoanalytic reflections on the "beaten wife syndrome." In M. Kirkpatrick (Ed.), Women's sexual experience: Explorations of the dark continent (pp. 263-267). New York: Plenum.

Bowker, L. H. (1983). Beating wife-beating. Lexington, MA: Lexington Books.

Breines, W., & Gordon, L. (1983). The new scholarship on family violence. Signs, 8(3), 490-531.

Brickman, J. (1984). Feminist, nonsexist, and traditional models of therapy: Implications for working with incest. Women and therapy, 3(1), 49-67.

Burgess, A. W., Groth, N., Holmstrom, L. H., & Sgroi, S. M. (1978). Sexual assault of children and adolescents. MA: Lexington Books.

Offers a pragmatic approach to intervention and treatment.

Carmen, E. H. (1980). Overview: The "wife beater's wife" reconsidered. American Journal of Psychiatry, 137, 1336-1346.

Carmen, E. H., Rieker, P. P., & Mills, T. (1984). Victims
     of violence and psychiatric illness. In P. P. Rieker
     & E. Carmen (Eds.), The gender gap in psychotherapy:
     Social realities and psychological processes
     (pp. 199-212). New York: Plenum. (Reprinted from
     American Journal of Psychiatry, 1976, 141, 378-383)

Constantino, C. (1981). Intervention with battered women:
     The lawyer-social worker team. Social Work, 26(6),
     456-461.

     Author explores factors behind the lack of effective-
     ness of legal and social work services with battered
     women and proposes a model of multidisciplinary inter-
     ventions. (CSWE)

Davis, L., & Carlson, B. (1981). Attitudes or service
     providers toward domestic violence. Social Work
     Research Abstracts, 17(4), 34-39.

     The attitudes of 500 social workers, health service
     providers, police officers and family court judges
     toward victims of domestic violence and their abusers
     gives evidence that most service providers blame the
     victim. (CSWE)

Department of Justice, Federal Bureau of Investigation.
     (1984). Uniform Crime Reports for 1983. Washington,
     DC: U.S. Government Printing Office.

Dobash, R. E., & Dobash, R. (1979). Violence against
     wives: A case against the patriarchy. New York:
     Free Press.

Donnerstein, E. (1980). Pornography and violence against
     women: Experimental studies. Annals of the New York
     Academy of Sciences, 347, 277-288.

Donnerstein, E. (1980). Aggressive erotica and violence
     against women. Journal of Personality and Social Psy-
     chology, 39(2), 269-277.

Dutton, D., & Painter, S. L. (1981). Traumatic bonding:
     The development of emotional attachments in battered
     women and other relationships of intermittent abuse.
     <u>Victimology: An International Journal</u>, <u>6</u>, 139-155.

     Using a behaviorist model, the authors point out that
     the beatings leave the women emotionally and physical-
     ly hurt and drained, in need of human comfort. Since
     the men who abused them are often still present and
     sometimes feeling guilty, they may extend some affec-
     tion to the needy women. The authors postulate the
     theory of "traumatic bonding," saying that it's not
     the abusive side of their abusers to which these women
     bond, but to the warmer, affectionate side which meets
     their needs for love and care.

Finkelhor, D., & Yllo, K. (1985). <u>License to rape</u>. New
     York: Holt, Rinehart & Winston.

Finkelhor, D., Gelles, R. J., Hotaling, G., & Straus, M.
     (1983). <u>The dark sides of families: Current family
     violence research</u>. Beverly Hills, CA: Sage.

Fleming, J. B. (1979). <u>Stopping wife abuse: A guide to the
     emotional, psychological, and legal implications...for
     the abused woman and those helping her</u>. New York:
     Anchor Press.

Fortune, M. M. (1983). <u>Sexual violence: The unmentionable
     sin</u>. New York: The Pilgrim Press.

Frieze, I. H. (1983). Investigating the causes and
     consequences of marital rape. <u>Signs</u>, <u>8</u>(3), 532-553.

Gee, P. W. (1983). Ensuring police protection for battered
     women: The <u>Scott v. Hart</u> suit. <u>Signs</u>, <u>8</u>(3), 554-567.

Gelles, R. J. (1979). <u>Family violence</u>. Beverly Hills, CA:
     Sage.

     This book provides an excellent treatment of the
     important issues of child abuse and marital violence.

Goffman, J. M. (1984). Batters anonymous: Self-help counseling for men who batter. San Francisco: Batterer's Anononymous Press.

Herman, J. (1981). Father-daughter incest. Professional Psychology, 12(1), 76-80.

Herman, J. (1981). Father-daughter incest. Cambridge, MA: Harvard University Press.

Herman, J. (1984). Sexual violence (Work in Progress, Working Paper No. 8). Wellesley, MA: The Stone Center for Developmental Studies at Wellesley College.

Herman, J., & Hirschman, L. (1984). Father-daughter incest. In P. P. Rieker & E. Carmen (Eds.), The gender gap in psychotherapy: Social realities and psychological processes (pp. 237-258). New York: Plenum. (Reprinted from Signs, 1977, 2[4], 735-756)

Herman, J., & Hirschman, L. (1984). Families at risk for father-daughter incest. In P. P. Rieker & E. Carmen (Eds.), The gender gap in psychotherapy: Social realities and psychological processes (pp. 259-264). New York: Plenum. (Reprinted from American Journal of Psychiatry, 1981, 138[7], 967-970)

Herrington, L. H. (1985). Victims of crime: Their plight, our response. American Psychologist, 40(1), 99-103.

Hilberman, E. (1984). Overview: The "wife-beater's" wife reconsidered. In P. P. Rieker & E. Carmen (Eds.), The gender gap in psychotherapy: Social realities and psychological processes (pp. 213-236). New York: Plenum. (Reprinted from American Journal of Psychiatry, 1980, 137[11], 1336-1347)

Jansen, M. A., & Meyers-Abell, J. (1981). Assertiveness training for battered women: A pilot program. Social Work, 26(2), 164-165.

This article describes a pilot program that provided basic communication skills and assertive training in a

supportive group environment and addressed some of the
problems confronting women who had been beaten by
boyfriends and husbands. (CSWE)

King, L. S. (1981). _Responding to spouse abuse: The mental
health profession_. Washington, DC: Center for Women
Policy Studies.

Martin, D. (1981). _Battered wives_. San Francisco: Volcano
Press.

Nelson, B. (1984). _Making an issue of child abuse_:
Political agenda setting for social problems.
Chicago: University of Chicago Press.

Response to the victimization of women and children.
(1984). [Special issue]. _Journal of the Center for
Women Policy Studies_. (2000 P St., N.W., Suite 508,
Washington, DC 20036 -- $30.00 per volume)

Roberts, A. R. (1984). _Battered women and their families_:
Intervention strategies and treatment programs. New
York: Springer.

Roberts, A. R. (1981). _Sheltering battered women: A
national study and service guide_. New York: Springer.

Rodino, P. (1985). Current legislation on victim
assistance. _American Psychologist, 40_(1), 104-106.

Rosewater, L. B. (1985). Schizophrenic, borderline or
battered? In L. B. Rosewater & L. E. Walker (Eds.),
A handbook of feminist therapy (pp. 215-225). New
York: Springer.

Russell, D. E. H. (1982). _Rape in marriage_. New York:
Macmillan.

Russell, D. E. H. (1984). _Sexual exploitation: Rape, child
sexual abuse, and workplace harassment_. Beverly
Hills, CA: Sage Publications.

Sametz, L. (1980). Children of incarcerated women. Social Work, 25(4), 298-303.

This article proposes ways of fostering the relationship between incarcerated women and their children. (CSWE)

Sonkin, D., Martin, D., & Walker, L. E. (1985). The male batterer: A treatment approach. New York: Springer.

Strauss, M. A., Gelles, R. J., & Steinmetz, S. K. (1980). Behind closed doors: Violence in the American family. New York: Anchor.

This is a summary of 8 years of research by this country's most accomplished family violence research team.

Stringer, D. M. (1979). Battered women. Beverly Hills: Sage.

Symonds, A. (1979). Violence against women: The myth of masochism. American Journal of Psychotherapy, 33(2), 161-173.

Thorman, G. (1980). Family violence. Springfield, IL: Charles C. Thomas.

This is a valuable book for those who provide services to the families of abused children and battered wives.

Walker, L. E. (1979). The battered woman. New York: Harper and Row.

Walker, L. E. (1984a). Battered women, psychology and public policy. American Psychologist, 39(10), 1178-1182.

Walker, L. E. (1984b). The battered woman syndrome. New York: Springer.

Walker, L. E. (1984c). Violence against women:
     Implications for mental health policy. In L. E.
     Walker (Ed.), Women and mental health policy
     (pp. 197-206). Beverly Hills, CA: Sage.

Warrior, B. (Ed.). (1982). Battered women's directory
     (8th ed.). Cambridge, MA: Warrior.

Weisheit, R. A. (1984). Women and crime: Issues and
     perspectives. Sex Roles, 11(7/8), 567-581.

Women and violence [Special issue]. (1983). Signs, 8(3).

L. Health

Abraham, G. E. <u>Premenstrual blues</u>. (Available from
      Optimax, Inc., P.O. Box 7000-280, Rolling Hills
      Estates, CA 90274).

Albino, J. E., & Tedesco, L. A. (1984). Women's health
      issues. In A. U. Rickel, M. Gerrard, & I. Iscoe,
      (Eds.), <u>Social and psychological problems of women</u>:
      <u>Prevention and crisis intervention</u> (pp. 157-172).
      New York: Hemisphere Publishing.

Boston Women's Health Book Collective. (Eds.). <u>Our bodies,
      ourselves</u> (3rd ed.). New York: Simon and Schuster.

Cooke, C. W., & Dworkin, S. (1979).   <u>The Ms. guide to a
      woman's health: The most up-to-date guide to women's
      health and well-being</u>. Garden City, NY: Anchor/
      Doubleday.

Dan, A., et al. (1980). <u>The menstrual cycle: Vol. 1.
      A synthesis of interdisciplinary research</u>. New York:
      Springer.

Debrovner, C. H. (Ed.). (1982). <u>Premenstrual tension</u>:
      <u>A multidisciplinary approach</u>. New York: Human
      Sciences Press.

Delaney, J., Lipton, M. J., & Toth, E. (1976). <u>The curse</u>:
      <u>A cultural history of menstruation</u>. New York: E. P.
      Dutton.

Delorey, C. (1984). Health care and midlife women. In G.
      Baruch & J. Brooks-Gunn (Eds.), <u>Women in midlife</u> (pp.
      277-301). New York: Plenum.

Eagan, A. (1983, October). The selling of premenstrual
      syndrome: Who profits from making PMS 'the disease of
      the '80s? <u>Ms. Magazine</u>.

Fee, E. (1983). <u>Women and health: The politics of sex in
      medicine</u>. Farmingdale, NY: Baywood Publishing.

Frankfort, E. (1972). <u>Vaginal politics</u>. New York: Quadrangle books.

Friedman, R. C., Hurt, S. W., Arnoff, M. S., & Clarkin, J. (1980). Behavior and the menstrual cycle. <u>Signs</u>, <u>5</u>(4), 719-738.

> The complex relationships that exist between behavior and the menstrual cycle are considered. Biological, psychological and sociocultural factors are given particular focus.

Golub, S. (1976). The effect of premenstrual anxiety and depression on cognitive function. <u>Journal of Personality and Social Psychology</u>, <u>34</u>(1), 99-104.

Golub, S. (Ed.). (1983a). <u>Lifting the curse of menstruation: A feminist appraisal of the influence of menstruation on women's lives</u>. New York: Haworth Press.

Golub, S. (Ed.). (1983b). <u>Menarche: An interdisciplinary view</u>. Lexington, MA: D. C. Heath.

Golub, S. (Ed.). (1983c). <u>Menarche: The transition from girl to woman</u>. Lexington, MA: Lexington Books.

Golub, S. (Ed.). (1984). Health care of the female adolescent [Special issue]. <u>Women and Health</u>, <u>9</u>(2/3).

Gonzalez, E. R. (1980). Premenstrual syndrome: An ancient woe deserving of modern scrutiny. <u>Journal of the American Medical Association</u>, <u>245</u>(14), 1393-96.

Hamilton, J. A., Alagna, S. W., & Sharpe, K. (In press). Cognitive approaches to the evaluation and treatment of premenstrual depression. In H. Osofsky (Ed.), Washington, DC: American Psychiatric Association Press.

Harrison, M. (1982). <u>Self-help for premenstrual syndrome</u>. Cambridge, MA: Matrix Press.

Harrison, M. Women in residence. Washington, DC: National
     Women's Health Network.

     Expose of OB/GYN care.

Kushner, R. Alternatives. Washington, DC: National Women's
     Health Network.

     New developments in the war on breast cancer.

Kutner, N. G. (1984). Women with disabling health condi-
     tions: The significance of employment. Women and
     health, 9(4), 21-31.

Lark, S. (1984). Premenstrual syndrome self-help book:
     A woman's guide to feeling good all month. Los
     Angeles: Forman.

Lauersen, N., & Whitney, S. (1973). It's your body:
     A woman's guide to gynecology. New York: Playboy
     Paperback.

Laws, S. (1983a). The sexual politics of pre-menstrual
     tension. Women's Studies International Forum, 6(1),
     19-31.

Laws, S. (1983b). Who needs PMT? A feminist approach to
     the politics of premenstrual tension. (Available from
     BWHBC, 465 Mt. Auburn St., Watertown, MA 02172. $5.00)

Moore, E. C. (1980). Women and health. Washington, DC:
     U.S. Government Printing Office.

National Women's Health Network. Plaintext doctor-patient
     checklist. Washington, DC: Author.

Napoli, M. (1982). Health facts. Washington, DC: National
     Women's Health Network.

     Alternative treatments for health problems.

National Women's Health Network. Plaintext doctor-patient
     checklist. Washington, DC: Author.

Neuhring, E. M., & Barr, W. E. (1980). Mastectomy: Impact
     on patients and families. Health and social work,
     5(1), 51-58.

     This article reviews the literature on the impact of
     breast cancer on patients' families or friends.
     (CSWE)

Parlee, M. B. (1983). The premenstrual syndrome.
     Psychological Bulletin, 83(6), 454-465.

Rubinow, D. R., & Roy-Byrne, P. (1984). Premenstrual
     syndromes: Overview from a methodological perspective.
     American Journal of Psychiatry, 141(2), 163-172.

Seaman, B. (1972). Free and female: The sex life of the
     contemporary woman. Washington, DC: National Women's
     Health Network.

Seaman, B., & Seaman, G. (1978). Women and the crisis in
     sex hormones. New York: Bantam Books.

Shuttle, P., & Redgrove, P. (1978). The wise wound: Eve's
     curse and everywoman. New York: Richard Marck
     Publishers.

Voda, A. M., with Tucker, J. (1984). Menopause me and you:
     A personal handbook for women. (Available from A. M.
     Voda, Ph.D., College of Nursing, University of Utah,
     25 South Medical Drive, Salt Lake City, UT 84112.
     $3.95 + $1.00 postage; 20+ copies: $3.25 + postage.)

Women and Disability Awareness Project. (1984). Building
     community: A manual exploring issues of women and
     disability. New York: Educational Equity Concepts.

M. Hysteria

The term hysteria comes with a long history of sexism and
misogyny attached to it. Although the concept is one
central to psychoanalytic understandings of female
personality, the term must be applied with caution.
Particularly as a descriptive term, it may be better
replaced with a behavior or symptom-based description.
Chodoff and Lyons's paper, cited below, is a useful guide to
understanding the problems with this aspect of nomenclature.
(L.S.B.)

Chodoff, P., & Lyons, H. (1958). Hysteria, the hysterical
    personality and personality and "hysterical"
    conversion. American Journal of Psychiatry, 114,
    734-743.

    The opinion is expressed that hysteria could usefully
    be considered as a caricature of femininity. This
    formulation supports the opinion that the displays of
    hysterical women represent an exaggeration of normal
    behavior under cultural pressures. An important cau-
    sative factor is the dominating and belittling expec-
    tations of men toward women.

Chodoff, P. (1974). The diagnosis of hysteria: An over-
    view. American Journal of Psychiatry, 131(10),
    1073-1078.

Chodoff, P. (1978). Psychotherapy of the hysterical perso-
    nality disorder. Journal of the American Academy of
    Psychoanalysis, 6(4), 497-510.

Chodoff, P. (1982). Hysteria and women. American Journal
    of Psychiatry, 139(5), 545-551.

    The author explores hysteria through the ages and
    concludes that the hysterical (hystriaic) personality
    is a caricature of femininity. It develops under the
    influences of cultural forces, particularly male domi-
    nation, and is not an attribute of women. He then

inquires whether the concept of a distinct femininity is itself a stereotype or is based in inborn personality differences in both the sexes.

Diacritics: A Review of Contemporary Criticism. (1983). A fine romance: Freud and Dora [Special issue].

Diacritics is a journal that is concerned primarily with criticism and is edited by the Department of Romance Studies at Cornell University. This volume is devoted to a critical assessment of Freud's case study of Dora. The leading paper is a dramatization of the case history of Dora by Helene Cixous, who had previously written of Dora in her novel Le portrait du soleil (1973) and in La jeune nee (1975). This piece of work is her formulation of feminist theory--published in collaboration with Catherine Clement. It is followed by three other interesting papers looking critically at Freud's case study of Dora. There is also included a good bibliography of books and articles (and one film) that are either directly concerned with Dora's case history or concerned in a more general way with the issues the case raises, e.g., the nature of hysteria, the mechanisms of transference, and the political bearings of psychoanalysis, particularly in relation to female sexuality.

Farber, L. (1966). Will and willfulness in hysteria. In L. Farber, The ways of the will. New York: Basic Books.

Hollender, M. (1971). The hysterical personality. Contemporary Psychiatry, 1(1), 17-24.

Hollender, M. (1972). Conversion hysteria: A post Freudian reinterpretation of 19th. century psychosocial data. Archives of General Psychiatry, 26, 311.

Hollender argues that hysterical symptoms appear when a person who is powerless and dependent can't cope with someone who is powerful and unassailable. Thus, he claims it's not surprising that women are more likely to show hysterical behavior, considering their inferior position in society.

Horowitz, M. J. (Ed.). (1977). Hysterical personality. New York: Jason Aronson.

Hunter, D. (1983). Hysteria, psychoanalysis, and feminism: The case of Anna O. Feminist Studies, 9(3), 464-488.

Jordan, B. T., & Kempler, S. (1970). Hysterical personality: An experimental investigation of sex-role conflict. Journal of Abnormal Psychology, 75(2), 172-176.

In this article 39 female "hysterical personalities" (Authors' quotation marks) and 39 nonhysterical females were tested by three measures for their response to various threats. The authors concluded that anxiety over inadequacy and sex-role competency in particular are significant variables affecting the behavior of the hysterical personality. (Walstedt)

Kendell, R. E. (1982). A new look at hysteria. In A. Roy (Ed.), Hysteria (pp. 27-36). New York: John Wiley.

Krohn, A., & Krohn, J. (1982). The nature of the oedipus complex in the Dora case. Journal of the American Psychoanalytic Association, 30(3), 555-578.

Lacan, J. (1983). Intervention on transference: Female sexuality. New York: Norton.

Lacan critically engages at a number of different levels the institution of psychoanalysis. Firstly, he develops his concept of the ego, of both the analyst and the patient, which he identifies as the point of resistance to the analytic treatment. He contrasts this concept with those theories which see the integration of the ego as the objective of an analytic process. Secondly, he re-opens the case of Dora and points to his theoretical thesis that the demands of the analyst (here, Freud himself) block the treatment at the crucial point of its encounter with sexual identity.

Lerner, H. E. (1953). The hysterical personality: A
     woman's disease. Comprehensive Psychiatry, 15,
     656-675.

     The author sees the hysterical personality, and parti-
     cularly its cognitive inadequacies, as based on the
     repression of healthy feminine intellectual curiosity
     in the interest of fulfilling the male requirements
     that women play dependent and infantile, or "attrac-
     tive female" roles.

Marmor, J. (1953). Orality in the hysterical personality.
     Journal of the American Psychoanalytic Association, 1,
     656-671.

Mowbray, C. T., Lanir, S., & Hulce, M. (Eds.). (1984).
     Section 3: Diagnoses applied to women: The evidence
     --Example: Hysteria. Women and Therapy, 3(3/4),
     99-104.

Ramas, M. (1980). Freud's Dora, Dora's hysteria: The
     negation of a woman's rebellion. Feminist Studies, 6,
     472-510.

Reubens, P. (1981). Hysteria: A feminist interpretation.
     Comprehensive Psychotherapy, 2, 68-83.

     Reubens believes that hysteria is still with us but
     reformulates its etiology. She contends that disso-
     ciation of impulses (both sexual and aggressive) leads
     to a limited sense of personal power. Thus for her,
     while the psychodynamic process involves instinctual
     drives, it is neither their repression nor the repres-
     sion of genital envy which causes the hysterical
     condition but rather the curtailment of the full being
     -in-the-world which inhibits full active living. This
     sense of powerlessness can be seen in both men and
     women although in men it tends to be more ego-dystonic.

Rose, J. (1978). Dora--fragment of an analysis. m/f. 2.

     Rose, who has translated some of Lacan's work and has
     been influenced by his theories, outlines in this
     paper some of the difficulties in the case of Dora.

The article speaks to the following issues: "the failure of the case and its relation to Freud's concept of femininity; the relation of changes in the concept of femininity to changes in that of analytic practice (transference); and then to the concept of the unconscious in its relation to representation (hysterical and schizophrenic language); how these changes made impossible any notion of the feminine which would be outside representation, the failure of the case of Dora being precisely the failure to articulate the relations between these two terms."

Roy, A. (Ed.) (1982). Hysteria. New York: John Wiley.

Satow, R. (1979). Where has all the hysteria gone? Psychoanalytic Review, 66(4), 463-477.

Slater, E. (1982). What is hysteria? In A. Roy (Ed.), Hysteria (pp. 37-40). New York: John Wiley.

Stone, M. (1980). Traditional psychoanalytic characterology reexamined in light of constitutional and cognitive differences between the sexes. Journal of the American Academy of Psychoanalysis, 8(3), 381-401.

Weintraub, M. I. (1983). Hysterical conversion reactions: A clinical guide to diagnosis and treatment. Jamaica, NY: Spectrum.

Wolowitz, H. (1972). Hysterical character and feminine identity. In J. Bardwick (Ed.), Readings on the psychology of women (pp. 307-314). New York: Harper & Row.

Woodruff, R. A., Goodwin, D. W., & Guze, S. B. (1982). Hysteria (Briquet's syndrome). In A. Roy (Ed.), Hysteria (pp. 117-129). New York: John Wiley.

N. Lesbianism

Lesbianism, one of several sexual orientations among women, raises a number of secondary emotional, social and political issues. The books and articles which follow highlight current thinking in this area. (N.A.)

Albro, J., & Tully, C. (1979). A study of lesbian life styles in the homosexual micro-culture and the heterosexual macro-culture. Journal of Homosexuality, 4(4), 341-344.

American Psychiatric Association. (1974). Positive statement on homosexuality and civil rights. American Journal of Psychiatry, 131, 497(c).

Beiger, R. (1984). Realities of gay and lesbian aging. Social Work, 29(1).

Beiger, R. (1982). The unseen minority: Older guys and lesbians. Social Work, 27(3), 236-242.

Bell, A., Weinberg, M., & Hammersmith, S. K. (1981). Sexual preference: Its development in men and women. Bloomington, IN: Indiana University Press.

Boswell, J. (1980). Christianity, social tolerance and homosexuality: Gay people in Western Europe from the beginning of the Christian era to the fourteenth century. Chicago: The University of Chicago Press.

Brown, R. (1973). Rubyfruit jungle. Plainfield, VT: Daughters, Inc.

Caldwell, M. A., & Peplau, L. A. (1984). The balance of power in lesbian relationships. Sex Roles, 10(7/8), 587-599.

Cass, V. (1979). Homosexual identity formation: A
     theoretical model. Journal of Homosexuality, 4(3),
     219-235.

     The author presents a six stage model of identity
     formation that may be of interest to those concerned
     with a psycho-sociological model of the process of
     being homosexual.

Chafetz, J., et al. (1974). A study of homosexual women.
     Social Work, 19(6), 714-23.

Clark, D. (1978). Loving someone gay. New York: Signet
     Books.

Cruikshank, M. (Ed.). (1982). Lesbian studies: Present
     and future. Old Westbury, NY: The Feminist Press.

Cruikshank, M. (Ed.). (1985). The lesbian path.
     San Francisco: Grey Fox Press.

Eisenbud, R. J. (1969). Female homosexuality: A sweet
     enfranchisement. In G. D. Goldman & D. S. Milman
     (Eds.), Modern woman (pp. 247-271). Springfield, IL:
     Charles C. Thomas.

Eisenbud, R. J. (1982). Early and later determinants of
     lesbian choice. The Psychoanalytic Review, 69(1),
     85-109.

     In this article the etiology of lesbianism is
     considered.

Ettorre, E. M. (1980). Lesbians, women and society.
     London: Routledge & Kegan Paul.

     This book presents an analysis of lesbianism as the
     phenomenon has developed from a "personal problem" or
     "individual deviance" to a social movement.

Fairchild, B., & Hayward, N. (1981). Now that you know:
     What every parent should know about homosexuality.
     New York: Harcourt Brace Jovanovich.

Freedman, J., & Doat, A. (1968). Deviancy: The psychology of being different. New York: Academic Press.

Gartrell, N. (1984a). Combating homophobia in the psychotherapy of lesbians. Women and therapy, 3(1), 13-30.

Gartrell, N. (1984b). Issues in the psychotherapy of lesbians. In P. P. Rieker & E. Carmen (Eds.), The gender gap in psychotherapy: Social realities and psychological processes (pp. 285-299). New York: Plenum. (Originally published under the title "Combatting homophobia in the psychotherapy of lesbians," Women and Therapy, 1984, 3(1).

Gonsiorek, J. (Ed.). (1982). Homosexuality and psychotherapy. New York: Haworth Press.

Goodman, B. (1977). The lesbian: A celebration of difference. New York: Out & Out Books.

Gundlach, R. H., & Reiss, B. F. (1968). Self and sexual identity in the female: A study of female homosexuals. In B. F. Reiss (Ed.), New directions in mental health (pp. 205-231). New York: Grune & Stratton.

Hanckel, F., & Cunningham, J. D. (1979). A way to love, a way of life: A young person's introduction to what it means to be gay. New York: Lothrop, Lee & Shepard.

Hidalgo, H., Peterson, T., & Woodman, N. J. (Eds.). (1985). Lesbian and gay issues: A resource manual for social workers. New York: Springer.

Kestenberg, J. S. (1962). Panel on theoretical and clinical aspects of overt female homosexuality reported by C. W. Socarides. Journal of the American Psychoanalytic Association, 10, 579-592.

Kirkpatrick, M., Roy, R., & Smith, K. (1976, August). A new look at lesbian mothers. Human Behavior, 60-61.

Kirkpatrick, M., Smith, K., & Roy, R. (1981). Lesbian
     mothers and their children: A comparative survey.
     American Journal of Orthopsychiatry, 51, 544-551.

Krieger, S. (1982). Lesbian identity and community: Recent
     social science literature. Signs, 8(1), 91-108.

Krieger, S. (1983). The mirror dance: Identity in a
     women's community. Philadelphia, PA: Temple
     University Press.

The lesbian issue [Special issue]. (1984). Signs, 9(4).

Lewis, S. (1979). Sunday's women: A report on lesbian life
     today. Boston: Beacon Press.

Loulan, J. (1984). Lesbian sex. San Francisco: Spinsters
     Ink.

Mandel, T., & Oline, P. (1977). Counseling the lesbian.
     In J. Money & H. Musaph (Eds.), Handbook of Sexology
     (pp. 1279-1286). Amsterdam: Elsevier/North-Holland
     Biomedical Press.

Martin, D., & Lyon, P. (1983). Lesbian/woman. New York:
     Bantam.

Martin, D., & Lyon, P. (1984). Lesbian women and mental
     health policy. In L. E. Walker (Ed.), Women and
     mental health policy (pp. 151-179). Beverly Hills,
     CA: Sage.

Marmor, J. (Ed.) (1980). Homosexual behavior: A modern
     reappraisal. New York: Basic Books.

Matza, D. (1969). Becoming deviant. Englewood Cliffs, NJ:
     Prentice-Hall.

McDougall, J. (1970). Homosexuality in women. In
     J. Chassequet-Smirgel (Ed.), Female sexuality
     (pp. 171-212). Ann Arbor, MI: University of Michigan
     Press.

Meyer, J. K. (1982). The theory of gender identity disorder. _Journal of the American Psychoanalytic Association_, _30_(2), 381-418.

Morin, S. F. (1977). Heterosexual bias in psychological research on lesbianism and male homosexuality. _American Psychologist_, _32_(8), 629-637.

Moses, A. E. (1978). _Identity management in lesbian women_. New York: Praeger.

Paul W. et al. (Eds.). (1982). _Homosexuality_. Beverley Hills, CA: Sage Publications.

Peplau, L. A., Cochran, S., Rook, K., & Padesky, C. (1978). Loving women: Attachment and autonomy in lesbian relationships. _Journal of Social Issues_, _34_(3), 7-27.

Psychology and the gay community [Special issue]. (1978). _Journal of Social Issues_, _34_(3).

Reiss, B. F. (1974). New viewpoints on the female homosexual. In V. Franks & V. Burtle (Eds.), _Women in therapy_ (pp. 191-214). New York: Brunner/Mazel.

Samois (pseud.). Eds.). (1981). _Coming to power_. San Francisco: Authors.

Schafer, S. (1976). Sexual and social problems of lesbians. _The Journal of Sex Research_, _12_(1), 50-69.

Shachar, S. A., & Gilbert, L. A. (1983). Working lesbians: Role conflicts and coping strategies. _Psychology of Women Quarterly_, _7_(3), 244-256.

Sharratt, S., & Bern, L. (1985). Lesbian couples and families: A co-therapeutic approach to therapy. In L. B. Rosewater & L. Walker (Eds.), _A handbook of feminist therapy_ (pp.91-99). New York: Springer.

Silverstein, C. (1977). _A family matter: A parents' guide to homosexuality_. New York: McGraw-Hill.

Socarides, C. (1978). Basic concepts: Female
    homosexuality. In C. Socarides (Ed.), <u>Homosexuality</u>
    (pp. 119-142). New York: Jason Aronson.

    Socarides reviews the psychoanalytic etiological his-
    tory of female homosexuality as pathological. He then
    focuses on the preoedipal issues involved, particular-
    ly those related to mother fixations, oral aggression
    and the underlying fear of afphanisis - the threat of
    total extinction. Further discussion is related to
    identity formation (in the homosexual woman) and mas-
    culine vs. feminine position(s). Socarides also at-
    tempts to review the multiple forms of female homo-
    sexuality in clinical groupings.

    Readers are cautioned that this book is extremely
    homophobic, and that this author's conceptualizations
    of homosexuality are inconsistent with the majority of
    scholarly knowledge on the topic. A particular
    problem is the reliance on a clinical sample only,
    thus leading to unfounded overgeneralizations to non-
    clinical populations. (L.S.B.)

<u>Sourcebook on lesbian/gay health care</u>. (1984). New York:
    The National Gay Health Education Foundation, Inc.
    From the First International Lesbian and Gay Health
    Conference. (Includes the Third AIDS Forum)

    This book presents speeches and excerpts from the
    Third AIDS Forum and the First International Lesbian
    and Gay Health conference. Some of the issues exa-
    mined are: alcoholism and chemical dependency, family,
    general health concerns, holistic health and healing,
    mental health issues. This sourcebook provides a
    bibliography on gay and lesbian health care issues.
    This book is published by and can be ordered from: The
    National Gay Health Education Foundation, Inc., P.O.
    Box 784, New York, N.Y. 10108.

Steinhorn, A. (1982). Lesbian mothers--The invisible
    minority: Role of the mental health worker. <u>Women and
    Therapy</u>, <u>1</u>(4), 35-48.

Steinhorn, A.   (1984).   On lesbian mothers.   Siecus Report,
     V. XII, 3.

Vida, G.   (Ed.).   (1978).   Our right to love: A lesbian
     resource book.   Englewood Cliffs, NJ: Prentice-Hall.

Weinberg, G.   (1973).   Society and the healthy homosexual.
     New York: Anchor Press.

Wolff, D. G.   (1979).   The lesbian community.   Berkely, CA:
     University of California Press.

Woodman, N. J., & Lenna, H. R.   (1980).   Counseling with gay
     men and women: A guide for facilitating positive life-
     styles.   San Francisco: Jossey-Bass.

O. Marriage and Divorce

Ambert, A. (1983). Separated women and remarriage
      behavior: A comparison of financially secure and
      financially insecure women. Journal of Divorce, 6(3),
      43-54.

Aslin, A. L. (1978). Counseling "single-again" (divorced
      and widowed women. In L. W. Harmon et al. (Eds.),
      Counseling women (pp. 230-240). Monterey, CA: Brooks/
      Cole.

Bernard, J. (1971). The paradox of happy marriage. In
      V. Gornick & B. Moran (Eds.), Woman in sexist society
      (pp. 85-98). New York: Basic Books.

      Though married women tend to describe themselves as
      happy, the author provides evidence for a greater
      prevalence of emotional disturbance among wives than
      among husbands. Problems inherent in the marital
      situation for females are discussed. (JSAS)

Bernard, J. (1982). The future of marriage. New Haven,
      CT: Yale University Press.

Cantor, D. W. (1982). Divorce: Separation or separation-
      individuation. The American Journal of
      Psychoanalysis, 42(4), 307-313.

Chiriboga, D. A., & Cutler, L. (1977). Stress responses
      among divorcing men and women. Journal of Divorce,
      1(2), 95-106.

Collins, S., & Bernstein, B. E. (1983). Women and the
      divorcing process: Therapist and lawyer collabora-
      tions. Women and therapy, 4(2), 49-60.

Cunningham, J. D., Braiker, H., & Kelley, H. H. (1982).
      Marital-status and sex differences in problems
      reported by married and cohabiting couples.
      Psychology of Women Quarterly, 6(4), 415-427.

Divorce and separation [Special issue]. (1976). <u>Journal of Social Issues</u>, <u>32</u>,(1).

Furstenberg, F., & Spanier, G. (1984). <u>Recycling the family: Remarrige after divorce</u>. Beverly Hills, CA: Sage Publications.

Gove, W. R., Hughes, M., & Style, C. B. (1983). Does marriage have positive effects on the psychological well-being of the individual? <u>Journal of Health and Social Behavior</u>, <u>24</u>(2), 122-131.

Hess, B. B., & Sussman, M. B. (Eds.). (1984). <u>Women and the family: Two decades of change</u>. New York: Haworth Press.

Laws, J. L. (1971). A feminist review of marital adjustment literature: The rape of the locke. <u>Journal of Marriage and Family</u>, <u>33</u>(3), 483-516.

Lessing, D. (1964). <u>A proper marriage</u>. New York: New American Library.

> Doris Lessing brilliantly portrays an unconventional girl in a socially approved conventional marriage. The girl cannot find a role model to combine a woman accepting femininity and motherhood and a woman who is also a person. The girl finds her role increasingly impossible and while still young leaves her child and husband for a harder less secure life. The book excellently depicts the sex role maladjustment experience by an increasing number of modern women.

Lief, H. I. (1982). The importance of marriage in mental health. <u>Psychiatric Annals</u>, <u>12</u>(7), 671-672.

Nadelson, C. C., & Notman, M. T. (1981). To marry or not to marry: A choice. <u>American Journal of Psychiatry</u>, <u>138</u>(10), 1352-56.

Spanier, G., & Thompson, L. (1984). <u>Parting: The aftermath of separation and divorce</u>. Beverly Hills, CA: Sage Publications.

Symonds, A. (1973). Phobias after marriage: Women's
     declaration of dependence. In J. B. Miller (Ed.),
     Psycho-analysis and women (pp. 287-300). New York:
     Brunner/Mazel. (Reprinted from American Journal of
     Psychoanalysis, 1971, 31[2], 144-152)

Visher, E. B., & Visher, J. S. (1979). Step-families:
     A guide to working with stepparents and stepchildren.
     New York: Brunner/Mazel.

Visher, E. B., & Visher, J. S. (1982). How to win as a
     stepfamily. New York: Dembner Books.

Zeiss, A. M., Zeiss, R. A., & Johnson, S. M. (1980). Sex
     differences in initiation of and adjustment to
     divorce. Journal of Divorce, 4(2), 21-33.

P. Masculinity-Femininity, Sex-roles, Androgyny, and Gender Schema

Androgyny [Special issue]. (1979). Sex Roles, 5(6).

Bem, S. L. (1975). Sex-role adaptability: One consequence of psychological androgyny. Journal of Personality and Social Psychology, 31(4), 634-643.

Bem, S. L. (1976). Probing the promise of androgyny. In A. G. Kaplan & J. P. Bean (Eds.), Beyond sex-role stereotypes: Reading towards a psychology of androgyny (pp. 48-62). Boston: Little, Brown.

Bem, S. L. (1977). On the utility of alternative procedures for assessing psychological androgyny. Journal of Consulting and Clinical Psychology, 45(2), 196-205.

A series of articles in which the concept of androgyny is explored. Bem has developed a measurement instrument (rating scale) which can be used to assess psychological androgyny. In her articles, she discusses her research findings with the possibility of there being an advantage to forsaking adherence to traditional sex-roles in favor of more androgynous behavior.

Bem, S. L. (1978). Beyond androgyny: Some presumptuous prescriptions for a liberated sexual identity. In J. Sherman & F. Denmark (Eds.), Psychology of women: Future directions of research. New York: Psychological Dimensions.

Bem, S. L. (1981). Gender schema theory: A cognitive account of sex typing. Psychological Review, 88(4), 354-364.

Bem, S. L., & Lenny, E. (1976). Sex-typing and the avoidance of cross-sex behavior. Journal of Personality and Social Psychology, 33(1), 48-54.

Berger, C. R. (1968). Sex differences related to self-esteem factor structure. _Journal of Consulting and Clinical Psychology, 32_(4), 442-446.

   Males appear to be more capable of maintaining self-esteem whatever the valuations of them by others, whereas females need to feel liked in order to maintain high levels of self-esteem.

Brooks-Gunn, J., & W. S. Mathews. (1979). _He and she: How children develop their sex-role identity_. Englewood Cliffs: Spectrum.

Butler, M., & Paisley, W. (Eds.). (1980). _Women and the mass media: Sourcebook for research and action_. New York: Human Sciences Press.

Condry, J. C. (1984). Gender identity and social competence. _Sex Roles, 11_(5/6), 485-511.

Datan, N., Antonovsky, A., & Maoz, B. (1981). _A time to reap: The middle age of women in five Israeli subcultures_. Baltimore: Johns Hopkins Press.

Deaux, K. (in press). From individual differences to social categories: Analysis of a decade's research on gender. _American Psychologist_.

Denmark, F. L., Shaw, J. S., & Ciali, S. D. (in press). The relationship between sex roles, living arrangements, and the division of household responsibilities. _Sex Roles_.

Doyle, J. A. (1983). _The male experience_. W. C. Brown.

Eagly, A. H., & Wood, W. (1982). Inferred sex differences in status as a determinant of gender stereotypes about social influence. _Journal of Personality and Social Psychology, 43_(5), 915-928.

Fleishman, E. G. (1983). Sex-role acquisition, parental behavior, and sexual orientation: Some tentative hypotheses. _Sex Roles, 9_(10), 1051-1059.

Fleishman, E. G. (1983). Sex-role acquisition, parental behavior, and sexual orientation: Some tentative hypotheses--A rejoinder. Sex Roles, 9(10), 1063-1065.

Garnets, L., & Pleck, J. H. (1979). Sex role identity, androgyny, and sex role transcendence: A sex role strain analysis. Psychology of Women Quarterly, 3(3), 270-283.

Gelb, L. (1973). Masculinity-femininity: A study in imposed inequality. In J. B. Miller (Ed.), Psychoanalysis and women (pp. 363-406). Baltimore: Penguin Books.

Gelb makes the point that many practitioners of psychoanalysis are guilty of making a significant contribution to the institutionalization of limiting and rigid male and female roles. While many males and females are currently striving toward competence and growth, psychoanalysts frequently advise women about the importance of passivity and dependency, and encourage men to "reestablish masculine identity." (JSAS)

Gould, L. (1978). A fabulous child's story. New York: Daughters Press.

Grady, K. E. (1979). Androgyny reconsidered. In J. H. Williams (Ed.), Psychology of Women: Selected readings. New York: W. W. Norton.

Greenglass, E. R. (1982). A world of difference: Gender roles in perspective. Toronto: John Wiley.

Gump, J. P. (1972). Sex-role attitudes and psychological well-being. Journal of Social Issues, 28(2), 79-92.

Sex-role concepts of 162 college women are explored in relationship to ego strength, happiness, and achievement plans. The majority of women believe it possible to assume the roles of wife and mother while concomitantly pursuing extra-familial interests. Neither happiness nor the establishing of relationships with men differentiated women traditional in sex-role orientation from women primarily interested in realizing their potential. Differences in ego strength were found to be associated with plans for marriage and career. Subjects who obtained the highest ego strength scores were actively pursuing both objectives. The latter finding suggests that ego strength may be negatively related to the adoption of the traditional female sex-role. AUTHOR ABSTRACT. JSAS

Heilbrun, A. B. Jr. (1968). Sex role, instrumental-expressive behavior and psychopathology in females. Journal of Abnormal Psychology, 73(2), 131-136.

Girls who were viewed as better adjusted, a concept related to goal-orientation, were more masculine than girls who were less well-adjusted. Masculine girls had a wider range of coping skills, because they were more able to be instrumental and expressive in contrast to highly feminine girls who were only capable of being expressive. Masculine girls were likely to identify with masculine mothers and/or masculine fathers, whereas the less well-adjusted feminine girls were highly identified with feminine mothers. JSAS

Heilbrun, C. G. (1973). Towards a recognition of androgyny. New York: Knopf.

Henley, N. M. (1977). Body Politics. Englewood Cliffs, NJ: Prentice-Hall.

Hinkle, B. (1920). On the arbitrary use of the terms masculine and feminine. Psychoanalytic Review, 7, 15-30.

(Note the date of this paper!)

Hoffman, D. M., & Fidell, L. S. (1979). Characteristics of androgynous, undifferentiated, masculine, and feminine middle-class women. Sex Roles, 5(6), 765-781.

Hubbard, R., & Lowe, M. (1979). Genes and gender II: Pitfalls in research on sex and gender. New York: Gordian Press.

Kaplan, A. G. (1976). Androgyny as a model of mental health for women. In A. G. Kaplan & J. P. Bean (Eds.), Beyond sex-role stereotypes. Boston: Little, Brown.

Kaplan, A. G. (Ed.). (1979). Psychological androgyny: Further considerations [Special issue]. Psychology of Women Quarterly, 3(3).

Kessler, D., & McKenna, W. (1985). Gender: An ethnomethodological approach. Chicago: University of Chicago Press.

LaBarbera, J. D. (1984). Seductive father-daughter relationships and sex roles in women. Sex Roles, 11(9/10), 941-951.

Laws, J. L. (1979). The second X: Sex role and social role. New York: Greenwood Press.

By concentrating on major roles of women that are constrained by sex role socialization, the author provides comprehensive coverage of work on the biological and sex roles of women. Her thorough and far-reaching study of professional literature contributes to an integrative analysis.

Lerner, H. E. (1974). Early origins of envy and devaluation of women: Implications for sex role stereotypes. Bulletin of the Menninger Clinic, 38(6), 538-553.

Maccoby, E. E., & Jackson, C. N. (1974). The psychology of sex differences. Stanford, CA: Stanford University Press.

Mayo, C., & Henley, N. M. (Eds.). (1981). Gender and nonverbal behavior. New York: Springer-Verlag.

Markus, H., Crane, M., Bernstein, S., & Siladi, M. (1982). Self-schemas and gender. Journal of Personality and Social Psychology, 42(1), 38-50.

O'Leary, V. E., Unger, R. K., & Wallston, B. S. (Eds.). (1985). Women, gender, and social psychology. Hillsdale, NJ: Lawrence Erlbaum Associates.

Parsons, J. E. (Ed.). (1980). The psychobiology of sex differences and sex roles. New York: McGraw-Hill.

Person, E. S., & Ovesey, L. (1983). Psychoanalytic theories of gender identity. Journal of the American Academy of Psychoanalysis, 11(2), 203-26.

Petersen, A. C. (1980). Biopsychosocial processes in the development of sex-related differences. In J. Parsons (Ed.), The psychobiology of sex differences and sex roles (pp. 31-55). New York: Hemisphere.

Pleck, J. H. (1981). The myth of masculinity. Cambridge, MA: MIT Press.

Psychological androgyny: Further considerations [Special issue]. (1979). Psychology of Women Quarterly, 3(3).

Richardson, B. L., & Wirtenberg, J. (1983). Sex role research: Measuring social change. New York: Praeger.

Rollins, J. C., & White, P. N. (1982). The relationship between mothers' and daughters' sex-role attitudes and self-concepts in three types of family environment. Sex Roles, 8(11), 1141-1155.

Ruble, T. L. (1983). Sex stereotypes: Issues of change in the 1970s. Sex Roles, 9(3), 397-402.

Rubin, L. B. (1984). Intimate strangers: Men and women together. New York: Harper & Row.

Russo, N. F. (in press). Sex role stereotyping, socialization, and sexism. In A. Sargent (Ed.), Beyond sex roles (rev. ed.). St. Paul: West Publishing Co.

Sherif, C. W. (1982). Needed concepts in the study of gender identity. Psychology of Women Quarterly, 6(4), 375-398.

Sherman, J. A., & Beck, E. (Eds.). (1979). The prism of sex: Essays in the sociology of knowledge. Madison, WI: University of Wisconsin Press.

Shields, S. A. (1975). Functionalism, Darwinism, and the psychology of women: A study in social myth. American Psychologist, 30(7), 739-754.

Signorella, M. L. (1984). Cognitive consequences of personal involvement in gender identity. Sex Roles, 11(9/10), 923-940.

Simari, C. G., & Baskin, D. (1983). Sex-role acquisition, parental behavior, and sexual orientation: Some tentative hypotheses--A critique. Sex Roles, 9(10), 1061-1062.

Singer, J. (1976). Androgyny: Toward a new theory of sexuality. New York: Anchor/Doubleday.

Slevin, K. F., & Wingrove, C. R. (1983). Similarities and differences among three generations of women in attitudes toward the female role in contemporary society. Sex Roles, 9(5), 609-624.

Spence, J. T., & Helmreich, R. L. (1978). Masculinity and femininity: Their psychological dimensions, correlates, and antecedents. Austin, TX: University of Texas Press.

The authors present data showing that masculinity and femininity do not relate negatively to each other and that masculinity-femininity co-existence holds for a large number of groups. Further the authors find that androgynous individuals (individuals with a co-existence of masculinity and femininity) display more self-esteem, social competence, and achievement orientation than individuals who are strong in either masculinity or femininity or are strong in neither.

Spence, J. T., & Helmreich, R. L. (1980). Masculine instrumentality and feminine expressiveness: Their relationship with sex role attitudes and behaviors. Psychology of Women Quarterly, 5(2), 147-163.

Spence, J. T., Deaux, K., & Helmreich, R. L. (1983). Sex roles in contemporary American society. In G. Lindzey & E. Aronson (Eds.), Handbook of social psychology (3rd ed.). Reading, MA: Addison-Wesley.

Spender, D. (Ed.). (1981). Men's studies modified: The impact of feminism on the academic disciplines. New York: Pergamon.

Taylor, M. C., & Hall, J. (1982). Psychological androgyny: A review and reformulation of theories, methods, and conclusions. Psychological Bulletin, 92(2), 347-366.

Tobach, E., & Rosoff, B. (Eds.). (1978). Genes and gender I: On hereditarianism and women. New York: Gordian Press.

Tobach, E., & Rosoff, B. (Eds.). (1980). Genes and gender III: Genetic determinism and children. New York: Gordian Press.

Unger, R. K. (1979). Toward a redefinition of sex and gender. American Psychologist, 34(11), 1085-1094.

Unger, R. K. (1981). Sex as a social reality: Field and laboratory research. Psychology of Women Quarterly, 5(4), 645-653.

Unger, R. K., & Denmark, F. (1975). Woman: Dependent or independent variable? New York: Psychological Dimensions.

Q. Masochism and Passivity

As is the case with hysteria, each of these terms carries
significant problems in its usage outside of a strictly
constructed psychoanalytic context. Several authors, among
them Caplan (cited below) have pointed out the lack of
awareness of female social realities that permeates the use
of this terminology. Sociol-cultural understandings of
female personality development may be of greater use in
comprehending the behaviors and ways of being that are
purportedly described by this wording. (L.S.B.)

Berliner, B. (1947). On some psychodynamics of masochism.
    Psychoanalytic Quarterly, 16, 459-471.

Bernstein, I. (1983). Masochistic pathology and feminine
    development. Journal of the American Psychoanalytic
    Association, 31(2), 467-486.

    Bernstein examines those aspects of feminine develop-
    ment that favor the development of masochistic reac-
    tions and character formations. He believes these are
    a result of failures of development which can occur in
    men as well as women. Case studies of several female
    masochistic patients are described and the author
    attempts to show how "by abandoning older mistaken
    concepts and applying recent advances in understanding
    feminine development, we are better able to recognize
    and treat pathological masochistic outcomes in women
    when they come for analysis."

Blum, H. P. (1977). Masochism, the ego ideal, and the
    psychology of women. In H. Blum (Ed.), Female
    psychology: Contemporary psychoanalytic views
    (pp. 157-191). New York: International Universities
    Press.

    In this paper, Blum finds Freud's early propositions
    of a masochistic and inferior female psychic structure
    with ego tendencies toward arrest and rigidity, rela-
    tive inability to sublimate, and a deficient superego
    to be incomplete and obsolete. Femininity is seen as

not being derived from a primary masculinity with
disappointed maleness, masochistic resignation to
fantasized inferiority, or compensation for fantasized
castration. Rather he proposes femininity is derived
from a positive feminine identification and individuation. He feels both parents are important in this
process of feminine individuation and foster and
orient a positive feminine identity, body image, and
ego ideal.

Caplan, P. J. (1984). The myth of women's masochism.
     American Psychologist, 39(2), 130-139.

     Theories about women's "natural" masochism are criti-
     cally reviewed, and it is demonstrated that (a) such
     theories are unnecessary because all of the phenomena
     that the notion of women's natural masochism is sup-
     posed to explain can be explained satisfactorily and
     fully by other means; and (b) the notion that women
     are naturally unconsciously masochistic does women a
     profound disservice. The concept of masochism per se
     is criticized, and an alternative interpretation for
     so-called masochistic behavior is proposed. (AUTHORS
     ABSTRACT)

Caplan, P. J. (1985). The myth of women's masochism.
     New York: Dutton.

Dweck, C. S., Davidson, W., Nelson, S., & Enna, B. (1978).
     Sex differences in learned helplessness: II. The
     contingencies of evaluative feedback in the classroom
     and III. An experimental analysis. Developmental
     Psychology, 14(3), 268-276.

Fried, E. (1971). Active/passive: The crucial
     psychological dimension. New York: Harper & Row.

     This book presents a contemporary psychoanalytic
     statement. (JSAS)

Gardiner, M. (1955). Feminine masochism and passivity.
    Bulletin of the Philadelphia Association of
    Psychoanalysis, 5, 44-59.

    Gardiner, in this early paper, took an important step
    away from the hypothesis proposed by Freud and later
    stressed by Deutsch that masochism and passivity are
    necessary for adult feminine sexual development and
    fulfillment. Instead, she points to masochism and
    passivity as regression from the genital phase and
    indicative of unresolved conflicts.

Hart, H. H. (1961). A review of the psychoanalytic
    literature on passivity. Psychiatric Quarterly, 35,
    331-352.

Huesmann, L. R. (Ed.). (1978). Learned helplessness as a
    model of depression [Special issue]. Journal of
    Abnormal Psychology, 87(1).

Kestenberg, J. S. (1980). The three faces of femininity.
    Psychoanalytic Review, 67(3), 313-335.

Lenzer, G. (1975). On masochism: A contribution to the
    history of a phantasy and its theory. Signs, 1(2),
    277-324.

Lerner, L. (1979). Masochism and the emergent ego. New
    York: Human Sciences.

Manalis, S. A. (1976). The psychoanalytic concept of
    feminine passivity: A comparative study of
    psychoanalytic and feminist views. Comprehensive
    Psychiatry, 17(1), 241-247.

Marcus, M. (1981). A taste for pain: On masochism and
    female sexuality. New York: St. Martin's Press.

Menaker, E. (1953). Masochism: A defense reaction of the
    ego. Psychoanalytic Quarterly, 22, 205-220.

    Using data from the analysis of adult patients,
    Menaker presents the following hypothesis: Masochistic
    self-devaluation originates at the oral level and it

is the outcome of traumatic deprivation. It is a
defense against experiencing this deprivation with its
anxiety and aggression, and it is a means of perpetua-
ting a bond to mother.

Meyer, J., & Dupkin, C. (1983). Sadomasochism. In
    W. Fann, I. Karacan, et al. (Eds.), Phenomenology and
    treatment of psychosexual disorders (Vol. 1)
    (pp. 13-22). New York: SP Medical & Scientific Books.

Newman, F., & Caplan, P. J. (1982). Juvenile female
    prostitution as gender-consistent response to early
    deprivation. International Journal of Women's
    Studies, 5(2), 128-137.

In a study on juvenile female prostitutes, the authors
found that the definition of masochism (enjoyment of
pain and humiliation) did not fit them; that this
definition of masochism is very different from both
the willingness to make do with less because one has
never had more and the willingness to endure the bad
in order to get the good. They also make the point
that certain behaviors would be labelled masochistic
depending on the sex of the person involved.

Norwood, R. (1985). Women who love too much. Los Angeles:
    J. P. Tarcher.

Panken, S. (1973). The joy of suffering: The
    psychoanalytic understanding of masochism. New York:
    Jason Aronson, Inc.

Parkin, A. (1980). On masochism enthralment: A
    contribution to the study of moral masochism.
    International Journal of Psychoanalysis, 61(P3),
    307-314.

Parkin disagrees with Freud's death instinct explanation for masochism and suggests instead that because
the pain is associated with something important and
pleasurable, it is to be endured or even sought. When
it is sought, what is being repeated is the experience
that with the pain comes pleasure in the form of a

sense of omnipotence, a feeling of being with the mother (a toxic introject), or a reaction formation to cover hatred and resentment of the mother.

Samois (pseud.). (Eds.). (1981). Coming to power. San Francisco: Authors.

Schad-Somers, S. (1982). Sadomasochism: Etiology and treatment. New York: Human Sciences Press.

Schafer, R. (1968). On the theoretical and technical conceptualization of activity and passivity. Psychoanalytic Quarterly, 37(2), 173-198.

This paper while not focusing directly on female development is helpful in conceptualizing activity and passivity. Schafer looks at these issues from five contexts: instinct theory, structural theory, object relations, subjective experience and trauma. Since passivity is often discussed as an issue in female psychology, this paper provides a new frame in which to study female development.

Schafer, R. (1984). The pursuit of failure and the idealization of unhappiness. American Psychologist, 39(4), 398-405.

A psychoanalytic account of unconscious mental processes involved in entrenched psychical suffering. Although disturbed ideal-self development appears to characterize both sexes, the unconscious active pursuit of failure seems more prevalent in men and the unconscious idealization of unhappiness in women. This relative sex difference is attributed to sexist influences on women, typical fantasies and problems of early development, and the analyst's interpretive activity that inevitably influences the dialogic construction of psychoanalytic life histories and that varies among and within schools of psychoanalytic thought. (AUTHORS ABSTRACT)

Schecter, D. (1981). Masochism in women: A psychodynamic analysis. In S. Klebanow (Ed.), <u>Changing concepts in psychoanalysis</u> (pp. 169-182). New York: Gardner Press.

Shainess, N. (1979). Vulnerability to violence: Masochism as process. <u>American Journal of Psychotherapy</u>, <u>33</u>(2), 174-189.

Shainess, N. (1984). <u>Sweet suffering: Woman as victim</u>. New York: Bobbs-Merril.

Smith, C. A., & Smith, C. J. (1980). Learned helplessness and preparedness in discharged mental patients. <u>Social Work Research and Abstracts</u>, <u>14</u>, 21-27.

Thompson, C. (1964). <u>On women</u>. New York: New American Library.

The author argues that women's "masochism also often proves to be a form of adaptation to an unsatisfactory and circumscribed life" (p. 133). She reminds the reader that Freud's theory of feminine masochism was based in part on fantasies of passive male homosexuals and suggests the error of equating such fantasies with the feelings of the average woman.

Thompson, C. (1973a). Cultural pressures in the psychology of women. In J. B. Miller (Ed.), <u>Psychoanalysis and women</u> (pp. 49-64). New York: Brunner/Mazel.

Thompson, C. (1973b). Some effects of the derogatory attitude toward female sexuality. In J. B. Miller (Ed.), <u>Psychoanalysis and women</u> (pp. 65-74). New York: Brunner/Mazel.

In these two articles the author refers to women's learned denial of their sexuality; that denial has incorrectly been interpreted by others as evidence of women's "natural masochism."

Waites, E. A. (1984). Female masochism and the enforced
    restriction of choice. In P. P. Rieker & E. Carmen
    (Eds.), The gender gap in psychotherapy: Social
    realities and psychological processes (pp. 139-150).
    New York: Plenum. (Reprinted from Victimology: An
    International Journal, 1977-1978, 2[3-4], 535-544)

R. Mothering

Adams, P. L., Milner, J. R., Schrepf, N. A. (1984).
    Fatherless children. New York: John Wiley & Sons.

Alexander, J., Kornfein, M. (1983). Changes in family
    functioning amongst nonconventional families.
    American Journal of Orthopsychiatry, 53(3), 408-417.

Alpert, J. L., & Richardson, M. S. (1980). Parenting.
    In L. W. Poon (Ed.), Aging in the 1980s: Psychological
    issues. Washington, DC: American Psychological
    Association.

Alpert, J. L., & Richardson, M. S. (1983). Parenting:
    Effects on parents, effect on children, and social
    policy implications. In M. F. Levy (Ed.),
    Contemporary research and theory in developmental
    psychology: A collection of award papers of the New
    York State Psychological Association. New York:
    Irvington Press.

Arcana, J. (1979). Our mothers daughters. San Francisco:
    Shameless Hussy Press.

Ashford, J. (Ed.). (1983). Whole birth catalogue: A
    sourcebook for choices in childbirth. Trumansburg,
    NY: Crossing Press.

Barnett, R. C., & Baruch, G. K. (1984). Mothers
    participation in child care: Patterns and consequences
    (Working Paper No. 137). Wellesley, MA: Wellesley
    College Center for Research on Women.

Bart, P. B. (1970). Mother Portnoy's complaints.
    TransAction, 8(1-2), 69-74.

    This article deals with adjustment problems of mothers
    in modern society, as well as some strategies for
    coping with such problems. (JSAS)

Bell, N., & Carver, W. (1980). A reevaluation of gender label effects: Expectant mothers' responses to infants. Child Development, 51(3), 925-927.

Belle, D. (1980). Mothers and their children: A study of low-income families. In C. Heckman (Ed.), The evolving female: Women in psychosocial context (pp. 74-91). New York: Human Sciences Press.

Benedek, T. (1970a). Parenthood during the life cycle. In E. J. Anthony & T. Benedek (Eds.), Parenthood, its psychology and psychopathology (pp. 185-206). Boston: Little, Brown.

Benedek takes the psychoanalytically-derived position that pregnancy is a critical phase in the life of women. Because pregnancy is assumed to be a normal condition, fears are often suppressed, only to become problematic later on. (JSAS)

Benedek, T. (1970b). Motherhood and nurturing. In E. J. Anthony & T. Benedek (Eds.), Parenthood, its psychology and psychopathology (pp. 153-165). Boston: Little, Brown.

Berlin, I. N. (1983). On conflict in nontraditional families: A clinical perspective. American Journal of Orthopsychiatry, 53(3), 436-438.

Bernard, J. (1974). The future of motherhood. New York: Dial Press.

Bernstein, D. (1978). Female identity synthesis. In A. Woland, (Ed.), Career and motherhood. New York: Human Sciences Press.

Burns, C. (in press). Stepmotherhood: How to survive without feeling frustrated, left out, or wicked. New York: Times Books.

Cassidy-Brinn, Hornstein, F., & Downer, C. (1984). Women-centered pregnancy and birth. Pittsburgh, PA: Cleis Press.

Chico, N. P., & Hartley S. F. (1981). Widening choices in motherhood of the future. Psychology of Women Quarterly, 6(1), 12-25.

Children of divorce [Special issue]. (1979). Journal of Social Issues, 35(4).

Chodorow, N. (1974). Family structure and feminine personality. In M. Z. Rosaldo & L. Lamphere (Eds.). Women, culture, and society (pp. 43-66). Stanford, CA: Stanford University Press.

This chapter includes a cross-cultural comparison of mother-daughter relationships that she unfortunately does not pursue in her book.

Chodorow, N. (1978). The reproduction of mothering: Psychoanalysis and the sociology of gender. Berkeley, CA: University of California Press.

Chodorow, a sociologist with a psychoanalytic perspective, analyzes gender development within a sociological model. Her thesis is that mothering is the outcome of a social environment which differs for, and is experienced differently by, female and male children and consequently leads to early sex differences in personality development. She notes that identity formation for girls takes place in the context of an ongoing relationship with mother which tends to fuse attachment and identity formation, while for boys the definition of themselves as masculine involves separating from mother. Chodorow points out that while sex differences in these early relationships exist, the Freudian psychoanalytic bias sees women's differences in development as deficiencies rather than differences (weaker ego boundaries, tendency to psychosis, etc.). The feminine personality is based more on retention of continuity with external relationships and less on repression of inner objects. Boys, not having identificatory objects so close, need to be taught role more consciously. Chodorow says, "women as mothers, produce daughters with mothering capacities and the desire to mother." By contrast, women as mothers (and men as not mothers) produce sons whose nurturant capacities and needs have been "curtailed and repressed." For Chodorow, an explanation of gender difference is a social and not a biological fact. Boys must separate from mother more rigidly than girls. Masculine personality involves denial of relation and connection. Chodorow speaks for relational rather than an autonomous self. Each sex is assigned one side of human experience. The child must become independent in relation to another who recognizes its independence. Outcome of struggle between autonomy and connectedness may often involve splitting and polarization. This struggle becomes institutionalized as gender identity.

Daniels, P., & Weingarten, K. (1983). <u>Sooner or later</u>: <u>The timing of parenthood in adult lives</u>. New York: Norton.

This book is about the relevance of timing both in the beginning and at subsequent moments in parents' and children's lives. The question here is not "whether?" but "when?" and how does the "when" work out across the life cycle. How does the timing of parenthood affect marriage as couples make room for their first child? As they enlarge the nest to include a second child? What are the implications for the ways in which women and men integrate the pleasures and cares of family life with the pleasures and cares of their work in the world? What difference does it make to be "older" or "younger" when children leave home? This book clearly indicates the complexities of adult life.

Dinnerstein, D. (1976). <u>The mermaid and the minotaur</u>. New York: Harper and Row.

Don, D., & Friedenberg, L. (1984). Mothering and the young child. In A. U. Rickel et al (Eds.), <u>Social and psychological problems of women</u> (pp. 45-58). New York: McGraw-Hill.

An interesting discussion of psychodynamics from an interactive perspective--effects from child to mother as well as mother to child.

Eiduson, B. T. (1983a). Children of the children of the 1960s: An introduction. American Journal of Orthopsychiatry, 53(3), 400-407.

Eiduson, B. T. (1983b). Conflict and stress in nontraditional families: Impact on children. American Journal of Orthopsychiatry, 53(3), 426-435.

Feldman, S. S., & Nash, S. C. (1984). The transition from expectancy to parenthood: Impact of the firstborn child on men and women. Sex Roles, 11(1/2), 61-78.

Flax, J. (1978). The conflict between nurturance and autonomy in mother-daughter relationships and within feminism. Feminist Studies, 4(2), 172-189.

Flax, drawing on an Freudian oedipal paradigm and on object relations theory, focuses on certain aspects of mother daughter relationships.

Fox, M. L. (1979). Unmarried adult mothers: A study of the parenthood transition from late pregnancy to two months postpartum. Unpublished doctoral dissertation, Boston University, Boston.

Friday, N. (1977). My mother/myself: The daughter's search for identity. New York: Delacorte Press.

A probing examination of the mother/daughter bond and the consequent development toward attaining independence and sexual womanhood.

Gerson, M., Alpert, J. L., & Richardson, M. S. (1984). Mothering: The view from psychological research. Signs, 9(3), 434-453.

Gladieux, J. D. (1978). Pregnancy, the transition to parenthood: Satisfaction with the pregnancy experience as a function of sex role conceptions, marital relationships, and social network. In W. B. Miller & L. F. Newman (Eds.), The first child and family formation (pp. 275-295). Chapel Hill: North Carolina Population Center.

Gongla, P. (1982). Single parent families: A look at families of mothers and children. <u>Marriage and Family Review</u>, <u>5</u>(2), 5-27.

Greenberg, S. (1979). <u>Right from the start: A guide to nonsexist childrearing</u>. Boston: Houghton Mifflin.

Gross, H. E., Bernard, J., Dann, A. J., Glover, N., Lorber, J., McClintock, M., Newton, N., & Rossi, A. S. (1979). Considering a biosocial perspective on parenting. <u>Signs</u>, <u>4</u>(4), 695-717.

This journal includes the seven reactions of seven important authors to Rossi's "A biosocial perspective on parenting." Some reactions reject Rossi's position. Others extend it. A reply by Rossi is included. These are thought-provoking articles. (See Rossi, 1977).

Hall, N. (1981). <u>The moon and the virgin: Reflections on the archetypal feminine</u>. New York: Harper & Row.

A feminist psychoanalytic consideration about mothers and daughters from a Jungian perspective.

Hammer, S. (1975). <u>Daughters and mothers, mothers and daughters</u>. New York: Quadrangle Book Co.

Hammer notes she is indebted to Chodorow's early work (1974) comparing more primitive communities and middle class Western civilization in the varying opportunities women have had to develop a clearer more defined sense of self.

Hare-Mustin, R. T., & Broderick, P. C. (1979). The myth of motherhood: A study of attitudes toward motherhood. <u>Psychology of Women Quarterly</u>, <u>4</u>(1), 114-128.

Heffner, E. (1978). <u>Mothering: The emotional experience of motherhood after Freud</u>. New York: Doubleday & Co.

Hirsch, M. (1981). Mothers and daughters: A review.
    Signs: Journal of Women in Culture and Society, 7(1),
    200-222.

    In 1976 Adrienne Rich demonstrated the absence of the
    mother-daughter relationship from theology, psychoanal-
    ysis, art, and sociology. Subsequently much focus
    has been given to the mother-daughter relationship.
    Hirsch accounts for this reversal and the subsequent
    centrality of the mother-daughter relationship in
    current feminist scholarship. The range and direction
    of exploration are deliniated. [Hirsch's review essay
    is an important one].

Jung, C. G. (1973). Psychological aspects of the mother
    archetype. In C. G. Jung, Four archetypes (pp. 75-
    110). Princeton, NJ: Bolligen.

Lamb, M. E. (Ed.). (1981). The role of the father in
    child development (2nd ed.). New York: John Wiley.

Lerner, L. (1982). Special book review. Chodorow's
    "Reproduction of mothering: An appraisal." The
    Psychoanalytic Review, 61(1), 151-162.

    Three discussants (Carol Nadelson, Jessica Benjamin,
    and Mary Brown Parlee) examine Chodorow's analysis and
    the implications of her recommendations for men and
    women to share more equally in parenting.

Longfellow, C., Zelkowitz, P., & Saunders, E. (1982). The
    quality of mother-child relationships. In D. Belle
    (Ed.), Lives in stress: Women and depression (pp. 163-
    176). Beverly Hills, CA: Sage.

Lorber, J., Coser, R. L., Rossi, A. S., & Chodorow, N.
    (1981). On The reproduction of mothering: A
    methodological debate. Signs, 6(3), 482-514.

Macklin, E., & Rubin, R. (1983). Contemporary families
    and alternative lifestyles: Handbook on research and
    theory. Beverly Hills, CA: Sage.

Nakamura, C. Y., McCarthy, S. J., Rothstein-Fisch, C., & Winges, L. D. (1981). Interdependence of child care resources and the progress of women in society. Psychology of Women Quarterly, 6(1), 26-40.

National Women's Health Network. Whole birth catalogue. Washington, DC: Author.

Odent, M. (1984). Birth reborn. New York: Pantheon.

Pogebrin, L. C. (1980). Growing up free: Raising your child in the 80s. New York: McGraw-Hill.

Rexford, M. T. (1976). Single mothers by choice: An exploratory study. Unpublished doctoral dissertation, California School of Professional Psychology, Los Angeles.

Rich, A. (1977). Of woman born: Motherhood as experience and institution. New York: Bantam.

Ross, M. E., & Ross, C. L. (1983). Mothers, infants and the psychoanalytic study of ritual. Signs, 9(1), 26-39.

In Freud's view, the oedipal phase is primarily of interest for what it tells of the relationship between sons and their fathers. He understands ritual and religion in general terms of the struggle between fathers and sons. This article suggests that these more positive elements can be comprehended within the psychoanalytic interpretation of ritual if interpretation is extended to include the preoedipal period of life and the preoedipal mother infant relationship.

Rossi, A. S. (1968). Transition to parenthood. Journal of Marriage and the Family, 30(1), 26-39.

Most studies of mother-child relationships have been concerned with the impact of mother on their children. There has unfortunately been a neglect of the effect on women of their children, the need to be a mother, the difficulties of the role transition, and maternal satisfaction. (JSAS)

Rossi, A. S. (1977). A biosocial perspective on parenting.
Daedelus, 106(2), 1-31.

In this important and controversial paper Rossi presents the thesis that the concept of egalitarianism
underlying current sociological research is inadequate
because it neglects our biological heritage. She
hypothesizes a biosocial perspective which emphasizes
the biological roots of what is learned and the
difference in the ease with which children of
different sexes learn.

Russo, N. F. (1976). The motherhood mandate. Journal of
Social Issues, 32(3), 143-153.

Russo, N. F. (1979a). Sex roles, fertility, and the
motherhood mandate: An overview. Psychology of Women
Quarterly, 4(1), 7-15.

Russo, N. F. (Ed.). (1979b). The motherhood mandate
[Special issue]. Psychology of Women Quarterly, 4(1).

Schlesinger, B. (1984). The one parent family:
Perspectives and annotated bibliography (5th ed.).
Toronto: University of Toronto Press.

Shure, M. B. (1984). Enhancing childrearing skills in
lower income women. In A. U. Rickel, M. Gerrard, &
I. Iscoe, (Eds.), Social and psychological problems of
women: Prevention and crisis intervention (pp. 121-
138). New York: Hemisphere Publishing.

Treblicot, J. (Ed.). (1984). Mothering: Essays in
feminist theory. Totowa, NJ: Rowman and Allenheid.

Weisskopf, W. C. (1980). Maternal sexuality and asexual
motherhood. Signs, 5(4), 766-782.

Wood, V., Traupmann, J., & Hay, J. (1984). Motherhood in
the middle years: Women and their adult children. In
G. Baruch & J. Brooks-Gunn (Eds.), Women in midlife
(pp. 227-244). New York: Plenum Press.

Wortis, R. P. (1971). The acceptance of the concept of the
    maternal role by behavioral scientists: Its effects on
    women. <u>American Journal of Orthopsychiatry</u>, <u>41</u>,
    733-746.

Yogev, S., & Vierra, A. (1983). The state of motherhood
    among professional women. <u>Sex Roles</u>, <u>9</u>(3), 391-396.

Zelkowitz, P. (1982). Parenting philosophies and
    practices. In D. Belle (Ed.), <u>Lives in stress: Women
    and depression</u> (pp. 154-162). Beverly Hills, CA:
    Sage.

Zimmerman, I. L., & Bernstein, M. (1983). Parental work
    patterns in alternative families: Influence on child
    development. <u>American Journal of Orthopsychiatry</u>,
    <u>53</u>(3), 418-425.

S. Narcissism

Lachmann, F. (1982a). Narcissism and female gender
     identity: A reformulation. The Psychoanalytic Review,
     69(1), 43-61.

Lachmann, F. (1982b). Narcissistic development. In
     D. Mendell (Ed.), Early female development: Current
     psychoanalytic views (pp. 227-248). New York: SP
     Medical and Scientific Books.

T. The Older Woman

(1981). Aging: A more difficult problem for women than for
    men? In H. J. Wershaw (Ed.), Controversial issues in
    gerontology (pp. 109-126). New York: Springer.

Barnett, R. C., & Baruch, G. K. (1978). Women in the
    middle years: A critique of research and theory.
    Psychology of Women Quarterly, 3(2), 187-197.

Barnett, R. C. (1979). Women in widowhood. In J. H.
    Williams (Ed.), Psychology of women. New York:
    W. W. Norton.

Block, M. R., Davidson, J. L., & Grambs, J. D. (1981).
    Women over forty: Visions and realities. New York:
    Springer.

    This volume is devoted to a factual presentation of
    the research about older women. It seeks to minimize
    prevailing myths and stereotypes.

Carey, G. (1977). The widowed: A year later. Journal of
    Counseling Psychology, 24, 125-133.

Datan, N. et al. (1981). A time to reap: The middle age
    of women in five Israeli subcultures. Baltimore:
    Johns Hopkins Press.

    A discussion of cultural influences on one's attitude
    about the aging process.

Davis, L. J., & Brody, E. M. (1979). Rape and older women:
    A guide to prevention and protection. Washington, DC:
    U.S. Department of Health and Human Services, National
    Center for the Prevention and Control of Rape.

Duffy, M. (1984). Aging and the family: Intergenerational
    psychodynamics. Psychotherapy, Theory, Research and
    Practice, 21(3), 342-346.

Gatz, M., Pearson, C., & Fuentes, M. (1984). Older women
    and mental health. In A. U. Rickel, M. Gerrard, &
    I. Iscoe, (Eds.), Social and psychological problems
    of women: Prevention and crisis intervention (pp. 273-
    299). New York: Hemisphere Publishing.

Gatz, M., Fuentes, M., & Pearson, C. (no date). Health and
    mental health of older women in the 1980's:
    Implications for psychologists. University of
    Southern California, Los Angeles, Department of
    Psychology.

Giele, J. Z. (Ed.). (1982). Women in the middle years:
    Current knowledge and directions for research and
    policy. New York: John Wiley.

    This book explores the differences and similarities
    between adult development in men and women. Evidence
    indicates that women focus more on the quality of
    their relationships. Men are more concerned with
    their individual achievements. Giele's treatment of
    women's work and family roles demonstrates how the
    lives of men and women are exhibiting greater "cross-
    over." The capacities of both to perform instrumental
    and affective roles has increased. At the end of the
    book Giele presents her theory which accounts for the
    paradoxical coexistence of sex differences and "cross-
    over" based on the role differentiation that accompa-
    nies modernization. A cross section of experts, psy-
    chologists, psychiatrists, anthropologists, and socio-
    logists contribute chapters to this book.

Lesnoff-Caravaglia, G. (Ed.). (1983). The world of the
    older woman: Conflicts and resolutions. New York:
    Human Sciences Press.

Neugarten, B. L. (1965). The awareness of middle age. In
    B. L. Neugarten (Ed.), Middle age and aging: A reader
    in social psychology (pp. 93-98). Chicago: University
    of Chicago Press.

Neugarten, B. L., & Kraines, R. (1965). Menopausal
    symptoms in women of various ages. Psychosomatic
    Medicine, 27(3), 266-273.

Porcino, J. (1983). <u>Growing older, getting better: A handbook for women in the second half of life</u>. Boston, MA: Addison-Welsey.

Rix, S. E. (1984). <u>Older women: The economics of aging</u>. Washington, DC: Women's Research and Education Institute of the Congressional Caucus for Women's Issues.

Rubin, L. B. (1981). <u>Women of a certain age: The midlife search for self</u>. New York: Harper & Row.

Seidler, S. (1984, March/April). Drug use and the elderly. <u>Network News</u>. (Available from the National Women's Health Network, Washington, DC).

Steuer, J. L. (1982). Psychotherapy with older women: Ageism and sexism in traditional practice. <u>Psychotherapy: Theory, Research and Practice</u>, <u>19</u>(4), 429-436.

Szinovacz, M. (Ed.). (1982). <u>Women's retirement: Policy implications of recent research</u>. Beverley Hills, CA: Sage Publications.

   The author defines special needs of retired women and implications for social policy.

U. S. Department of Health, Education and Welfare. (1979). <u>Elderly and psychoactive drugs</u>. Washington, DC: Author.

Wasmuth, M. (1979). <u>Counseling older women: An annotated bibliography</u>. Boston: Womanspace.

White House Mini-Conference on Older Women. (1981). <u>Growing numbers, growing forces: A report from the White House Mini-Conference on Older Women</u>. Des Moines, IA: Author.

U. Phobias

Chambless, D. L., & Goldstein, A. J. (1980). Anxieties:
     Agoraphobia and hysteria. In A. M. Brodsky & R. T.
     Hare-Mustin (Eds.). Women and psychotherapy: An
     assessment of research and practice (pp. 113-134).
     New York: Guilford Press.

Fodor, I. G. (1974). The phobic syndrome in women:
     Implications for treatment. In V. Franks & V. Burtle
     (Eds.), Women in therapy (pp. 132-168). New York:
     Brunner/Mazel.

Goldstein, A. J. (1973). Learning theory insufficiency in
     understanding agoraphobia--a plea for empiricism.
     Proceedings of the First Meeting of the European
     Association for Behavior Therapy and Behavior
     Modification. Munich, Germany: Urban & Schwarzenburg.

Hafner, R. J. (1977). The husbands of agoraphobic women
     and their influence on treatment outcome. British
     Journal of Psychiatry, 131, 289-294.

Mathews, A. M., Gelder, M. G., & Johnston, D. W. (1981).
     Agoraphobia--Nature and treatment. New York: The
     Guilford Press.

Mowbray, C. T., Lanir, S., & Hulce, M. (Eds.). (1984).
     Section 3: Diagnoses applied to women: The evidence
     --Example Agoraphobia. Women and Therapy, 3(3/4),
     91-94.

Symonds, A. (1971). Phobias after marriage--Women's
     declaration of dependence. American Journal of
     Psychoanalysis, 31(2), 144-152.

V. Rape and Incest

Amir, M. (1971). Patterns in forcible rape. Chicago:
University of Chicago Press.

Amir presents and refutes myths about rape, and pro-
ceeds to take a phenomenological approach to the experience. Psychological and sociological approaches to
the systematic investigation of rape are explored.
(JSAS)

Atkeson, B. M., Calhoun, K. S., et al. (1982). Victims of
rape: Repeated assessment of depressive symptoms.
Journal of Consulting and Clinical Psychology, 50(1),
96-102.

Bart, P. B. (1981). A study of women who were raped and
avoided rape. Journal of Social Issues, 37(4),
123-137.

Bart, P. B., & O'Brien, P. H. (1984). Stopping rape:
Effective avoidance strategies. Sex Roles, 10(1),
83-101.

Becker, J. V., Skinner, L. J., & Abel, G. G. (1983).
Sequelae of sexual assault: The survivor's
perspective. In J. G. Greer & I. R. Stuart (Eds.),
The sexual aggressor: Current perspectives in
treatment (pp. 240-266). New York: Van Nostrand-
Rheinhold.

Becker, J. V., Skinner, L. J., Abel, G. G., Axelrod, R., &
Cichon, J. (1984). Sexual problems of sexual assault
survivors. Women and Health, 9(4), 5-20.

Breines, W., & Gordon, L. (1983). The new scholarship on
family violence. Signs, 8(3), 490-531.

Brownmiller, S. (1975). Against our will: Men, women, and
rape. New York: Simon and Schuster.

Brownmiller's primary thesis is that rape is a world-
wide social mechanism, with a long history, by which

men oppress and control women -- rather than a random
act by troubled or atypical men. Rape is primarily an
act of power, not of sex. (JSAS)

Burgess, A. W., & Holmstrom, L. H. (1974a). Rape trauma
    syndrome. American Journal of Psychiatry, 131(9),
    981-986.

The "rape trauma syndrome" described in this article
was based on an analysis of reactions by 99 adult
female victims of forcible rape. In general, the
victims of rape studies here experienced a long period
of anxiety, and recurrent attacks of panic. The acute
phase involved disorganization, with fear as the pre-
dominant symptom, and somatic symptoms were present
during the first several weeks. The long-term reorga-
nization appeared to involve a reintegration of self.
However, none of the women displayed psychotic reactions, and all returned to previous levels of functioning within a few months. The authors described 3
distinct ways in which the victims responded to the
rape trauma, and provided strategies for dealing with
each. (JSAS)

Burgess, A. W., & Holmstrom, L. H. (1974b). Rape: Victims
    of crisis. Bowie, MD: Robert J. Brady.

Burgess, A. W., & Holmstrom, L. H. (1978). Recovery from
    rape and prior life stress. Research in Nursing and
    Health, 1(4), 165-174.

Calhoun, K. S., & Atkeson, B. M. (in press). Treatment of
    victims of sexual assault. Elmsford, NY: Pergamon.

Calhoun, K. S., Atkeson, B. M., & Ellis, E. M. (1981).
    Social adjustment in victims of sexual assault.
    Journal of Consulting and Clinical Psychology, 49,
    705-712.

Calhoun, K. S., Atkeson, B. M., & Resick, P. A. (1982). A
    longitudinal examination of fear reactions in victims
    of rape. Journal of Counseling Psychology, 29(6),
    655-661.

Cann, A., Calhoun, L. G., Selby, J. W., et al. (1981).
    Rape: A contemporary overview and analysis. Journal
    of Social Issues, 37(4), 1-4.

Coates, D., & Winston, T. (1983). Counteracting the
    deviance of depression: Peer support groups for
    victims. Journal of Social Issues, 39(2), 169-194.

Colao, F., & Hunt, M. (1983). Therapists coping with
    sexual assault. In J. H. Robbins & R. J.Siegel
    (Eds.), Women changing therapy (pp. 205-214).
    New York: Haworth press.

Courtois, C. A. (1980). Studying and counseling women with
    past incest experience. Victimology, 5(2-4), 322-334.

Courtois, C. A., & Watts, D. L. (1982). Counseling adult
    women who experienced incest in childhood or
    adolescence. Personnel and Guidance Journal, 60(5),
    275-279.

Davis, L. J., & Brody, E. M. (1979). Rape and older women:
    A guide to prevention and protection. Washington, DC:
    U.S. Department of Health and Human Services, National
    Center for the Prevention and Control of Rape.

Department of Justice, Federal Bureau of Investigation.
    (1984). Uniform Crime Reports for 1983. Washington,
    DC: U.S. Government Printing Office.

Ellis, E. M., Atkeson, B. M., & Calhoun, K. S. (1981). An
    assessment of long-term reaction to rape. Journal of
    Abnormal Psychology, 90(3), 263-266.

Ellis, E. M., Atkeson, B. M., & Calhoun, K. S. (1982). An
    examination of differences between multiple-and
    single-incident victims of sexual assault. Journal of
    Abnormal Psychology, 91(3), 221-224.

Ellis, E. M., Calhoun, K. S., & Atkeson, B. M. (1980)
    Sexual dysfunction in victims of rape: Victims may
    experience a loss of sexual arousal and frightening
    flashbacks even one year after the assault. Women and
    Health, 5(4), 39-47.

Fine, M. (1983-1984). Coping with rape: Critical perspectives on consciousness. <u>Imagination, Cognition and Personality</u>, <u>3</u>(3), 249-267.

Forman, B. D. (1980). Cognitive modification of obsessive thinking in a rape victim: A preliminary study. <u>Psychological Reports</u>, <u>47</u>(3, pt.1), 817-822.

Forman, B. D. (1980). Psychotherapy with rape victims. <u>Psychotherapy: Theory, Research and Practice</u>, <u>17</u>(3), 304-311.

Forman, B. D. (1983). Assessing the impact of rape and its significance in psychotherapy. <u>Psychotherapy: Theory, Research and Practice</u>, <u>20</u>(4), 515-519.

Frank, E. (1981). Past psychiatric symptoms and the response to sexual assault. <u>Comprehensive Psychiatry</u>, <u>22</u>(5), 479-487.

Frank, E., & Stewart, B. D. (1983). Treating depression in victims of rape. <u>Clinical Psychologist</u>, <u>36</u>(4), 95-98.

Frieze, I. H. (1983). Investigating the causes and consequences of marital rape. <u>Signs</u>, <u>8</u>(3), 532-553.

Gager, N., & Schurr, C. (1976). <u>Sexual assault: Confronting rape in America</u>. New York: Grosset & Dunlap.

In this book, Gager and Schurr have presented the results of their research on the causes, nature and effects of rape. While they write that the psychological consequences of being raped must not be minimized and must certainly not be compounded by cruel, indifferent or inhumane treatment following the rape by medical or law enforcement officials, they also point out that "rape must not be considered a lifetime burden, and we should guard against making 'permanent' victims of females who are assaulted . . . (It is important that we avoid unconsciously reinforcing) concepts of rape as irrevocably 'staining.' 'damaging,' and 'soiling' women . . . Righteous anger must not blind us to the healthy possibilities of individual assimilation." (JSAS)

Gatz, M., Pearson, C., & Fuentes, M. (1984). Social and psychological problems of women: Prevention and crisis intervention. Washington, DC: Hemisphere.

Greenacre, P. (1952). The prepuberty trauma in girls. In Trauma, growth and personality (pp.204-223). New York: International Universities Press.

Halpern, S. (1981). The mythology of rape. In P. Russianoff (Ed.), Women in crisis (pp. 145-147). New York: Human Sciences Press.

Herman, J. (1981). Father-daughter incest. Professional Psychology, 12(1), 76-80.

Herman, J., & Hirschman, L. (1981). Families at risk for father-daughter incest. American Journal of Psychiatry, 138(7), 967-970.

Herrington, L. H. (1985). Victims of crime: Their plight, our response. American Psychologist, 40(1), 99-103.

Holmes, K. (1981). Services for victims of rape: A dualistic practice model. Social Casework, 62(1), 30-39.

This article outlines an expanded practice model for helping rape victims that uses crisis intervention and advocacy. (CSWE)

James, J (1981). Prostitution and sexual violence. In P. Russianoff (Ed.), Women in crisis (pp. 176-217). New York: Human Sciences Press.

Janoff-Bulman, R. (1982). Esteem and control bases of blame: "Adaptive" strategies for victims versus observers. Journal of Personality, 50(2), 180-192.

Johnson, A. G. (1980). On the prevalance of rape in the
    United States. Signs, 1980, 6(1), 136-146.

Katan, A. (1973). Children who were raped. Psychoanalytic
    Study of the Child, 28, 208-224.

    Katan studied six adult patients who were assaulted in
    early childhood. Her study indicates that the long-
    term effects of rape in childhood, if untreated, are
    severe problems in self-esteem, anxiety about men, and
    aggression.

Kilpatrick, D. G., Resnick, P. A., & Veronen, L. J. (1981).
    Effects of rape experiences: A longitudinal study.
    Journal of Social Issues, 37(1), 105-122.

Krulewitz, J. E. (1983). Reactions to rape victims:
    Effects of rape circumstances, victim's emotional
    response, and sex of helper. Journal of Counseling
    Psychology, 29(6), 645-654.

Lott, B., Reilly, M. E., & Howard, D. R. (1982). Sexual
    assault and harassment: A campus community case study.
    Signs, 8(2), 296-319.

Malamuth, N. (1981). Rape proclivity among males. Journal
    of Social Issues, 37(4), 138-157.

Miller, A. (1984). Thou shalt not be aware: Society's
    betrayal of the child. New York: Farrar, Strauss &
    Giroux.

Nadelson, C. C., Notman, M. T., Zackson, H. et al. (1982).
    A follow-up study of rape victims. American Journal
    of Psychiatry, 139(10), 1266-1270.

O'Hare, J., & Taylor, K. (1983). The reality of incest.
    In J. H. Robbins, & R. J. Siegel (Eds.), Women
    changing therapy (pp. 215-230). New York: Haworth
    Press.

Orlando, J. A., & Koss, M. P. (1983). The effects of sexual victimization on sexual satisfactions: A study of the negative-association hypothesis. <u>Journal of Abnormal Psychology</u>, <u>92</u>(1), 104-106.

President's Task Force on Victims of Crime (1983). <u>Final report</u>. Washington, DC: U. S. Government Printing Office.

Rada, R. (1977). <u>Clinical aspects of the rapist</u>. New York: Grune & Stratton.

Rada, R. (1983). Rape. In W. Fann, Karacan, I. (Eds.). <u>Phenomenology and treatment of psychosexual disorders</u>. New York: SP Medical and Scientific Books.

Rape [Special issue]. (1981). <u>Journal of Social Issues</u>, <u>37</u>(4).

Reactions to victimization [Special issue]. (1983). <u>Journal of Social Issues</u>, <u>39</u>(2).

Resick, P. A., Calhoun, K. S., et al. (1981). Social adjustment in victims of sexual assault. <u>Journal of Consulting and Clinical Psychology</u>, <u>49</u>(5), 705-712.

Riger, S., & Gordon, M. T. (1981). The fear of rape: A study in social control. <u>Journal of Social Issues</u>, <u>37</u>(4), 71-92.

Riger, S., & Gordon, M. T. (1984). The impact of crime on urban women. In A. U. Rickel, M. Gerrard, & I. Iscoe, (Eds.), <u>Social and psychological problems of women</u>: <u>Prevention and crisis intervention</u> (pp. 139-156). New York: Hemisphere Publishing.

Rodino, P. (1985). Current legislation on victim assistance. <u>American Psychologist</u>, <u>40</u>(1), 104-106.

Rush, F. (1980). <u>The best kept secret: Sexual abuse of children</u>. Englewood Cliffs, NJ: Prentice-Hall.

Russell, D. E. H. (1984). Sexual exploitation: Rape, child sexual abuse, and workplace harassment. Beverly Hills, CA: Sage Publications.

Russell, D. E. H., & Howell, N. (1983). The prevalence of rape in the United States revisited. Signs, 8(4), 688-695.

Russell, D. E. H. (1983). Rape in marriage. New York: Collier.

Sanday, P. R. (1981). The socio-cultural context of rape: A cross-cultural study. Journal of Social Issues, 37(4), 5-27.

Sandiford, K., & Burgess, A. W. (1984). Shattered night. New York: Warner Books.

Scheppele, K. L., & Bart, P. B. (1983). Through women's eyes: Defining danger in the wake of sexual assault. Journal of Social issues, 37(2), 63-80.

Schuker, E. (1979). Psychodynamics and treatment of sexual assault victims. Journal of the American Academy of Psychoanalysis, 7(4), 553-573.

This paper discusses myths and facts about sexual assault; common reactions of those who work with rape victims, the rape trauma syndrome, an approach to immediate and short term treatment, and the long-term effects of sexual assault and related treatment issues.

Silver, R. L., Boon, C., & Stones, M. H. (1983). Searching for meaning in misfortune: Making sense of incest. Journal of Social Issues, 39, 81-101.

Sunday, S. S. R., & Tobach, E. (Eds.). (in press). Genes and gender: Vol. 1. Violence against women: A critique of the sociobiology of rape. New York: Gordian Press.

Sutherland, S., & Scherl, D. S. (1970). Patterns of
        responses among victims of rape. American Journal of
        Orthopsychiatry, 40(3), 503-511.

        The 13 rape victims interviewed here were 18 to 24
        years of age age, and all were young white girls who
        had moved into lower income communities in order to do
        something "meaningful." The reactions to the assault
        by these victims followed a pattern: (1) acute
        distress, (2) denial of adverse effects and pseudo-
        adjustment, and (3) depression and the desire to
        verbalize to a supportive other. (JSAS)

VanBuskirk, S. S., & Cole, C. F. (1983). Characteristics
        of eight women seeking therapy for the effects of
        incest. Psychotherapy: Theory, Research and Practice,
        20(4), 503-514.

Vernon, L. J., & Best, C. L. (1983). Assessment and
        treatment of rape-induced fear and anxiety. Clinical
        Psychologist, 36(4), 99-101.

Warner, C. G., & Braen, G. R. (Eds.). (1982). Management
        of the physically and emotionally abused: Emergency
        assessment, intervention and counseling. Norwalk, CT:
        Appleton-Century-Crofts.

White, P. N., & Rollins, J. C. (1981). Rape: A family
        crisis. Family Relations, 30(1), 103-109.

Wooley, M. J., & Vigilanti, M. A. (1984). Psychological
        separation and the sexual abuse victim.
        Psychotherapy, Theory, Research and Practice,
        21(3), 347-352.

W. Reproductive Issues

Adler, N. (1981). Sex roles and unwanted pregnancy in
    adolescent and adult women. Professional Psychology,
    12(1), 56-66.

Allison, J. R. (1984). Roles and role conflict of women in
    infertile couples. In P. P. Rieker & E. Carmen
    (Eds.), The gender gap in psychotherapy: Social
    realities and psychological processes (pp. 151-166).
    New York: Plenum. (Reprinted from Psychology of Women
    Quarterly, 1979 4[1], 97-113)

Arms, S. (1984). Immaculate deception: A new look at women
    and childbirth. Hadley, MA: Bergin & Garvey
    Publishing, Inc.

Arney, W. R. (1983). Power and the profession of
    obstetrics. Chicago: University of Chicago Press.

Atkinson, A. K., & Rickel, A. U. (1984). Depression in
    women: The postpartum experience. In A. U. Rickel,
    M. Gerrard, & I. Iscoe (Eds.), Social and
    psychological problems of women: Prevention and
    crisis intervention (pp. 197-218). New York:
    Hemisphere Publishing.

Bardwick, J. M. (1970). Psychological conflict and the
    reproductive system. In J. M. Bardwick, E. Douvan, M.
    S. Horner, & D. Gutman (Eds.), Feminine personality
    and conflict (pp. 3-28). Belmont, CA: Brooks/Cole.

    Bardwick writes that "women are their bodies," and
    that the expression and gratification of self-esteem
    needs, and feelings, are made primarily through the
    reproductive system which also, in turn, affects the
    needs, moods and conflicts of women. "Menstruation,
    pregnancy, childbirth, lactation, and menopause are
    all periods of normal crisis for women and should be
    understood as such." (JSAS)

Barker, G. H. (1983). Your search for fertility: A sympathetic guide to achieving pregnancy for childless couples. New York: William Morrow.

Bibring, G. L. (1959). Some considerations of the psychological processes in pregnancy. Psychoanalytic Study of The Child, 14, 113-121.

Bibring argues that for all women, whatever their prior level of personal adjustment, pregnancy is a period of developmental crisis. The individual makes the transition to a new developmental stage. During this transition emotional turmoil may occur. (JSAS)

Blum, B. L. (Ed.). (1980). Psychological aspects of pregnancy, birthing, and bonding. New York: Human Sciences Press.

Bresnick, E., & Taymor, M. L. (1979). The role of counseling in infertility. Fertility and sterility, 32(2), 154-156.

Coleman, A., & Coleman, L. (1973). Pregnancy: The psychological experience. New York: Seabury Press.

Debrovner, C. H. (Ed.). (1982). Premenstrual tension: A multidisciplinary approach. New York: Human Sciences Press.

Delaney, J., Lipton, M. J., & Toth, E. (1976). The curse: A cultural history of menstruation. New York: E. P. Dutton.

Ehrenreich, B., & English, D. (1978). For her own good: 150 years of the experts' advice to women. Garden City, NY: Anchor/Doubleday.

Friedman, R. C., et al. (1980). Behavior and the menstrual cycle. Signs, 5(4), 719-738.

Gath, D., & Cooper, P. J. (1982). Hysterectomy and psychiatric disorder: I. Levels of psychiatric morbidity before and after hysterectomy. British Journal of Psychiatry, 140, 335-342.

Gerrard, M., McCann, L., & Geis, B. D. (1984). The
     antecedents and prevention of unwanted pregnancy.
     In A. U. Rickel, M. Gerrard, & I. Iscoe (Eds.), Social
     and psychological problems of women: Prevention and
     crisis intervention (pp. 85-102). New York:
     Hemisphere Publishing.

Golub, S. (Ed.). (1983a). Lifting the curse of
     menstruation: A feminist appraisal of the influence of
     menstruation on women's lives [Special issue]. Women
     and Health, 8(2/3).

Golub, S. (Ed.). (1983b). Menarche: An interdisciplinary
     view. Lexington, MA: D. C. Heath.

Golub, S. (Ed.). (1983c). Menarche: The transition from
     girl to woman. Lexington, MA: Lexington Books.

Goodman, M. (1980). Toward a biology of menopause. Signs,
     5(4), 739-753.

Greenberg, R., & Fisher, S. (1983). Freud and the female
     reproductive process: Tests and issues. In J. Masling
     (Ed.), Empirical studies of psychoanalytic theories
     (Vol. 1, pp. 251-281). Hillsdale, NJ: Lawrence Erl-
     baum Associates.

Greenwood, S. (1984). Menopause, naturally (Preparing for
     the second half of life). San Francisco, CA: Volcano
     Press.

Grossman, F. K., Eichler, L. S., & Winickoff, S. A. (1980).
     Pregnancy, birth and parenthood: Adaptations of
     mothers, fathers and infants. San Francisco, CA:
     Jossey-Bass.

This book, written by clinical psychologists, is the
result of a longitudinal study that focused on the
experience of pregnancy and the first year postpartum
of 84 couples. The goals of the study were (1) to
increase understanding of the process of childbearing,
including the contributions and interactions of
mother, father, and infant as the family develops; (2)

to identify those factors early in pregnancy that are
predictive of adaptational problems later on - factors
that can become the focus for programs of preventive
intervention; and (3) to compare the experience of
first-time parents with that of couples who are al-
ready parents. Each chapter includes a review of the
relevant literature, a description of factors predictive of the adaptation range of mother, father, and
baby, and some qualitative description of the experiences of pregnancy, labor, and the first year of
parenthood.

Haire, D. (1972). The cultural warping of childbirth.
Minneapolis, MN: International Childbirth Education
Association Special Report.

Harrison, M. (1982). Women in residence. New York: Random
House.

Expose of OB/GYN care.

Harrison, M. (1985). Self-help for premenstrual syndrome.
Washington, DC: National Women's Health Network.

Keith, L. G. with Kent, D. R., Berger, G. S., & Brittain, J.
R. (1980). The safety of fertility control. New
York: Springer.

Kestenberg, J. S. (1977). Regression and reintegration in
pregnancy. In H. Blum (Ed.), Female psychology:
Contemporary psychoanalytic views (pp. 213-250).
New York: International Universities Press.

Eight psychoanalytic case histories of expectant
parents scored before, during and after pregnancy.
Regression in pregnancy drew on earlier inner-genital
phases (Kestenberg, 1956a, 1956a, 1968b, 1975). This
does not support the original Freudian hypothesis that
the wish for a child is derived either from pregenital
or phallic drives.

Kipper, D. A., Zigler-Shani, Z., Serr, D. M., & Insler, V. (1977). Psychogenic infertility, neuroticism and the feminine role: A methodological inquiry. <u>Journal of Psychosomatic Research</u>, <u>21</u>, 353-358.

Koeske, R. (1981). Theoretical and conceptual complexities in the design and analysis of menstrual cycle research. In P. Konmenich, M. McSweeney, J. Noack et al. (Eds.), <u>The menstrual cycle</u> (Vol. 2). New York: Springer.

Kraft, A. D., Palombo, J., Mitchell, D., Dean, C., Meyers, S., & Schmidt, A. W. (1980). The psychological dimensions of infertility. <u>American Journal of Orthopsychiatry</u>, <u>50</u>(4), 618-628.

Leifer, M. (1980). Pregnancy. <u>Signs</u>, <u>5</u>(4), 754-765.

    Much psychological research continues to report on women having reproductive difficulties or psychiatric problems. In this essay, Leifer reviews studies assessing the responses of normal women to salient aspects of pregnancy.

Magnus, E. M. (1980). Sources of maternal stress in the postpartum period: A review of the literature and an alternative view. In J. E. Parsons (Ed.), <u>The psychology of sex differences and sex roles</u>. Washington, DC: Hemisphere Publishing Co.

Mazor, M. D., & Simons, H. F. (Eds.). (1984). <u>Infertility: Medical, emotional, and social considerations</u>. New York: Human Sciences Press.

McKeever, P. (1984). The perpetuation of menstrual shame: Implications and directions. <u>Women and Health</u>, <u>9</u>(4), 33-47.

Menning, B. E. (1977). <u>A guide for the childless couple</u>. Englewood Cliffs, NJ: Prentice-Hall.

Morgan, S. (1982). <u>Coping with hysterectomy</u>. New York: Dial Press.

Nadelson, C. C., & Notman, M. T. (1984). Reproductive
    advancements: Theory, research applications, and
    psychological issues. In L. E. Walker (Ed.), Women
    and mental health policy (pp. 117-134). Beverly
    Hills, CA: Sage Publications.

National Women's Health Network. Plaintext pregnancy/
patient checklist. Washington, DC: Author.

Notman, M. T., & Nadelson, C. C. (1980). Reproductive
    crisis. In A. M. Brodsky & R. T. Hare-Mustin (Eds.),
    Women and psychotherapy: An assessment of research and
    practice (pp. 307-338). New York: Guilford.

Oakley, A. (1980). Women confined: Towards a sociology of
    childbirth. New York: Schocken.

Parlee, M. B. (1978). Psychological aspects of
    menstruation, childbirth, and menopause. In J. A.
    Sherman & F. L. Denmark (Eds.), The psychology of
    women: Future directions in research. New York:
    Psychological Dimensions.

Parlee, M. B. (1984). Reproductive issues, including
    menopause. In G. Baruch & J. Brooks-Gunn (Eds.),
    Women in midlife (pp. 303-313). New York: Plenum
    Press.

Phillips, R. N., Thornton, J., & Gleicher, N. (1982).
    Physician bias in caesarean sections. Journal of
    the American Medical Association, 248, 1082.

Reitz, R. (1984). Menopause: A positive approach. New
    York: Viking/Penguin.

    Exercise, nutrition, sex, alternatives to estrogen
    replacement.

Robertson, J. (1980). A treatment model for post-partum
    depression. Canada's Mental Health, 28(2), 16-17.

Rothman, B. K. (1982). In labor: Women and power in the
    birthplace. New York: W. W. Norton.

Rubinow, D. R., & Byrne, P. (1984). Premenstrual
     syndromes: Overview from a methodological perspective.
     American Journal of Psychiatry, 141(2), 163-172.

Russo, N. F. (1979). Overview: Sex roles, fertility and
     the motherhood mandate. Psychology of Women Quarterly,
     4(1), 7-15.

Scully, D., & Bart, P. B. (1973). A funny thing happened
     on the way to the orifice: Woman in gynecology
     textbooks. American Journal of Sociology, 78(4),
     1045-1050.

Seaman, B. (1980). Doctors' case against the pill (rev.
     and updated ed.). New York: Doubleday.

Seaman, B., & Seaman, G. (1978). Women and the crisis in
     sex hormones. New York: Bantam.

Seibel, M. M., & Taymor, M. L. (1982). Emotional aspects
     of infertility. Infertility and Sterility, 37,
     137-145.

Seiden, A. M. (1976). Overview: Research on the psychology
     of women I. Gender differences and sexual and
     reproductive life. American Journal of Psychiatry,
     133(9), 955-1007.

VanArkel, W. G., Ament, A. J., & Bell, N. (1980). The
     politics of home delivery in The Netherlands.
     Birth and the Family Journal, 7(2), 101-112.

Young, D. (1982). Changing childbirth: Family birth in the
     hospital. Rochester, NY: Childbirth Graphics.

Zaslaw, M. J., & Pedersen, F. A. (1981). Sex role
     conflicts and the experience of childbearing [Special
     issue]. Professional Psychology, 12(1), 47-55.

X. Sexuality

Anderson, B. L. (1983). Primary orgasmic dysfunction: Diagnostic considerations and review of treatment. Psychological Bulletin, 93(1), 105-136.

Barbach, L. G. (1975). For yourself: The fulfillment of female sexuality. New York: Signet.

Barbach, L. G. (1980). Women discover orgasm: A therapist guide to new treatment approach. New York: Free Press.

Barbach, L. G., & Flaherty, M. (1980). Group treatment of situationally orgasmic women. Journal of Sex and Marital Therapy, 6(1), 19-29.

Belzer, E. G. (1981). Orgasmic expulsions of women: A review and heuristic inquiry. Journal of Sex Research, 17(1), 1-12.

Butler, C. (1976). New data about female sexual response. Journal of Sex and Marital Therapy, 2(1), 40-46.

This paper reports on a 195-subject pilot study of female sexual response based on a naturalistic questionnaire method. The questionnaire used in the study is described, and the data obtained are discussed and integrated with established research and theory. Discussion of findings focuses on the relatively low frequency with which women actually experience orgasm in sexual relations and the need to understand the reasons. The concept of the normality of a varied capacity for orgasm is presented in contrast to the usual tendency to evaluate female responses by male standards.

Chesney, A. P., Blakeney, P. E., Chan, F. A., & Cole, C. M. (1981). The impact of sex therapy on sexual behavior and marital communication. Journal of Sex and Marital Therapy, 7(1), 70-79.

Clower, V. L. (1975). Significance of masturbation in
    female sexual development and function. In I. Marcus
    & J. J. Francis (Eds.). Masturbation: From infancy
    to senescence (pp. 107-143). New York: International
    Universities Press.

    In this paper Clower discusses masturbation throughout
    female development tracing the development of female
    identity in body image and genital function. Her
    discussion revises the classical phallocentric views
    of female development substituting a female perspec-
    tive, particularly with regard to the "phallic" phase.

deBruijn, G. (1982). From masturbation to orgasm with
    a partner: How some women bridge the gap--and why
    others don't. Journal of Sex and Marital Therapy,
    8(2), 151-167.

Dekker, J., & Everaerd, W. (1983). A long-term follow-up
    study of couples treated for sexual dysfunctions.
    Journal of Sex and Marital Therapy, 9(2), 99-113.

Everaerd, W., & Dekker, J. (1981). A comparison of sex
    therapy and communication therapy: Couples complaining
    of orgasmic dysfunction. Journal of Sex and Marital
    Therapy, 7(4), 278-289.

Gillespie, W. H. (1969). Concepts of vaginal orgasm.
    International Journal of Psycho-analysis, 50(4),
    495-497.

Glenn, J., & Kaplan, E. (1968). Types of orgasm in women:
    A critical review and redefinition. Journal of The
    American Psychoanalytic Association, 16(3), 549-564.

    Authors discuss the problems of defining different
    types of orgasm and offer some ideas for a basis of
    such definition. They also point to the importance of
    the location of the orgastic experience as a useful
    starting point for associations that lead to under-
    standing of latent meaning of orgasm.

Harris, H. (1979). Some linguistic considerations related to the issue of female orgasm. The Psychoanalytic Review, 66(2), 187-200.

Within the context of female orgasm, Harris is among the first to identify linguistic issues relevant to woman and society. Implications for psychotherapeutic theory and practice are suggested.

Heiman, M. (1968). Female sexuality: Introduction. Journal of The American Psychoanalytic Association, 16(3), 565-568.

The studies of Masters and Johnson and the interpretation by Sherfey are discussed. The author concludes that these studies compel us to examine orgasm within the context of woman's genetic inheritance, constitutional endowment and psychosexual development.

Heiman, M. (1977). Sleep orgasm in woman. In H. Blum (Ed.), Female psychology: Contemporary psychoanalytic views (pp. 285-304). New York: International Universities Press.

Heiman formulates the hypothesis that the nursing situation may provide sensations in the vagina for the baby girl. The author further suggests that the sensations are not the result of mechanical stimulation but of a "resonance" phenomenon whereby the infant's genitals are stimulated from within. The formulations are highly speculative and are based mainly on data obtained from the analysis of one woman, but it does provide a beginning step in understanding the female orgasm.

Heiman, J. R., & LoPiccolo, J. (1983). Clinical outcome of sex therapy: Effects of daily versus weekly treatment. Archives of General Psychiatry, 40(4), 443-449.

Hite, S. (1981). The Hite report: A study of male sexuality. New York: Ballantine.

Jayne, C. (1981). A two-dimensional model of female sexual
     response. Journal of Sex and Marital Therapy, 7(1),
     3-30.

Kirkpatrick, M. (Ed.). (1980). Women's sexual development:
     Explorations of inner space. New York: Plenum.

     This volume is the fifth of Notman and Nadelson's
     Women in context: Development and stresses series. It
     is a collection of papers representing a variety of
     professional points of view on contemporary issues
     regarding female sexual development. [Psychiatrists,
     psychologists, sociologists, psychoanalysts, nurses,
     educators, and feminist activists are represented.]

Kirkpatrick, M. (1982). Women's sexual experience:
     Explorations of the dark continent. New York: Plenum.

     The sixth volume of Notman and Nadelson's Women in
     context: Development and stresses series provides an
     examination and explanation of women's sexual experi-
     ence from the woman's perspective. Papers in this
     volume come from many sources--academic, experiential,
     journalistic and personal.

Kohut, H. (1978). A note on female sexuality. In P.
     Ornstein (Ed.), Search for the self (pp. 783-792).
     New York: International Universities Press.

Kuriansky, J. B., & Sharpe, L. (1981). Clinical and
     research implications of the evaluation of women's
     group therapy for anorgasmia: A review. Journal of
     Sex and Marital Therapy, 7(4), 268-277.

Kuriansky, J. B., Sharpe, L., & O'Conner, D. (1982). The
     treatment of anorgasmia: Long-term effectiveness of a
     short-term behavioral group therapy. Journal of Sex
     and Marital Therapy, 8(1), 29-43.

Lampl-de Groot, J. (1933). Problems of femininity.
     Psychoanalytic Quarterly, 2, 489-518.

Laws, J. L. (1980). Female sexuality through the life
    span. In P. B. Baltes & D. G. Bruin (Eds.), Life-span
    development and behavior. New York: Academic Press.

Loulan, J. (1984). Lesbian sex. San Francisco: Spinsters
    Ink.

Luria, Z., & Meade, R. G. (1984). Sexuality and the
    middle-aged woman. In G. Baruch & J. Brooks-Gunn
    (Eds.), Women in midlife (pp. 371-397). New York:
    Plenum Press.

Marcus, I. (1975). Masturbation: From infancy to
    senescence. New York: International Universities
    Press.

    The author presents a collection of 19 papers on the
    role of masturbation in human development. Topics
    include oral autoerotic and autoaggressive behaviors,
    anal masturbation, precocious sexuality, issues speci-
    fic to female sexuality, cultural factors, the role of
    fantasies, and masturbation in literature.

Miller, P. Y., & Fowlkes, M. R. (1980). Social and
    behavioral constructions of female sexuality. Signs,
    5(4), 783-800.

Montgrain, N. (1983). On the vicissitudes of female sexua-
    lity: The difficult path from "anatomical destiny" to
    psychic representation. International Journal of
    Psychoanalysis, 64(2), 169-186.

Moore, B. (1961). Frigidity in woman. Journal of the
    American Psychoanalytic Association, 9, 571-584.

Moore, B. (1964). Frigidity: A review of psychoanalytic
    literature. Psychoanalytic Quarterly, 33(3), 323-349.

    Moore's review of the literature indicates that the
    compromise nature of frigidity as a symptom has not
    been clarified. It is suggested that the erotic needs
    of some women find gratification in the biological
    function of motherhood and specific orgiastic dis-
    charge is not required. Further attention needs to be

focused on differentiating conflict-free, normal frigid women from those in whom frigidity is clearly pathological.

Moore, B. (1977). Psychic representation and female orgasm. In H. Blum, (Ed.), <u>Female psychology: Contemporary psychoanalytic views</u> (pp.305-330). New York: International Universities Press.

Staying within the current psychoanalytic frame, Moore contends that there is remarkable concurrence between this frame and the recent anatomical and physiological studies of Masters and Johnson and Sherfey. The paper has complex theoretical theses. Some hypotheses presented are: (1) Psychic rather than physical satisfaction seems to determine most women's preference for coitally induced orgasm, despite the fact that clitorally induced orgasms may be equally or more intense. This preference is based on ego maturation influenced by self- and object representations which contribute to female identity centered on woman's anatomy; (2) A clitoral myth should not replace a vaginal myth. Both sensation and cathexis of different female parts will vary during different developmental periods; (3) Psychoanalytic treatment should focus on the cathexis of coitus and the achievement of intrapsychic change sufficient to improve the object relationship rather than the desirable intensity and localization of orgastic experience.

Moulton, R. (1966). Multiple factors in frigidity. In J. Masserman (Ed.), <u>Science and psychoanalysis</u> (Vol. 10). Grune & Stratton.

Moulton, R. (1973). Sexual conflicts of contemporary women. In E. W. Wittenberg (Ed.), <u>Interpersonal exploration in psychoanalysis</u>. New York: Basic Books.

Person, E. S. (1980). Sexuality as the mainstay of
        identity: Psychoanalytic perspectives. Signs, 5(4),
        605-630.

        This paper aims to evaluate psychoanalytic paradigms
        in order to see their implications for a contextual
        theory of female sexuality. Person's position is that
        sexuality must be understood not only in terms of its
        source, but also in its relationship to the mainte-
        nance of identity.

Schaefer, L. C.   (1973). Women and sex: Sexual experience
        and reactions of a group of thirty women as told to
        a female psychotherapist. New York: Pantheon.

Sexual behavior: Social psychological issues [Special
        issue]. (1977). Journal of Social Issues, 33(2).

Sherfey, M. J. (1966). The evolution and nature of female
        sexuality in relation to psychoanalytic theory.
        Journal of The American Psychoanalytic Association,
        14(1), 28-128.

        Sherfey uses the findings of Masters and Johnson to
        dispute the theory of the shift of cathexis from the
        clitoris to the vagina. The two parts are of the same
        functional unit. She also asserts that the woman's
        capacity for sexual stimulation is superior to that of
        man. She further asserts the embryonic primacy of the
        female and contradicts the theory of innate bisexuali-
        ty. This is a controversial paper which has been
        subjected to a number of critical discussions (see
        Benedek, Kestenberg, Heiman in Discussion of Mary June
        Sherfey [1968], Journal of The American Psychoanalytic
        Association, 16[3]).

Sherfey, M. J. (1972). The nature and evolution of female
        sexuality. New York: Random House.

Stimpson, C. R., & Person, E. S. (Eds.). (1981). Women:
        Sex and sexuality. Chicago: University of Chicago
        Press.

Vance, C. S. (Ed). (1984). _Pleasure and danger: Exploring female sexuality_. Boston: Routledge and Kegan Paul.

Waterman, C. K., & Chiauzzi, E. J. (1982). The role of orgasm in male and female sexual enjoyment. _Journal of Sex Research_, _18_(2), 146-159.

Weisberg, M. (1981). A note on female ejaculation. _Journal of Sex Research_, _17_(1), 90-91.

Weisskopf, S. (1980). Maternal sexuality and asexual motherhood. _Signs_, _5_(4), 766-782.

   This essay confronts the powerful and pervasive ideology of asexual motherhood. The belief is that good mothers do not have sexual feelings in relationship to children. Weisskopf argues that many women have internalized this ideology of asexual motherhood which leads to psychological pain.

Williams, J. H. (1982). _Psychology of women_ (2nd ed.). New York: W. W. Norton.

Women: Sex and sexuality [Special issue]. (1980). _Signs_, _5_(4).

Y. Women Alone

Adams, M.   (1971). The single woman in today's society:
     A reappraisal. _American Journal of Orthopsychiatry,_
     _41,_ 776-786.

Barrett, C. J.   (1977). Review essay: Women in widowhood.
     Signs, _2_(4), 856-868.

     Barrett discusses the stress of widowhood including
     dealing with grief and loneliness and the impaired
     physical and mental health that often accompanies this
     stress.

Caldwell, R. A., Bloom, B. L., & Hodges, W. F.   (1984).
     Sex differences in separation and divorce: A
     longitudinal perspective. In A. U. Rickel, M.
     Gerrard, & I. Iscoe, (Eds.), _Social and psychological_
     problems of women: Prevention and crisis intervention
     (pp. 103-120). New York: Hemisphere Publishing.

Chamberlin, J.   (1979).   _On our own: Patient controlled_
     alternatives to the mental health system. New York:
     McGraw-Hill Book Co.

Gigy, L. L.   (1980). Self-concept of single women.
     Psychology of Women Quarterly, _5_(2), 321-340.

Greenglass, E. R., & Devins, R.   (1982). Factors related
     to marriage and career plans in unmarried women. _Sex_
     Roles, _8_(1), 57-71.

Pearce, D., & McAdoo, H.   (1981). _Women and children, alone_
     and in poverty. Washington, DC: National Advisory
     Council on Economic Opportunity.

Silverman, P. R.   (1981). _Helping women cope with grief._
     Beverly Hills, CA: Sage Publications.

Z. Women and Work

Allington, D. E., & Troll, L. E. (1984). Social change and equality: The roles of women and economics. In G. Baruch & J. Brooks-Gunn (Eds.), Women in midlife (pp. 181-202). New York: Plenum Press.

Applegarth, A. (1977). Some observations on work inhibitions in women. In H. Blum (Ed.), Female psychology (pp. 251-268). New York: International Universities Press.

Astin, H. S. (1978). Patterns of women's occupations. In J. Sherman, & F. Denmark (Eds.), Psychology of women: Future directions of research (pp. 258-283). New York: Psychological Dimensions.

Barnett, R. C. (1982). Multiple roles and well-being: A study of mothers of preschool age children. Psychology of Women Quarterly, 7(2), 175-178.

Barnett, R. C. (1984). Women, work, and stress: In search of a research paradigm (Working Paper No. 135). Wellesley, MA: Wellesley College Center for Research on Women.

Baruch, G. K., Barnett, R. C., & Rivers, C. (1983). Lifeprints: New patterns of love and work for today's women. New York: McGraw-Hill.

   Based on a major three-year study of American women funded by the NSF, Lifeprints attempts to define what is important in creating a sense of self-fulfillment for women. The authors explore such questions as: What role do children play in a woman's sense of who she is? Is work merely of marginal importance in a woman's life? Does a woman risk major stress and disease if she takes on both a high-powered career and a family life?

Beyond nine to five: Sexual harassment on the job [Special issue]. (1982). Journal of Social Issues, 38(4).

Blumstein, P., & Schwartz, P. (1983). American couples:
    Money, work and sex. New York: Morrow.

Chernesky, R. H. (1979). A guide for women managers: A
    review of the literature. Administration in Social
    Work, 3(1), 91-97.

    The author reviews the current literature on women in
    management. The author believes that external versus
    internal barriers are preventing women from advancing
    in management. (CSWE)

Cherry, F., & Deaux, K. (1978). Fear of success versus
    fear of gender-inappropriate behavior. Sex Roles,
    4(1), 97-101.

Cohen, S., Kamarek, T., & Mermelstein, R. (1983). A global
    measure of perceived stress. Journal of Health and
    Social behavior, 24(4), 385-396.

Crosby, F. J. (1982). Relative deprivation and working
    women. New York: Oxford University Press.

Crull, P. (1982). Stress effects of sexual harassment on
    the job. American Journal of Orthopsychiatry, 52(3),
    539-544.

Curlee, M., & Raymond, F. (1978). The female admini-
    strator: Who is she? Administration in Social Work,
    2(3), 307-318.

    This article describes the 'roles' that males cast
    female administrators into that may hamper their
    effectiveness. (CSWE)

Deal, T., & Kennedy, A. (1982). Corporate cultures: The
    rites and rituals of corporate life. Reading, MA:
    Addison-Wesley.

Development and the sexual division of labor [Special issue].
    (1981). Signs, 7(2).

Douvan, E. (1976). The role of models in women's
     professional development. Psychology of Women
     Quarterly, 1(1), 5-20.

Eccles, J. S., & Hoffman, L. W. (in press). Sex roles,
     socialization, and occupational behavior. In H. W.
     Stevenson & A. E. Siegel (Eds.), Research in child
     development and social policy (Vol. 1). Chicago:
     University of Chicago Press.

Ferber, M. A. (1982). Women and work: Issues of the 1980s.
     Signs, 8(2), 273-295.

Filer, R. K. (1983). Sexual differences in earnings: The
     role of individual personalities and tastes. Journal
     of Human Resources, 18(1), 82-99.

Fishman, P. (1978). Interaction: The work women do.
     Social Problems, 25(4), 397-406.

Galinsky, E. (1985). Family life and corporate policies.
     In M. Yogman & T. B. Brazelton (Eds.), Stresses and
     supports for families. Boston: Harvard University
     Press.

Gold, M. E. (1983). A dialogue on comparable worth. New
     York: ILR Press (New York State School of Industrial
     & Labor Relations, Cornell University).

Goldberg, A. S., & Shiflett, S. (1981). Goals of male and
     female college students: Do traditional sex
     differences still exist? Sex Roles, 7(12), 1213-1222.

Greenfeld, S., Greiner, L., & Wood, M. M. (1980). The
     "feminine mystique" in male-dominated jobs: A compari-
     son of attitudes and background factors of women in
     male-dominated versus female-dominated jobs. Journal
     of Vocational Behavior, 17(3), 291-309.

Greenglass, E. R., & Devins, R. (1982). Factors related to
     marriage and career plans in unmarried women. Sex
     Roles, 8(1), 57-71.

Harragan, B. L. (1978). Games mother never taught you. New York: Warner Communications.

Josefowitz, N. (1980). Paths to power. New York: Addison-Wesley.

Kamerman, S. B., Kahn, A. J., & Kingston, P. W. (1984). Maternity policies and working women. New York: Columbia University Press.

Kirk, R. J. (1981, September). Alternative work schedules experimental program: Interim report to the President and the Congress. Washington, DC: U.S. Office of Personnel Management, Office of Compensation Program Development.

The labor of women: Work and family [Special issue]. (1979). Signs, 4(4).

Lockheed, M. E., & Hall, K. P. (1976). Conceptualizing sex as a status characteristic: Applications to Leadership Training Strategies. Journal of Social Issues, 32(3), 111-124.

Menaker, E. (1979). Some inner conflicts of women in a changing society. In A. Roland & B. Harris (Eds.), Career and motherhood: Struggle for a new identity. New York: Human Sciences Press.

Largely ignoring the classical Freudian view, Menaker adopts an ego psychological frame. She stresses that guilt originated in the girl's rejection of the mother implied by her separation from her. When the girl then counteridentifies with the mother's lack of self-fulfillment and depressed self-image, this conflict becomes the root of the woman's anxiety about motherhood and career.

Mogul, K. M. (1979). Women in midlife: Decisions, rewards and conflicts related to work and careers. American Journal of Psychiatry, 136(9), 1139-1143.

Mott, F. L. (Ed.). (1982). The employment revolution:
     Young American women in the 1970s. Cambridge, MA:
     MIT Press.

Mowbray, C. T., Lanir, S., & Hulce, M. (Eds.). (1984).
     Section 6: Prevention of mental health problems for
     women in the work place. Women and Therapy, 3(3/4),
     185-192.

National Research Council Committee on Occupation
     Classification and Analysis. (1981). Women, work,
     and wages. Washington, DC: National Academy Press.

Nieva, V. F., & Gutek, B. A. (1981). Women and work:
     A psychological perspective. New York: Praeger.

     The data and commentary in this book are multidisci-
     plinary while the viewpoint is primarily psychologi-
     cal. Some of the topics considered are: social, his-
     torical, and economic context for the study of women
     and work; career choice; determinants of decision to
     work; relationship of work and family life; social
     change and working women. Two psychological themes
     which recur are sex-role stereotyping and the demand
     of sex-role-congruent behavior.

Nollen, S. D. (1982). New work schedules in practice:
     Managing time in a changing society. New York: Van
     Nostrand Reinhold.

O'Farrell, B. (1982). Women and nontraditional blue collar
     jobs in the 1980s.: An overview. In P. A. Wallace
     (Ed.), Women in the workplace (pp. 135-165). Boston:
     Auburn House.

O'Leary, V. E. (1974). Some attitudinal barriers to
     occupational aspirations in women. Psychological
     Bulletin, 81(11), 809-826.

Person, E. S. (1982). Women working: Fears of failure,
     deviance and success. Journal of the American Academy
     of Psychoanalysis, 10(1), 67-84.

Riger, S., & Galligan, P. (1980). Women in management: An exploration of competing paradigms. <u>American Psychologist</u>, <u>35</u>(10), 902-910.

Rohrlich, J. (1982). <u>Work and love: The crucial balance</u>. New York: Crown Press.

Roland, A., & Harris, B. (Eds.). (1979). <u>Career and motherhood: Struggles for a new identity</u>. New York: Human Sciences Press.

In this book the difficulties and solutions that today's women are encountering in living these dual roles are explored. Recognized authorities (mostly psychoanalysts) discuss the historical and psychological forces that have shaped women's attitudes and roles in the past and consider how contemporary women are now overcoming this legacy.

Russell, D. E. H. (1984). <u>Sexual exploitation: Rape, child sexual abuse, and workplace harassment</u>. Beverly Hills, CA: Sage Publications.

Sales, E., & Frieze, I. H. (1984). Women and work: Implications for mental health. In L. E. Walker (Ed.), <u>Women and mental health policy</u> (pp. 229-246). Beverly Hills, CA: Sage.

Schafer, R. (1984). The pursuit of failure and the idealization of unhappiness. <u>American Psychologist</u>, <u>39</u>(4), 398-405.

Solomon, L. J. (1984). Working women and stress. In C. M. Brody (Ed.), <u>Women therapists working with women: New theory and process of feminist therapy</u> (pp.135-143). New York: Springer.

Stiver, I. (1983). <u>Work inhibitions in women: Clinical considerations</u>. (Work in Progress, Working Paper No. 3). Wellesley, MA: The Stone Center for Developmental Studies at Wellesley College.

Stueve, A., & O'Donnell, L. (1984). Interactions between daughters and aging parents: Conditions and consequences of daughters' employment (Working Paper No. 146). Wellesley, MA: Wellesley College Center for Research on Women.

Symonds, A. (1978). The psychodynamics of expansiveness in the success oriented woman. American Journal of Psychoanalysis, 38(3), 195-205.

Task Force on Getting, Keeping and Changing Jobs, Division 35 of the American Psychological Association. (1984). Getting, keeping and changing jobs. (Available from Suzanna Rose, Task Force Chair, Department of Psychology, University of Missouri-St. Louis, St. Louis, MO 63121. Copies are $3.75 each, including postage).

Tebbets, R. (1982). Work: Its meaning for women's lives. In D. Belle (Ed.), Lives in stress: Women and depression (pp. 83-95). Beverly Hills, CA: Sage.

Tittle, C. K. (1981). Careers and family: Sex roles and adolescent life plans. Beverly Hills, CA: Sage.

Tresemer, D. (1976). The cumulative record on research of fear of success. Sex Roles, 2(3), 217-236.

Verbrugge, L. (1983). Work satisfaction and physical health. Journal of Community Health, 7(4), 262-282.

Waldron, I., Herold, J., Dunn, D., & Staum, R. (1982). Reciprocal effects of health and labor force participation among women: Evidence from two longitudinal studies. Journal of Occupational Medicine, 24, 126-132.

Wheeler, A., Lee, E. S., & Loe, H. (1983). Employment, sense of well-being, and use of professional services among women. American Journal of Public Health, 73(8), 908-911.

Women as managers [Special issue]. (1979). Sex Roles, 5(5).

Women's Bureau, U. S. Department of Labor. (1983).
    Twenty facts about women workers. Washington, DC:
    U.S. Government Printing Office.

Woods, N. F., & Hulka, B. S. (1979). Symptom reports and
    illness behavior among employed women and homemakers.
    Journal of Community Health, 5(1), 36-45.

PART IV

MENTAL HEALTH ISSUES

As women become more vigorous members of society, the mental health issues which have confronted them for generations are being more openly acknowledged, assessed, and treated. (N.A.)

Al-Issa, I. (1979). The psychopathology of women. Englewood Cliffs, NJ: Prentice-Hall.

Al-Issa, I. (1983). Gender and psychopathology. New York: Academic Press.

American Psychiatric Association. (1984). The homeless mentally ill. Washington, DC: Author.

Bachrach, L. (1984). Deinstitutionalization and women: Assessing the consequences of public policy. American Psychologist, 39(10), 1171-1177.

Bassuk, E. L., Rubin, L., & Lauriat, A. (1984). Is homelessness a mental problem? American Journal of Psychiatry, 141(12), 1546-1550.

Baxter, E., & Hopper, K. (1982). The new mendicancy: Homeless in New York City. American Journal of Ortho-psychiatry, 52(3), 393-408.

Belle, D. (1980). Who uses the mental health facilities? In M. Guttentag, S. Salasin, & D. Belle (Eds.), The mental health of women (pp.1-20). New York: Academic Press.

Belle, D. (1984) Inequality and mental health: Low income and minority women. In L. E. Walker (Ed.), Women and mental health policy (pp. 135-150). Beverly Hills, CA: Sage.

Belle, D. with Longfellow, C., Makosky, V., Saunders, E., & Zelkowitz, P. (1981). Income, mothers' mental health, and family functioning in a low income population. In American Academy of Nursing, The impact of changing resources on health policy (pp. 28-37). Kansas City, MO: American Nurses' Association.

Belle, D., & Goldman, J. (1980). Patterns of diagnoses received by men and women. In M. Guttentag, S. Salasin, & D. Belle (Eds.), The mental health of women. New York: Academic Press.

Bernard, J. (1984). Women's mental health in times of transition. In L. E. Walker (Ed.), Women and mental health policy (pp. 181-195). Beverly Hills, CA: Sage.

Bernardez, T. (1984). Prevalent disorders of women: Attempts toward a different understanding and treatment. Women and Therapy, 3(3/4), 17-28.

Brandenburg, J. B. (1982). Sexual harassment in the university: Guidelines for establishing a grievance procedure. Signs, 8(2), 320-336.

Brandwein, R. A., & Wheelock, A. E. (1978). A new course model for content on women's issues in social work education. Journal of Education for Social Work, 14(3), 20-26.

This article describes both the process of developing a new course on women and the course content. (CSWE)

Brown, L. S. (1984). Media psychology and public policy. In L. E. Walker (Ed.), Women and mental health policy (pp. 281-294). Beverly Hills, CA: Sage.

Carmen, E. H., Russo, N. F., & Miller, J. B. (1984). Inequality and women's mental health: An overview. In P. P. Rieker & E. Carmen (Eds.), The gender gap in psychotherapy: Social realities and psychological processes (pp. 17-41). New York: Plenum. (Reprinted from American Journal of Psychiatry, 1981, 138[10], 17-41)

Center for Women's Policy Studies. (1984, January/
    February). Response. Washington, DC: Author.

Cicchinelli, L. F., Belle, J. C., Dittmar, N. D.,
    Manzanares, D. L., Sackette, K. L., & Smith, G.
    (1981). Factors influencing the deinstitutional-
    ization of the mentally ill: A review and analysis.
    Denver, CO: University of Denver, Denver Research
    Institute.

Cromwell, P. E. (1975). Women and mental health--A
    bibliography. Rockville, MD: Division of Scientific
    and Technical Information, National Institute of
    Mental Health.

Cummings, N. A. (1984). Professional psychology's response
    to women's mental health needs. In L. E. Walker
    (Ed.), Women and mental health policy (pp. 295-305).
    Beverly Hills, CA: Sage.

Cypress, B. K. (1980). Characteristics of visits to female
    and male physicians: The national ambulatory medical
    care survey, 1977 (Vital and Health Statistics Series
    13, No. 49). Hyattsville, MD: National Center for
    Health Statistics.

Dailey, D. M. (1980). Are social workers sexists? A
    replication. Social Work, 25(1), 46-50.

    The author replicates a previous study and finds
    contradictory results. However, both studies find
    presence of bias in professional objectivity. (CSWE)

Department of Health & Human Services. (1984). Helping the
    homeless: A resource guide. Washington, DC: Author.

Department of Health & Human Services. (1984). The
    homeless: Background, analysis and options.
    Washington, DC: Author.

Department of Housing & Urban Development. (1984). A
    report to the Secretary on the homeless and emergency
    shelters. Washington, DC: Author.

Dohrenwend, B., & Dohrenwend, B. S. (1976). Sex
    differences and psychiatric disorders. American
    Journal of Sociology, 81(6), 1447-1454.

Ezell, H. F., & Charles, A. O. (1980). An empirical
    inquiry of variables impacting women in management in
    public social service organizations. Administration
    in Social Work, 4(4), 53-70.

    Responses of male, female managers in public social
    service organizations are analysed to determine their
    attitudes concerning the impact of certain variables
    which may negatively or positively affect the initial
    movement of women into managerial positions, women
    functioning as managers, and the promotion of women in
    the management hierarchy in public social service
    organizations. (CSWE)

Fidell, L. S. (1981). Disabled women: Sexism without the
    pedestal. Journal of Sociology and Social Welfare, 8,
    233-248.

Franks, V. (1979). Gender and psychotherapy. In E. J.
    Gomberg & V. Franks (Eds.), Gender and disordered
    behavior: Sex differences in psychopathology (pp.
    453-485). New York: Brunner/Mazel.

Franks, V., & Rothblum, E. D. (1983). The stereotyping of
    women: Its effects on mental health. New York:
    Springer.

    In this volume the authors point to the contribution
    of sex role stereotypes to the prevalence of diagnos-
    tic symptomatology of depression, agoraphobia, sexual
    dysfunction. They also discusses the special problems
    of living for women leading to obesity, lack of asser-
    tiveness and violence against women.

Gomberg, E. S., & Franks, V. (1979). Gender and disordered behavior. New York: Brunner/Mazel.

This book brings together a range of papers, which lead to a better understanding of the relationship of gender and disordered behavior. Some chapters emphasize empirical findings, while some integrate findings and develop hypotheses. The areas covered in the book include: life crisis, problem behaviors, and functional disorders.

Gove, W. R. (1972). The relationship between sex roles, mental illness and marital status. Social Forces, 51(1), 34-44.

Gove, W. R. (1979). Sex differences in the epidemiology of mental disorder: Evidence and explanations. In E. J. Gomberg & V. Franks (Eds.), Gender and disordered behavior: Sex differences in psychopathology (pp. 23-68). New York: Brunner/Mazel.

Gove, W. R. (1980a). Mental illness and psychiatric treatment among women. Psychology of Women Quarterly, 4(3), 345-362.

Gove, W. R. (1980b). Mental illness and psychiatric treatment among women: A rejoinder to Johnson. Psychology of Women Quarterly, 4(3), 372-376.

Gove, W. R., & Tudor, J. (1973). Adult sex roles and mental illness. American Journal of Sociology, 78, 812-835.

Greenglass, E. R. (1982). A world of difference: Gender roles in perspective. Toronto: John Wiley.

Guttentag, M. (1980). Personality and psychopathology. New York: Academic Press.

Guttentag, M., & Salasin, S. (1976). Women, men, and mental health. In L. A. Carter & A. F. Scott (Eds.), Women and men: Changing roles, relationships and perceptions. New York: Aspen Institute.

Guttentag, M., & Secord, P. F. (1983). Too many women?
    The sex ratio question. Beverly Hills, CA: Sage.

Guttentag, M., Salasin, S., & Belle, D. (Eds.). (1980).
    The mental health of women. New York: Academic Press.

Halleck, S. L. (1984). Editorial: Morality in Medicine.
    In P. P. Rieker & E. Carmen (Eds.), The gender gap
    in psychotherapy: Social realities and psychological
    processes (pp. 15-16). New York: Plenum. (Reprinted
    from Contemporary Psychiatry, 1983, 2[2], 86)

Hamilton, J. A., & Conrad, C. (in press). Toward a
    developmental psychopharmacology: The physiological
    basis of age, gender, and hormonal effects on drug
    responsivity. In J. Call (Ed.), Handbook of child
    psychiatry.

Hamilton, J. A., & Conrad, C. (in press). Guidelines for
    avoiding methodological and policymaking biases in
    gender-related health research. Report submitted to
    the Public Health Service Task Force on Women's
    Health.

Harris, B., & Lightner, J. (1980). The image of women in
    abnormal psychology: Professionalism versus psycho-
    pathology. Psychology of Women Quarterly, 4(3),
    396-411.

Hilberman, E., & Russo, N. F. (1978). Mental health and
    equal rights: The ethical challenge for psychiatry.
    Psychiatric Opinion, 1978, 15(8), 11-19.

Howell, E., & Bayles, M. (Eds.). (1981). Women and mental
    health. New York: Basic Books.

The editors indicate that there is a growing awareness
of the need for knowledge and training to counteract
the prevalence of gender-role bias that often affects
the treatment of female clients. They indicate that
the training should include: (1) a raising of consciousness of one's own and others' sexist attitudes
and practices; (2) specific attention to concepts of
feminine development which have implications for

treatment; and (3) attention to some of the special treatment needs of women clients, such as abortion counseling, rape counseling, and treatment of battered women.

The Association for Women in Psychology. (1985). An international feminist mental health agenda. Washington, DC: Author.

Johnson, M. (1980). Mental illness and psychiatric treatment among women: A response. Psychology of Women Quarterly, 4(3), 363-371.

Kafka, M. S., Davenport, Y., Gold, P., Susman, E., Tallman, J., Waxler, C., & Yang, H. Y. (1981, February). Interim report of the adhoc committee to evaluate the differential impact of the NIMH intramural program on men and women. Washington, DC: National Institute of Mental Health.

Kaplan, M. (1983). A woman's view of DSM-III. American Psychologist, 38(7), 786-792.

Kessler, R., & McRae, J. (1981). Trends in the relationship between sex and psychological distress: 1957-1976. American Sociological Review, 46(4), 443-452.

Kessler, S., & McKenna, W. (1985). Gender: An ethnomethodological approach. Chicago: University of Chicago Press.

Kettere, R. F., Bader, B. C., & Levy, M. R. (1980). Strategies and skills for promoting mental health. In R. H. Price, B. C. Bader, & J. Monahan (Eds.), Sage annual reviews of community mental health: Vol. 1. Prevention and mental health: Research, policy, and practice. Beverly Hills, CA: Sage.

Kinney, E. L., Trautmann, J., Gold, J. A., Vessey, E. S. & Zelis, R. (1981). Underrepresentation of women in new drug trials. Annals of Internal Medicine, 95(4), 495-499.

Klerman, G. L., London, P., Michels, R., & Sharfstein, S.
    (1983). The efficacy of psychotherapy as the basis
    for public policy. American Psychologist, 38(8),
    929-934.

Lear, J. G. (1983). Women's health and public policy:
    1976-1982. In I. Tinker (Ed.), Women in Washington:
    Advocates for public policy (pp. 148-162). Beverly
    Hills, CA: Sage.

Lennane, K. J., & Lennane, R. J. (1981). Alleged
    psychogenic disorders in women--A possible
    manifestation of sexual prejudice. The New England
    Journal of Medicine, 95, 495-499.

Levine, I. S. (1984). Homelessness: Its implications for
    mental health policy and practice. Psychological
    Rehabilitation Journal, 8, 6-16.

Logan, D. D., & Kaschak, E. (1980). The relationship of
    sex, sex role, and mental health. Psychology of Women
    Quarterly, 4(4), 573-580.

Lowe, M., & Hubbard, R. (Eds.). (1983). Woman's nature:
    Rationalizations of inequality. Elmsford, NY:
    Pergamon.

Miller, J. B. (1982). Women and power: Some psychological
    dimensions (Working paper no. 1). Wellesley, MA: The
    Stone Center, Wellesley College.

Miller, J. B. (1984a). The effects of inequality on
    psychology. In P. P. Rieker & E. Carmen (Eds.),
    The gender gap in psychotherapy: Social realities and
    psychological processes (pp. 17-44). New York:
    Plenum. (Reprinted from Psychiatric Opinion, 1978,
    15[8], 29-32)

Miller, J. B. (1984b). Women's mental health issues:
    Moving forward with awareness and program alter-
    natives. Women and Therapy, 3(3/4), 29-35.

Mowbray, C. T., & Chamberlain, P. (1985). Sex differences among the long-term mentally disabled. Manuscript submitted for publication.

Mowbray, C. T., Lanir, S., & Hulce, M. (Eds.). (1984). Section 1: Sex differences in women's mental health problems and their causes: The evidence. Women and Therapy, 3(3/4), 5-16.

Mowbray, C. T., Lanir, S., & Hulce, M. (Eds.). (1984). Section 7: Conclusions. Women and Therapy, 3(3/4), 193-196.

Naierman, N. (1979). Sex discrimination in health and human development services (Contract No. HEW-100-78-0137). Cambridge, MA: Abt Associates.

National Association of Social Workers. (1983). Membership survey shows practice shifts. NASW NEWS, 28.

Olmeda, E. L., & Parron, D. L. (1981). Mental health of minority women: Some special issues. Professional Psychology, 12(1), 103-111.

Perry, S. (1983). The National Center for Health Care Technology: Assessment of psychotherapy for policymaking. American Psychologist, 38(8), 924-928.

President's Commission on Mental Health, Special Populations Subpanel on the Mental Health of Women. (1978). Report to the President (Vol. 3). Washington, DC: U.S. Government Printing Office.

Price, R. P., Foster, S. A., Curtis, C., & Behling, J. (1979). Student and faculty perceptions of women's content in the curriculum. Journal of Education for Social Work, 15(3), 51-57.

    This study reports data on the differences in percep-
    tions of content related to women among various groups
    in a school of social work, and their recommendations
    for curriculum modification. (CSWE)

Report of the Public Health Service Task Force on Women's Health Issues. (1985). <u>Public Health Reports</u>, <u>100</u>(1), 73-106.

Quinn, K. (1984). The killing ground: Police powers and psychiatry. <u>Women and Therapy</u>, <u>3</u>(3/4), 71-77.

Rice, D., & Cugliani, A. (1980). Health status of American women. <u>Women and Health</u>, <u>5</u>(1), 5-22.

Rosenfield, S. (1982). Sex roles and societal reactions to mental illness: The labeling of "deviant" deviance. <u>Journal of Health and Social Behavior</u>, <u>23</u>(1), 18-24.

Rosenman, L., & Ruckdeschel, R. (1981). Catch 1234B: Integrating material on women into the social work research curriculum. <u>Social Work</u>, <u>17</u>(2), 5-11.

This article maintains that sexual bias extends to research as it does to other areas of the social work curriculum. The ways that bias has affected conduct and teaching of research are examined and recommendations that would facilitate integration of the women's perspective into research are suggested. (CSWE)

Rubenstein, H. (1981). Women in organizations: A review of research and some implications for teaching social work practice. <u>Journal of Education for Social Work</u>, <u>17</u>(3), 20-27.

This article reviews the research on women employed in organizations and finds that women are in double jeopardy. First there are barriers to the advancement of women and secondly, as women advance they either do not receive or they lose the organizational and interpersonal rewards that accompany the advancement of men. Implications for teaching social work practice at the MSW level are discussed. (CSWE)

Rushford, K. B., O'Toole, A., Urbelis, D. P., Pearlstein, A.
     V., Pittcatsouphes, M., Stone, G., Arkway, C., &
     Veeder, N. W. (1980). Attitudes toward women's
     professional achievement among social work students
     and recent graduates. Journal of Education for Social
     Work, 16(2), 49-54.

     This study attempted to ascertain whether negative
     attitudes toward the achievement and success of women
     currently exist in the social work profession. The
     sample studied were 343 students in MSW programs and
     alumnae. (CSWE)

Russo, N. F. (1984a). Women in the mental health delivery
     system: Implications for policy, research, and
     practice. In L. Walker (Ed.), Women and mental health
     policy (pp. 21-42). Beverly Hills, CA: Sage.

Russo, N. F. (1984b). Women in the American Psychological
     Association. Washington, DC: American Psychological
     Association.

Russo, N. F. (Ed.). (1985). Developing a national agenda
     to address women's mental health needs. Washington,
     DC: American Psychological Association.

Russo, N. F., & Denmark, F. L. (1984). Women, psychology,
     and public policy: Selected issues. American
     Psychologist, 39(10), 1161-1165.

Russo, N. F., & Olmeda, E. L. (1983). Women's utilization
     of outpatient psychiatric services: Some emerging
     priorities for rehabilitation psychologists.
     Rehabilitation Psychology, 28(3), 141-155.

Russo, N. F., Olmeda, E., Stapp, J., & Fulcher, R. (1981).
     Women and minorities in psychology. American
     Psychologist, 36(11), 1315-1363.

Russo, N. F., & Sobel, S. B. (Eds.). (1981a). Sex roles,
     equality and mental health [Special issue].
     Professional Psychology, 12(1).

Russo, N. F., & Sobel, S. B. (1981b). Sex differences in the utilization of mental health facilities. <u>Professional Psychology</u>, <u>12</u>(1), 7-19.

Russo, N. F., & VandenBos, G. R. (1980). Women in the mental health delivery system. In W. H. Silverman (Ed.), <u>Community mental health: A sourcebook for board and professionals and advisory board members</u>. New York: Praeger.

Sales, E., Shore, B. K., & Bolitho, F. (1980). When mothers return to school: A study of women completing an MSW program. <u>Journal of Education for Social Work</u>, <u>16</u>(1), 57-65.

This article presents data from a study that examined the characteristics, role difficulties and role satis- factions of a group of women with children who recently completed an MSW program. The dominant theme was one of rewarding, ego-enhancing and easy movement through training and subsequently into professional positions. (CSWE)

Smith, C. A., & Smith, C. J. (1980). Learned helplessness and preparedness in discharged mental patients. <u>Social Work Research and Abstracts</u>, <u>14</u>, 21-27.

Sobel, S. B., & Russo, N. F. (1981a). Equality, public policy, and professional psychology. <u>Professional Psychology</u>, <u>12</u>(1), 171-179.

Sobel, S. B., & Russo, N. F. (Eds.). (1981b). Sex roles, equality, and mental health [Special issue]. <u>Professional Psychology</u>, <u>12</u>(1).

Solomon, Z., & Bromet, E. (1982). The role of social factors in affective disorder: An assessment of the vulnerability model of Brown and his colleagues. <u>Psychological Medicine</u>, <u>12</u>(1), 123-130.

Stephenson, S., & Walker, L. E. (1980). Psychotropic drugs and women. <u>Bioethics Quarterly</u>, <u>2</u>.

Stone, A. A. (1984). Presidential address: Conceptual ambiguity and morality in modern psychiatry. In P. P. Rieker & E. Carmen (Eds.), The gender gap in psychotherapy: Social realities and psychological processes (pp. 5-14). New York: Plenum. (Reprinted from American Journal of Psychiatry, 1980, 137[8], 887-891)

Stringer, D. M., & Welton, N. R. (1984). Female psychologists in policymaking positions. In L. E. Walker (Ed.), Women and mental health policy (pp. 43-58). Beverly Hills, CA: Sage.

Subpanel on the Mental Health of Women. (1978). Report to the President (Vol. 3). Washington, DC: U.S. Government Printing Office.

Subpanel on the Mental Health of Women, President's Commission on Mental Health. (1979). Task Panel Report. Vol. III, Appendix 1022-1116. Washington, DC: U.S. Government Printing Office.

Test, M. A., & Berlin, S. B. (1981). Issues of special concern to chronically mentally ill women. Professional Psychology: Research and Practice, 12(1), 136-145.

Thompson, E. G. (1984). Women in inpatient facilities: Impressions and reflections. Women and Therapy, 3(3/4), 51-56.

Thorne, B. (1984). A social perspective on women's mental health problems. Women and Therapy, 3(3/4), 45-50.

Thorne, B., Kramarae, C., & Henley, N. M. (1983). Language, gender and society: Opening a second decade of research. In B. Thorne, C. Kramarae, & N. Henley (Eds.), Language gender and society (pp. 7-24). Rowley, MA: Newbury House.

Thurer, S. (1983). Deinstitutionalization and women: Where the buck stops. Hospital and Community Psychiatry, 34(12), 1162-1163.

Waites, E. A. (1982). Fixing women: Devaluation, idealization and female fetish. Journal of the American Psychoanalytic Association, 30(2), 435-459.

Walker, L. E. (Ed.). (1984). Women and mental health policy. Beverly Hills, CA: Sage Publications.

Walker, L. E. (1984). Violence against women: Implications for mental health policy. In L. E. Walker (Ed.), Women and mental health policy (pp. 197-206). Beverly Hills, CA: Sage.

Wallen, J., Waitzkin, H., & Stoekle, J. D. (1979). Physician stereotypes about female health and illness. Women and Health, 4(2), 135-146.

Wallis, L. A., & Frings, J. (1984). National Institutes of Health gender staffing patterns. New York: Regional Council for Women in Medicine, Inc.

Weiss, S., Buscher, M., Shannon, R., Sample, K., & Eidskess, P. (1984). Alcohol, Drug Abuse and Mental Health Administration Women's Council Report to the Administrator: 1983-1984. Washington, DC: U.S. Department of Health and Human Service.

Widom, C. S. (Ed.). (1984). Sex roles and psychopathology. New York: Plenum.

Women's Task Force. (1982). For better or worse? Women and the mental health delivery system. Lansing, MI: Michigan Department of Mental Health.

Zuckerman, E. (1979). Changing directions in the treatment of women. Rockville, MD: National Institute of Mental Health.

PART V

SEX ROLE ISSUES IN PSYCHOTHERAPY AND SUPERVISION

The relationship between therapist and patient and supervisor and supervisee reflect gender role issues vis-a-vis sexuality, dependency, and aggression which can also be noted in other structured, close dyadic relationships. Recently, these sex role issues in therapy and supervision have begun to be addressed in curriculum development and in mental health policy. (N.A.)

A. Psychotherapeutic Issues

From the <u>American Psychologist</u>, December 1978, pp. 1122-1123.

Guidelines for Therapy with Women

TASK FORCE ON SEX BIAS AND SEX ROLE STEREOTYPING IN PSYCHOTHERAPEUTIC PRACTICE

The APA Task Force on Sex Bias and Sex Role Stereotyping in Psychotherapeutic Practice was charged with investigating sexism in psychotherapy and recommending corrective actions (American Psychological Association, 1975). It was specifically directed to "be concerned with psychotherapeutic practices as they affect women." To address this particular concern, the task force developed the "Guidelines for Therapy with Women" for use in training and in continuing professional practice. The task force recognizes that other subgroups in our society may well be subjected to similar mistreatment in psychotherapy, and consequently many of the guidelines also may be useful to these groups.

The task force method was to survey women psychologists as consumers and practitioners to learn
what they considered sexism in therapy to be
(American Psychological Association, 1975). The
therapist behaviors described fall into four
general categories: (1) fostering traditional sex
roles, (2) bias in expectations and devaluation
of women, (3) sexist use of psychoanalytic concepts, and (4) responding to women as objects,
including seduction of female clients. From
these categories and their respective subthemes,
the task force developed 13 general guidelines
for ethical and effective psychotherapy with
women. . . . (Brodsky et al., 1978).

1. The conduct of therapy should be free of
constrictions based on gender-defined roles, and
the options explored between client and
practitioner should be free of sex role
stereotypes. . . .

2. Psychologists should recognize the reality, variety, and implications of sex-discrimi-
natory practices in society and should facilitate
client examination of options in dealing with
such practices. . . .

3. The therapist should be knowledgeable
about current empirical findings on sex roles,
sexism, and individual differences resulting from
the client's gender-defined identity. . . .

4. The theoretical concepts employed by the
therapist should be free of sex bias and sex role
stereotypes. . . .

5. The psychologist should demonstrate
acceptance of women as equal to men by using
language free of derogatory labels. . . .

6. The psychologist should avoid establishing the source of personal problems within the

client when they are more properly attributable
to situational or cultural factors. . . .

7. The psychologist and a fully informed
client mutually should agree upon aspects of the
therapy relationship such as treatment modality,
time factors, and fee arrangements. . . .

8. While the importance of the availability
of accurate information to a client's family is
recognized, the privilege of communication about
diagnosis, prognosis, and progress ultimately
resides with the client, not with the therapist.
. . .

9. If authoritarian processes are employed as
a technique, the therapy should not have the
effect of maintaining or reinforcing stereotypic
dependency of women. . . .

10. The client's assertive behaviors should be
respected. . . .

11. The psychologist whose female client is
subjected to violence in the form of physical
abuse or rape should recognize and acknowledge
that the client is the victim of a crime. . . .

12. The psychologist should recognize and
encourage exploration of a woman client's sexuality and should recognize her right to define her
own sexual preferences. . . .

13. The psychologist should not have sexual
relations with a woman client nor treat her as a
sex object. . . .

REFERENCES

American Psychological Association. Report of
     the Task Force on Sex Bias and Sex-Role
     Stereotyping in Psychotherapeutic Practice.
     American Psychologist, 1975, 30, 1169-1175.

Brodsky, A. M., Holroyd, J. C., Payton, C. R.,
     Rubinstein, E. A., Rosenkranz, P., Sherman,
     J. A., Zell, F., Cummings, T., & Suber, C. J.
     Source materials for nonsexist therapy.
     JSAS Catalog of Selected Documents in
     Psychology, 1978, 3, 40. (Ms. No. 1685)

Acosta, F. (1980). Self-described reasons for premature
     termination of psychotherapy by Mexican American,
     Black American, and Anglo-American patients.
     Psychological Reports, 47(2), 435-443.

Alyn, J. H., & Becker, L. A. (1984). Feminist therapy with
     chronically and profoundly disturbed women. Journal
     of Counseling Psychology, 31(2), 202-208.

American Psychological Association. (1975). Report of the
     task force on sex biases and sex-role stereotyping in
     psychotherapeutic practice. American Psychologist,
     30, 1165-1175.

American Psychological Association. (1977a). Standards for
     providers of psychological services (rev. ed.).
     Washington, DC: Author.

American Psychological Association. (1977b). Ethical
     standards of psychologists. APA Monitor, 3, 22-23.

American Psychological Association. (1978a). Division 17
     Ad Hoc Committee on Women. Principles concerning the
     counseling and psychotherapy of women. Counseling
     Psychologist, 8(1), 21.

American Psychological Association. (1978b). Guidelines
     for therapy with women. American Psychologist, 33,
     1122.

American Psychological Association. (1979). Some
     information on feminist therapy and counseling women.
     Washington, DC: Author.

American Psychological Association. (1981a). Ethical principles of psychologists (revised). American Psychologist, 36, 633-638.

American Psychological Association. (1981b). Report of the Division 17 Committee on Women Task Force on Training for Counseling Women. (Available from Mary Sue Richardson, Department of Counselor Education, New York University, New York, NY 10003.)

American Psychological Association Division 17 Committee on Women. (1983). Rationale and implementation of the principles concerning the counseling/psychotherapy of women. Unpublished manuscript.

Armitage, K. J., Schneiderman, L. J., & Bass, R. A. (1980). Response of physicians to medical complaints in men and women. International Journal of Women's Studies, 3(2), 111-116.

Armstrong, L. Homefront. Washington, DC: National Women's Health Network.

Domestic violence and its relation to law and therapy.

Barnett, R. C. (1984). The anxiety of the unknown-- Choice, risk, responsibility: Therapeutic issues for today's adult women. In G. Baruch & J. Brooks-Gunn (Eds.), Women in midlife (pp. 341-357). New York: Plenum.

Barrett, C. J., Berg, P. I., Eaton, M., & Pomeroy, E. (1974). Implications of women's liberation for the future of psychotherapy. Psychotherapy: Theory, Research, and Practice, 11(1), 11-15.

Beavers, R. W. (1977). Psychotherapy and growth: A Family systems perspective. New York: Brunner/Mazel.

Benjamin, J. (1984). The convergence of psychoanalysis and feminism: Gender identity and autonomy. In C. M. Brody (Ed.), Women therapists working with women: New theory and process of feminist theory (pp. 37-45). New York: Springer.

Berger, M. (1984). Men's new family roles: Some implications for therapists. In P. P. Rieker & E. Carmen (Eds.), The gender gap in psychotherapy: Social realities and psychological processes (pp. 319-332). New York: Plenum. (Reprinted from The Family Coordinator, 1979, 28[4], 638-646)

Berliner, L. (1983). Impact of sexual assault and therapeutic intervention. In Sexual assault: Representing the victim. Seattle: Northwest Women's Law Center.

Bernardez, T. (1983). Women's groups. In M. Rosenbaum (Ed.), Handbook of short-term therapy groups (pp. 119-138). New York: McGraw-Hill.

Bernstein, A. E., & Warner, G. M. (1985). Women treating women: Case material from women treated by female psychoanalysts. New York: International Universities Press.

Beutler, L. E. (1979). Values, beliefs, religion and the persuasive influence of psychotherapy. Psychotherapy: Theory, Research and Practice, 16(4), 432-440.

Billingsley, D. (1977). Sex bias in psychotherapy: An examination of the effects of client sex, client pathology, and therapist sex on treatment planning. Journal of Consulting and Clinical Psychology, 45(12), 250-256.

Blechman, E. A. (1980). Behavior therapies. In A. M. Brodsky & R. T. Hare-Mustin (Eds.), Women and psychotherapy (pp. 217-244). New York: Guilford Press.

Blechman, E. A. (1983). Behavior therapy with women. New York: Guilford Press.

Borman, L. D. (1982). Introduction--Helping people to help themselves - Self-help and prevention. Prevention in Human Services 1, 3-15.

Bornstein, P. H., & Bornstein, M. T. (1985). Marital therapy: A behavioral-communications approach. Elmsford, NY: Pergamon Press.

Bosma, B. J. (1975). Attitudes of women therapists toward women clients, or a comparative study of feminist therapy. Smith College Studies in Social Work, 46, 53-54.

Bouhoutsos, J. C. (1984). Sexual intimacy between psychotherapists and clients: Policy implications for the future. In L. E. Walker (Ed.), Women and mental health policy (pp. 207-228). Beverly Hills, CA: Sage.

Bouhoutsos, J. C., Holroyd, J. C., Lerman, H., Forer, B., & Greenberg, M. (1983). Sexual intimacy between psychotherapists and patients. Professional Psychology: Research and Practice, 14(2), 185-196.

Brodsky, A. M. (1973). The consciousness-raising group as a model of therapy with women. Psychotherapy: Theory, Research and Practice, 10(1),24-29.

Brodsky, A. M. (1977). Countertransference issues and the woman therapist: Sex and the student therapist. The Clinical Psychologist, 30(2), 12-14.

Brodsky, A. M. (1980). A decade of feminist influence on psychotherapy. Psychology of Women Quarterly, 4(3), 331-344.

Brodsky, A. M., & Hare-Mustin, R. T. (Eds.). (1980a). Women and psychotherapy: An assessment of research and practice. New York: Guilford Press.

Based on an American Psychological Association project supported by the NIMH, this volume brings together researchers and practitioners, representing a spectrum of approaches, and focusing on: gender differences in

therapy, traditional approaches, high prevalence disorders among women, crisis intervention and alternative or non-traditional approaches.

Brodsky, A. M., & Hare-Mustin, R. T. (1980b).
     Psychotherapy and women: Priorities for research. In
     A. M. Brodsky & R. T. Hare-Mustin (Eds.), Women and
     psychotherapy (pp. 385-409). New York: The Guilford
     Press.

Brody, C. M. (Ed.). (1984a). Women therapists working
     with women: New theory and process of feminist theory.
     New York: Springer.

Brody, C. M. (1984b). Authenticity in feminist therapy.
     In C. M. Brody (Ed.), Women therapists working with
     women: New theory and process of feminist theory
     (pp. 11-21). New York: Springer.

Brody, C. M. (1984c). Feminist therapy with minority
     clients. In C. M. Brody (Ed.), Women therapists
     working with women: New theory and process of
     feminist theory (pp. 109-115). New York: Springer.

Brooks, V. R. (1981). Sex and sexual orientation as
     variables in therapists' biases and therapy outcomes.
     Clinical Social Work Journal, 9(3), 198-210.

Broverman, I., Broverman, D., Clarkson, F., Rosenkrantz, P.,
     & Vogel, S. (1970). Sex role stereotypes and
     clinical judgments of mental health. Journal of
     Counseling and Clinical Psychology, 34(1), 1-7.

A double standard of mental health appeared to exist
among mental health practitioners participating in
this study. The concept of mental health for an
adult, sex unspecified, was the same as for a healthy
male. Standards for an adult mentally healthy woman
were lower.

Brown, C. R., & Hellinger, M. L. (1975). Therapists' attitudes toward women. Social Work, 20(4), 266-270.

This study reveals differences in attitudes of female and male therapists toward women. Female/contemporary, male/traditional. (CSWE)

Brown, L. S. (1984). Finding new language: Getting beyond analytic verbal shorthand in feminist therapy. Women and therapy, 3(1), 73-80.

Butler, C. (1973). Genetic psychoanalysis: The dual method. Psychotherapy: Theory, Research, and Practice, 10(1), 74-77.

Butler, S. E., & Zelen, S. (1977). Sexual intimacies between psychotherapists and their patients. Psychotherapy: Theory, Research and Practice, 14(2), 143-145.

Cammaert, L. P. (1984). New sex therapies: Policy and practice. In L. E. Walker (Ed.), Women and mental health policy (pp. 247-266). Beverly Hills, CA: Sage.

Chesler, P. (1971). Patient and patriarch: Woman in the psychotherapeutic relationship. In V. Gornick & B. K. Moran (Eds.), Women in sexist society (pp. 362-392). New York: Basic Books.

Chesler, P. (1972). Women and madness. New York: Doubleday.

Cole, N. S. (1981). Bias in testing. American Psychologist, 36(10), 1067-1077.

Collier, H. (1982). Counseling women: A guide for therapists. New York: Free Press.

The author provides therapists with sensitive approaches to specific problems of female patients and clients. She has included women in the world of work, career counseling, women and their bodies, abuse, minority women, lesbians and female offenders. She includes extensive bibliography.

Cooperstock, R. (1978). Sex differences in psychotropic drug use. Social Science and Medicine, 12(3-B), 179-186.

Cottler, L. B., & Robins, L. (1983). The prevalence and characteristics of psychoactive medication use in a general population study. Psychopharmacology Bulletin, 19(4), 746-751.

Cowan, G. (1976). Therapist judgments of clients' sex-role problems. Psychology of Women Quarterly, 1(2), 115-124.

Dahlberg, C. C. (1970). Sexual contact between patient and therapist. Contemporary Psychoanalysis, 6(2), 107-124.

Davenport, J., & Reims, N. (1978). Theoretical orientation and attitudes toward women. Social Work, 23(4), 306-310.

    The authors study associations between the theoretical orientations of clinicians and their attitudes toward women's roles. (CSWE)

Davidson, V. (1984). Psychiatry's problem with no name: Therapist-patient sex. In P. P. Rieker & E. Carmen (Eds.), The gender gap in psychotherapy: Social realities and psychological processes (pp. 361-368). New York: Plenum. (Reprinted from American Journal of Psychoanalysis, 1977, 37, 43-50)

Davidson, C. V., & Abramowitz, S. I. (1980a). Sex bias in clinical judgment: Later empirical returns. Psychology of Women Quarterly, 4(3), 377-395.

Davidson, C. V., & Abramowitz, S. I. (Eds.). (1980b). Woman as patient [Special issue]. Psychology of Women, 4(3).

DeKraai, M. B., & Sales, B. D. (1984). Confidential communications of psychotherapists. Psychotherapy, Theory, Research and Practice, 21(3), 293-318.

DeLeon, P., VandenBos, G. R., & Cummings, N. A. (1983). Psychotherapy--Is it safe, effective and appropriate? The beginning of an evolutionary dialogue. <u>American Psychologist</u>, <u>38</u>(8), 907-911.

Delk, J. L. (1977). Differentiating sexist from nonsexist therapist, or my analogue can beat your analogue. <u>American Psychologist</u>, <u>32</u>(10), 890-893.

Dimidjian, V. J. (1982). A biographical study of the psychosocial developmental issues in the lives of six female psychotherapists in their thirties. <u>Women and therapy</u>, <u>1</u>(1), 27-44.

Dudley, G. R., & Rawlins, M. (Eds.). (1985). Psychotherapy with ethnic minorities [Special issue]. <u>Psychotherapy: Theory, Research, Practice</u>, <u>22</u>.

Edelwich, J., & Brodsky, A. M. (1982). <u>Sexual dilemmas for the helping professional</u>. New York: Brunner/Mazel.

Eichenbaum, L., & Orbach, S. (1984). Feminist psychoanalysis: Theory and practice. In C. M. Brody (Ed.), <u>Women therapists working with women: New theory and process of feminist theory</u> (pp. 46-55). New York: Springer.

Ellison, C. R. (1984). Harmful beliefs affecting the practice of sex therapy with women. <u>Psychotherapy, Theory, Research and Practice</u>, <u>21</u>(3), 327-334.

Escamilla-Mondanaro, J. (1977). Lesbians and therapy. In E. Rawlings & D. Carter (Eds.), <u>Psychotherapy for women: Treatment toward equality</u> (pp. 256-265). Springfield, IL: Charles C. Thomas.

Fabrikant, B. (1974). The psychotherapist and the female patient: Perceptions, misperceptions and change. In V. Franks & V. Burtle (Eds.), <u>Women in therapy</u> (pp. 83-109). New York: Brunner/Mazel.

Federation of Organizations for Professional Women.   (1981).
    Women and psychotherapy: A consumer handbook.
    Washington, DC: Author.

Feldman-Summer, J., & Jones, G. (1984). Psychological
    impacts of sexual contact between therapists or other
    health care practitioners and their clients.
    Manuscript submitted for publication.

Ferrerya, S., & Hughes, K. Table manners. Washington,
    DC: National Women's Health Network.

    A guide to pelvic exams for disabled women and health
    care professionals.

Fine, M., & Asch, A. (1981). Disabled women: Sexism
    without the pedestal. Journal of Sociology and Social
    Welfare, 8, 233-248.

Fodor, I. G. (1985). Assertiveness training for the 80's:
    Moving beyond the personal. In L. B. Rosewater & L.
    E. Walker (Eds.), A handbook of feminist therapy (pp.
    257-265). New York: Springer.

Fodor, I. G., & Rothblum, E. D. (1984). Strategies for
    dealing with sex-role stereotypes. In C. M. Brody
    (Ed.), Women therapists working with women: New theory
    and process of feminist theory (pp. 86-95). New York:
    Springer.

Franks, V. (1979). Gender and psychotherapy. In E.
    Gomberg & V. Franks (Eds.), Gender and disordered
    behavior (pp. 453-485). New York: Brunner/Mazel.

Franks, V., & Burtle, V. (Eds.). (1974). Women in
    therapy: New psychotherapies for a changing society.
    New York: Brunner/Mazel.

    These authors consider the impact of feminism on the
    practice of mental health professionals. In particu-
    lar the treatment of the female phobia, the female
    depressive, female alcoholic, female homosexual and
    female in mental hospitals are considered.

Franks, V., & Rothblum, E. D. (1983). The stereotyping of women: Its effects on mental health. New York: Springer.

Friedman, S. S., Gans, L., Gottlieb, N., Nesselson, C. (1979). A woman's guide to therapy. Englewood Cliffs, NJ: Prentice-Hall.

Gartrell, N. (1984). Issues in the psychotherapy of lesbians. In P. P. Rieker & E. Carmen (Eds.), The gender gap in psychotherapy: Social realities and psychological processes (pp. 285-299). New York: Plenum. (Originally published under the title "Combatting homophobia in the psychotherapy of lesbians," Women and Therapy, 1984, 3[1])

Gechtman, L., Pope, K. S/, & Bouhoutsos, J. Sexual intimacy between social workers and their clients. Manuscript in preparation.

Gibbs, M. S. (1984). The therapist as imposter. In C. M. Brody (Ed.), Women therapists working with women: New theory and process of feminist theory (pp. 22-33). New York: Springer.

Gilbert, L. A. (1980). Feminist therapy. In A. M. Brodsky & R. T. Hare-Mustin (Eds.), Women and psychotherapy (pp. 245-265). New York: The Guilford Press.

Gilbert, L. A., Waldroop, J. A., & Deutsch, C. J. (1981). Masculine and feminine stereotypes and adjustment: A reanalysis. Psychology of Women Quarterly, 5(5, suppl.), 790-794.

Gonsiorek, J. (1984). Observations on male victims and same-sex involvement in sexual exploitations of clients by therapists. Minneapolis: Walk-In Counseling Center.

Greene, L. R. (1980). On terminating psychotherapy: More evidence of sex-role related counter transference. Psychology of Women Quarterly, 4(4), 548-557.

Greenspan, M. (1983). A new approach to women and therapy. New York: McGraw-Hill.

Gurman, A. S., & Klein, M. H. (1980). Marital and family conflicts. In A. M. Brodsky & R. T. Hare-Mustin (Eds.), Women and psychotherapy (pp. 159-188). New York: The Guilford Press.

Haas, L. J., & Fennimore, D. (1983). Ethical and legal issues in professional psychology: Selected works, 1970-1981. Professional Psychology: Research and Practice, 14, 540-548.

Halbreich, U., Asnis, G., & Goldstein, S. (1984). Sex differences in response to psychopharmacological interventions in humans. Psychopharmacology Bulletin, 20(3), 526-530.

Hall, J., & Hare-Mustin, R. T. (1983). Sanctions and the diversity of ethical complaints against psychologist. American Psychologist, 38(6), 714-729.

Hamilton, J. A., & Parry, B. (1983). Sex-related differences in clinical drug response: Implications for women's health. Journal of the American Medical Women's Association, 38, 126-132.

Hare-Mustin, R. T. (1978). A feminist approach to family therapy. Family Process, 17(2), 181-194.

Hare-Mustin, R. T. (1981). The philosophical basis of psychiatric ethics. In S. Bloch & P. Chodoff (Eds.), Psychiatric ethics. Oxford, England: Oxford University Press.

Hare-Mustin, R. T. (1983). An appraisal of the relationship between women and psychotherapy--80 years after the case of Dora. American Psychologist, 38(5), 593-601.

This article reviews the relationship of women and psychotherapy. It suggests that the pervasive unhappiness of many women became a subject for psychotherapy, yet clinical theories of development have been inadequate in terms of women's experiences. Criticisms of psychotherapy from women's perspective have focused on sex role bias and recently on the lack of understanding of disorders of high prevalence and special problems of women. Research to date has not resolved these criticisms. If psychotherapy is to serve women more effectively, new treatment models are needed as well as more sophisticated research to explicate those disorders of high prevalence for women. (AUTHORS' ABSTRACT)

Hare-Mustin, R. T. (1984). A feminist approach to family therapy. In P. P. Rieker & E. Carmen (Eds.), The gender gap in psychotherapy: Social realities and psychological processes (pp. 301-318). New York: Plenum. (Reprinted from Family Process, 1978, 17[2], 181-194)

Hare-Mustin, R. T., & Hall, J. (1981). Procedures for responding to ethics complaints against psychologists. American Psychologist, 36(12), 1494-1505.

Harvey, J., & Parks, M. (Eds.). (1982). Master lecture series: Vol. 1. Psychotherapy research and behavior change. Washington, DC: American Psychological Association.

Holroyd, J. C. (1976). Psychotherapy and women's liberation. The Counseling Psychologist, 6(2), 22-28.

Holroyd, J. C. (1983). Erotic contact as an instance of sex-biased therapy. In J. Murray & P. Abrahamson (Eds.), Handbook of bias in psychotherapy.

Holroyd, J. C., & Bouhoutsos, J. (1984). <u>Sources of bias
    in reporting effects of sexual contact with patients</u>.
    Manuscript submitted for publication.

Holroyd, J. C., & Brodsky, A. M. (1977). Psychologists'
    attitudes and practices regarding erotic and nonerotic
    physical contact with patients. <u>American
    Psychologist</u>, <u>32</u>(10), 843-849.

Hopkins, T. J. (1980). A conceptual framework for
    understanding the three "isms"--racism, ageism,
    sexism. <u>Journal of Education for Social Work</u>, <u>16</u>(2),
    63-70.

    This article conducts a comparative analysis of the
    three major "isms" and attempts to specify their
    similarities and differences. (CSWE)

Hoppe, R. B. (1984). The case for or against diagnostic
    and therapeutic sexism. <u>Women and Therapy</u>, <u>3</u>(3/4),
    129-136.

Imes, S., & Clance, P. R. (1984). Treatment of the
    imposter phenomenon in high-achieving women. In C. M.
    Brody (Ed.), <u>Women therapists working with women: New
    theory and process of feminist theory</u> (pp. 69-85).
    New York: Springer.

Israel, J. (1979). A feminist works with non-traditional
    clients. <u>Smith College Journal-School of Social Work</u>,
    <u>6</u>, 20-22.

Israel, J. (1984). Feminist therapy. <u>Women and Therapy</u>,
    <u>3</u>(3/4), 157-161.

Jakubowski, P. (1978). Facilitating the growth of women
    through assertive training. In L. W. Harmon et al.
    (Eds.), <u>Counseling women</u> (pp. 106-122). Monterey, CA:
    Brooks/Cole.

Jarett, L. R., & Everhart, D. (1983). Effect of sex of
    patient and clinician on mental status descriptions of
    attractiveness. <u>Psychotherapy: Theory, Research and
    Practice</u>, <u>20</u>(4), 468-475.

Johnson, M. (Ed.). (1982). Research on teaching psychology of women. Psychology of Women Quarterly, 7(1), 96-104.

Johnson, M., & Richardson, M. S. (1984). Counseling women. In S. Brown & R. Lent (Eds.), Handbook of Counseling Psychology. New York: John Wiley.

Johnson, M., & Scarato, A. M. (1979). A knowledge base for counselors of women. Counseling Psychologist, 8(1), 14-16.

Jones, A., & Seagull, A. (1977). Dimensions of the relationship between the black client and the white therapist: A theoretical overview. American Psychologist, 32(10), 850-855.

Jordan, H., Surrey, J. L., & Kaplan, A. G. (1982). Women and empathy. Wellesley, MA: Stone Center Working Papers Series.

Kahn, S. E., & Theurer, G. (in press). Graduate education and evaluation in counseling women: A case study. In L. B. Rosewater & L. E. Walker (Eds.), A handbook of feminist therapy: Women's issues in psychotherapy. New York: Springer.

Kaplan, A. G. (1979). Toward an analysis of sex-role related issues in the therapeutic relationship. Psychiatry, 42(2), 112-120.

Kaplan, A. G. (1984). Female or male therapists for women: New formulations. (Work in Progress, Working Paper No. 5). Wellesley, MA: The Stone Center for Developmental Studies at Wellesley College.

Kaplan, A. G., & Yasinski, L. (1980). Psychodynamic perspectives. In A. M. Brodsky & R. T. Hare-Mustin (Eds.), Women and psychotherapy (pp. 191-215). New York: The Guilford Press.

Kaplan, M. (1983a). A woman's view of DSM-III. American Psychologist, 38(7), 786-792.

Kaplan, M.   (1983b).   The issue of sex bias in DSM-III:
     Comments on the articles by Spitzer, Williams, and
     Kass. American Psychologist, 38(7), 802-803.

Kaplan, M.   (1984).   Toward an analysis of sex-role-related
     issues in the therapeutic relationship. In P. P.
     Rieker & E. Carmen (Eds.), The gender gap in
     psychotherapy: Social realities and psychological
     processes (pp. 349-360). New York: Plenum.
     (Reprinted from Psychiatry, 1979, 42[5], 112-120)

Kass, F., Spitzer, R. L., & Williams, J. B.   (1983).   An
     empirical study of the issue of sex bias in the
     diagnostic criteria of DSM-III Axis II Personality
     Disorder. American Psychologist, 38(7), 799-801.

Kirsch, B.   (1974).   Consciousness-raising groups as therapy
     for women and women in therapy. New York: Brunner/
     Mazel.

Kirshner, L. A.   (1978).   Effects of gender on psychotherapy.
     Comprehensive Psychiatry, 19(1), 79-82.

Klerman, G. L.   (1983).   The efficacy of psychotherapy as
     the basis for public policy. American Psychologist,
     38(8), 929-934.

Kravetz, D.   (1980).   Consciousness-raising and self-help.
     In A. M. Brodsky & R. T. Hare-Mustin (Eds.), Women and
     psychotherapy (pp. 267-283). New York: The Guilford
     Press.

Kravetz, D., Marecek, J., & Finn, S. E.   (1983).   Factors
     influencing women's participation in consciousness-
     raising groups. Psychology of Women Quarterly, 7(3),
     257-271.

Kutza, E.   (in press).   Benefits for the disabled: How
     beneficial for women? Sociology and Social Welfare.

Kwower, J.   (1980).   Transference and counter-transference
     in homosexuality. American Journal of Psychotherapy,
     34(1), 72-80.

Ladd, F. (1984). Women's institutions as growth environments. (Work in Progress, Working Paper No. 6). Wellesley, MA: The Stone Center for Developmental Studies at Wellesley College.

Laing, M. (1984). A community college approach to meeting the needs of women. Women and Therapy, 3(3/4), 169-173.

LaPointe, K. A., & Rimm, D. C. (1980). Cognitive, assertive, and insight-oriented group therapies in the treatment of reactive depression in women. Psychotherapy: Theory, Research and Practice, 17(3), 312-321.

Lerman, H. E. (Ed.). (1984). Bibliography on sexual intimacies between psychotherapist and patients (sponsored by the Association of Women Psychologists and the American Psychological Association's Division 29's Committee on Women). (Available from D. Patricia Hannigan, 120 Newport Centre Drive #200, Newport Beach, CA 92660 -- $10.50 per copy)

Lerner, H. E. (1982). Special issues for women in psychotherapy. In M. T. Notman & C. C. Nadelson (Eds), The woman patient: Vol. 3. Aggression, adaptations and psychotherapy (pp. 273-286). New York: Plenum.

Lerner, H. E. (1984). Special issues for women in psychotherapy. In P. P. Rieker & F. Carmen (Eds.), The gender gap in psychotherapy: Social realities and psychological processes (pp. 271-284). New York: Plenum.

Lieberman, M., & Borman, L. D/ (Eds.). (1979). Self-help groups for coping with crisis: Origins, members, processes. San Francisco: Jossey-Bass.

Lorion, R. P., & Broughan, K. G. (1984). Differential needs and treatment approaches for women in psychotherapy. In A. U. Rickel, M. Gerrard, & I. Iscoe, (Eds.), Social and psychological problems of women: Prevention and crisis intervention (pp. 239-252). New York: Hemisphere Publishing.

Maffeo, P. A. (1979). Thoughts on Stricker's "Implications of research for psychotherapeutic treatment of women. American Psychologist, 34(8), 690-695.

Marciniak, D. (1984). A stress management training program for low income women. Women and Therapy, 3(3/4), 163-168.

Marecek, J., & Johnson, M. (1980). Gender and the process of therapy. In A. Brodsky & R. Hare-Mustin (Eds.), Women and psychotherapy (pp. 67-93). New York: Guilford Press.

    This article reviews studies in three areas: the influence of the therapist's and the client's gender on the process of therapy; the influence of sex-role stereotyping on therapists' behavior toward women; and the incidence of sexist statements and actions during the course of therapy.

Marecek, J., & Kravetz, D. (1979). Women and mental health: A review of feminist change efforts. Psychiatry, 40(4), 323-329.

Margolin, G., Fernandez, V., Talovic, S., & Onorato, R. (1983). Sex role considerations and behavioral marital therapy: Equal does not mean identical. Journal of Marital and Family Therapy, 9(2), 131-145.

McMahon, S. L. (1980). Women in marital transition. In A. M. Brodsky & R. T. Hare-Mustin (Eds.), Women and psychotherapy (pp. 365-382). New York: The Guilford Press.

Midlarsky, E. (1977). Women, psychopathology, and psycho-therapy: A partially annotated bibliography. Washington, DC: Journal Supplement Abstract Service (JSAS), American Psychological Association.

Miller, J. B. (1976). Women and power. Wellesley, MA: Stone Center Working Papers Series.

Miller, J. B. (1981). Intimacy: Its relation to work and family. Journal of Psychiatric Treatment and Evaluation, 3(2), 121-129.

Miller, J. B. (1983). The construction of anger in women and men. (Work in Progress, Working Paper No. 4). Wellesley, MA: The Stone Center for Developmental Studies at Wellesley College.

Mogul, K. M. (1982). Overview: The sex of the therapist. Journal of Psychiatry, 139(1), 1-11.

Moses, A. E., & Hawkins, R. O., Jr. (1982). Counseling lesbian women and gay men: A life-issues approach. St. Louis, MO: C. V. Mosley.

Mowbray, C. T. (1984). Case study: Women and the health care system--patients or victims? Women and Therapy, 3(3/4), 137-140.

Mowbray, C. T., Lanir, S., & Hulce, M. (Eds.). (1984). Summary and recommendations: Eliminating sexist treatment. Women and Therapy, 3(3/4), 109-120.

Mowbray, C. T., Lanir, S., & Hulce, M. (Eds.). (1984). Summary and recommendations: Medical treatment and medication practices. Women and Therapy, 3(3/4), 141-147.

Mowbray, C. T., Lanir, S., & Hulce, M. (Eds.). (1984). Summary and recommendations: Advancing innovative mental health programs for women. Women and Therapy, 3(3/4), 175-184.

Mulvey, A., & Dohrenwend, B. S. (1984). The relation of stressful life events to gender. In A. U. Rickel, M. Gerrard, & I. Iscoe, (Eds.), Social and psychological problems of women: Prevention and crisis intervention (pp. 219-238). New York: Hemisphere Publishing.

Mundy, J. (1974). Feminist therapy with lesbians and other women. Homosexual Counseling Journal, 1, 154-159.

Murray, J., & Abramson, P. (Eds.). (1983). Bias in psychotherapy. New York: Praeger.

Myers, M. F. (1982). The professional woman as patient: A review and an appeal. Canadian Journal of Psychiatry, 27(3), 236-240.

Nadelson, C. C., Notman, M. T., Arons, E., & Feldman, J. The pregnant therapist. American Journal of Psychiatry, 131(10), 1107-1111.

Nathans, J. (1982). Borderline personality: A new psychiatric syndrome or another example of male disapproval of female behavior. ERIC Resources in Education, 17(3), 26. (ERIC Document Reproduction Service No. ED 208 268)

New England Association for Women in Psychology. (Eds.). (1983). Current feminist issues in psychotherapy. New York: Haworth Press.

Notman, M. T. (1984). Reflections and perspectives on therapeutic issues for today's adult women. In G. Baruch & J. Brooks-Gunn (Eds.), Women in midlife (pp. 359-369). New York: Plenum.

Notman, M. T., & Nadelson, C. C. (1982). The woman patient: Vol. 3. Aggression, adaptations and psychotherapy. New York: Plenum.

Novara, R. (1984). Women and mental health: A community viewpoint. Women and Therapy, 3(3/4), 57-62.

Orlinsky, D. E., & Howard, K. I. (1976). The effects of sex of therapist on the therapeutic experience of women. <u>Psychotherapy: Theory, Research, and Practice</u>, <u>13</u>(1), 82-88.

This study demonstrates that the sex of the therapist and client interact in complex ways that single-variable studies miss. For example, young unmarried women clients are more likely to feel comfortable and helped by women therapists. On the other hand, older married women clients are more likely to report satisfaction from male therapists.

Orlinsky, D. E., & Howard, K. I. (1978). The relation of process to outcome in psychotherapy. In S. L. Garfield & A. E. Bergin (Eds.), <u>Handbook of psychotherapy and behavior change: On empirical analysis</u> (2nd ed.). New York: John Wiley.

Orlinsky, D. E., & Howard, K. I. (1980). Gender and psychotherapeutic outcome. In A. Brodsky & R. Hare-Mustin (Eds.), <u>Women and psychotherapy</u> (pp. 3-34). New York: The Guilford Press.

Orlinsky and Howard have found evidence that therapist gender has an effect on outcome of treatment in specific ways. Their data show, for example, that female therapists do better than male therapists with female patients presenting anxiety reaction or schizophrenia. They also found that the female patient's life status interacts with therapist gender: single women do better with female therapists and single female parents do better with male therapists.

Osmond, H., Franks, V., & Burtle, V. (1974). Changing views of women and therapeutic approaches: Some historic considerations. In V. Franks & V. Burtle (Eds.), <u>Women in therapy</u> ((pp. 3-24). New York: Brunner/Mazel.

Oyster-Nelson, C. K., & Cohen, L. H. (1981). The extent of sex bias in clinical treatment recommendations. <u>Professional Psychology: Research and Practice</u>, <u>12</u>(4), 508-515.

Parloff, M. B., Woskow, P. R., & Wolfe, B. E. (1978). Research on therapist attitudes in relation to process and outcome. In S. L. Garfield & A. E. Bergin (Eds.), Handbook of psychotherapy and behavior change. New York: Wiley.

Payn, N., & Wakefield, J. (1982). The effect of group treatment of primary orgasmic dysfunction on the marital relationship. Journal of Sex and Marital Therapy, 8(2), 135-150.

Person, E. (1983). Women in therapy: Therapist gender as a variable. International Review of Psychoanalysis, 10(2), 193-204.

Pleck, J. H. (1976). Sex role issues in clinical training. Psychotherapy: Theory, Research and Practice, 13(1), 17-19.

Pope, K. S., & Bouhoutsos, J. (1984). Sexual intimacy between marriage and family therapists and clients. Manuscript in preparation.

Pope, K. S., Levenson, H., & Schover, L. R. (1979). Sexual intimacy in psychology training: Results and implications of a national survey. American Psychologist, 34, 682-689.

Radov, C. G., Masnick, B. R., & Hauser, B. B. (1977). Issues in feminist therapy: The work of a women's study group. Social Work, 22(6), 507-509.

Rawlings, E. I., & Carter, D. K. (Eds.). (1977). Psychotherapy for women: Treatment toward equality. Springfield, IL: Charles C. Thomas.

Among the first books written primarily for practicing psychotherapists and counselors, this book examines the ways in which sexism influences the theories and practices of psychotherapists and presents models for helping women to develop as complete and equal people.

Richardson, M. S., & Johnson, M. (1984). Counseling women. In S. Brown & R. Lent (Eds.), Handbook of counseling psychology. New York: John Wiley.

Rickel, A. U., Gerrard, M., & Iscoe, I. (Eds.). (1984). Social and psychological problems of women: Prevention and crisis intervention. New York: McGraw-Hill.

Riddle, D., & Song, B. (1978). Psychotherapy with lesbians. Journal of Social Issues, 34(3), 84-100.

Rieker, P. P., & Carmen, E. H. (1983). Teaching value clarification: The example of gender and psychotherapy. American Journal of Psychiatry, 140(4), 410-415.

Rieker, P. P., & Carmen, E. H. (Eds.). (1984a). The gender gap in psychotherapy: Social realities and psychological processes. New York: Plenum.

Rieker, P. P., & Carmen, E. H. (1984b). Teaching value clarification: The example of gender and psychotherapy. In P. P. Rieker & E. Carmen (Eds.), The gender gap in psychotherapy: Social realities and psychological processes (pp. 337-348). New York: Plenum. (Reprinted from American Journal of Psychiatry, 1983, 140[4], 410-415)

Rivero, E. M., & Bordin, E. S. (1980). Initiative behavior of male and female therapists in first interviews with females. Journal of Consulting and Clinical Psychology, 48(1), 124-125.

Robbins, J. H. (1982). Woman experience: Organizing a seminar on feminist therapy. Women and therapy, 1(1), 45-54.

Robbins, J. H., & Siegel, R. J. (Eds.). (1983). Women changing therapy: New assessments, values and strategies in feminist therapy [Special double issue]. Women and therapy, 2(2/3).

Rochlin, M. (1981-82). Sexual orientation of the therapist and therapeutic effectiveness with gay clients. Journal of Homosexuality, 7, 21-29.

Rodolfa, E., & Hungerford, L. (1982). Self-help groups: A referral resource for professional therapists. Professional Psychology, 13, 345-353.

Rosewater, L. B. (1984). Feminist therapy: Implications for practitioners. In L. E. Walker (Ed.), Women and mental health policy (pp. 267-279). Beverly Hills, CA: Sage.

Rosewater, L. B. (1985). Feminist interpretations of traditional testing. In L. B. Rosewater & L. E. Walker (Eds.), A handbook of feminist therapy (pp. 266-273). New York: Springer.

Rosewater, L. B., & Walker, L. E. (Eds.). (1985). A handbook of feminist therapy. New York: Springer.

Rubin, C. (1980). Notes from a pregnant therapist. Social Work, 25(3), 210-215. (CSWE)

This article outlines the reactions of a pregnant therapist to her patients as well as the reactions of patients to the pregnant therapist. (CSWE)

Schlachet, B. C. (1984). Female role socialization: The analyst and the analysis. In C. M. Brody (Ed.), Women therapists working with women: New theory and process of feminist theory (pp. 56-65). New York: Springer.

Schoener, G., Milgrom, J. H., & Gonsiorek, J. (1984). Sexual exploitation of clients by therapists. Women and Therapy, 3(3/4), 63-70.

Schover, L. R., & LoPiccolo, J. (1982). Treatment effectiveness for dysfunctions of sexual desire. Journal of Sex and Marital Therapy, 8(3), 179-197.

Schwartz, M. C. (1975). Casework implications of a
     worker's pregnancy. Social Casework, 56(1). 27-34.

     The writer of this article has chosen one maturation
     crisis, a first pregnancy, in order to study its
     effect on the casework relationship from the perspec-
     tive of both the worker and the client. (CSWE)

Seiden, A. M. (1976). Overview: Research on the psychology
     of Women: II. Women in families, work, and
     psychotherapy. The American Journal of Psychotherapy,
     133(10), 1111-1123.

Seidler-Feller, D. (1985). A feminist critique of sex
     therapy. In L. B. Rosewater & L. E. Walker (Eds.),
     A handbook of feminist therapy (pp. 119-130). New
     York: Springer.

Serban, G. (1981). Sexual activity in therapy: Legal and
     ethical issues. American Journal of Psychotherapy,
     35(1), 76-85.

Sheridan, K. (1983). The evolving role of women in society:
     A fact for research and psychotherapy. Psychotherapy:
     Theory, Research and Practice, 20(4), 464-467.

Sherman, J. A. (1980). Therapist attitudes and sex-role
     stereotyping. In A. M. Brodsky & R. T. Hare-Mustin
     (Eds.), Women and psychotherapy (pp. 35-66). New
     York: The Guilford Press.

     Over fifty studies of therapists' attitudes toward
     women and sex-role stereotyping of women, especially
     in their role as patient, are reviewed. Half of the
     studies of attitudes toward women among therapists and
     counselors showed men to be more conservative than
     women, particularly with regard to working with
     others. A woeful lack of up-to-date information about
     the psychology of women among therapists was noted.

Sherman, J. A., Koufacos, C., & Kenworthy, J. A.   (1978).
     Therapists: Their attitudes and information about
     women.   Psychology of Women Quarterly, 2(4), 299-313.

     These authors, in their survey, find less bias toward
     women than earlier reports suggested. There is still
     evidence, however, that therapists have inadequate
     knowledge about women's psychological and physiologi-
     cal functioning.

Sherman, S. N.   (1976).   The therapist and changing sex
     roles. Social Casework, 57(2), 93-96.

     The author presents some interesting challenges to
     therapists that have resulted from changing sex roles.
     (CSWE)

Siegel, R. J.   (1982).   The long-term marriage: Implications
     for therapy. Women and therapy, 1(1), 3-11.

Smith, A., & Siegel, R.   (1985).   Feminist therapy:
     Redefining power for the powerless. In L. B.
     Rosewater & L. E. Walker (Eds.), A handbook of
     feminist therapy (pp. 13-21).   New York: Springer.

Smith, M.   (1980).   Sex bias in counseling and psychotherapy.
     Psychological Bulletin, 87(2), 392-407.

Smith, S.   (1984).   The sexually abused patient and the
     abusing therapist: A study in sadomasochistic
     relationships. Psychoanalytic Psychology, 1, 89-98.

     This paper describes cases in which the sexual contact
     between therapist and patient becomes injurious and
     traumatic for the patient. It explores the possible
     conscious and unconscious motives of the therapist and
     relates those issues to the background of the patient.

Sobel, S. B., & Cummings, N. A.   (1981).   The role of
     professional psychologists in promoting equality.
     Professional Psychology, 12(1), 171-179.

Stearns, B., Penner, L., & Kimmel, E. (1980). Sexism among psychotherapists: A case not yet proven. Journal of Consulting and Clinical Psychology, 48(4), 548-550.

Steinhorn, A. (1979). Lesbian adolescents in residential treatment. Social Casework Family Service of America, 60(8), 494-498.

Steinmann, A. (1974). Cultural Values, female role expectancies, and therapeutic goals: Research and interpretation. In V. Franks & V. Burtle (Eds.), Women in therapy (pp. 51-82). New York: Brunner/ Mazel.

Stephenson, P. S. (1973). Modern woman: Implications for psychotherapy. Canadian Psychiatric Association Journal, 18(1), 79-82.

Stephenson, P. S., & Walker, G. (1981). The psychiatrist-woman patient relationship. In E. Howell & M. Bayes (Eds.), Women and mental health (pp. 113-130). New York: Basic Books.

Steuer, J. L. (1982). Psychotherapy with older women: Ageism and sexism in traditional practice. Psychotherapy: Theory, Research and Practice, 19(4), 429-436.

Stone, A. A. (1984). Sexual misconduct by psychiatrists: The ethical and clinical dilemma of confidentiality. In P. P. Rieker & E. Carmen (Eds.), The gender gap in psychotherapy: Social realities and psychological processes (pp. 369-374). New York: Plenum. (Reprinted from American Journal of Psychiatry, 1982, 140[2], 195-197)

Stricker, G. (1977). Implications of research for psychotherapeutic treatment of women. American Psychologist, 32(1), 14-22.

Strouse, J. (1974). Women and analysis. New York: Grossman Publishers.

Sturdivant, S. (1980). _Therapy with women: A feminist philosophy of treatment_. New York: Springer.

Surrey, J. L., Kaplan, A. G., & Jordan, J. (1983). _Women and empathy_. (Work in Progress, Working Paper No. 2). Wellesley, MA: The Stone Center for Developmental Studies at Wellesley College.

Task Force on Consumer Issues in Psychotherapy of the Association for Women in Psychology and the Division of the Psychology of Women of the American Psychological Association. (1985). _Women and psychotherapy: A consumer handbook_ (rev. ed.). Washington, DC: Federation of Organization for Professional Women. (Available from FOPW, 1825 Connecticut Avenue, N.W., Suite 403, Washington, DC 20009 by sending a self-addressed mailing label and $3.75 per copy plus $1.25 for postage and handling [prepaid orders only]).

Tennov, D. (1973). Feminism, psychotherapy and professionalism. _Journal of Contemporary Psychotherapy, 5_(2), 107-111.

Tennov, D. (1976). _Psychotherapy: The hazardous cure_. Garden City, NY: Anchor Press.

Thorne, B., & Yalom, M. (Eds.). (1982). _Rethinking the family: Some feminist questions_. New York: Longman.

Todres, R. (1982). Professional attitudes, awareness and use of self-help groups. In L. Borman, L. Borck, R. Hess, & F. Pasquale (Eds.), _Helping people to help themselves: Self-help and prevention_. New York: The Haworth Press.

Trotman, F. K. (1984). Psychotherapy with black women and the dual effects of racism and sexism. In C. M. Brody (Ed.), _Women therapists working with women: New theory and process of feminist theory_ (pp. 96-108). New York: Springer.

Turkel, A. R. (1976). The impact of feminism on the practice of a woman analyst. The American Journal of Psychoanalysis, 36(2), 119-126.

Turner, B., & Troll, L. E. (1982). Sex differences in psychotherapy with older people. Psychotherapy: Theory, Research and Practice, 19(4), 419-428.

Underwood, M. M., & Underwood, E. D. (1976). Clinical observations of a pregnant therapist. Social Work, 21(6), 512-517.

The authors discuss the treatment of adults by a pregnant therapist and emphasize the themes that may emerge at specific points during the pregnancy. (CSWE)

Van Buskirk, S., & Cole, C. F. (1983). Characteristics of eight women seeking therapy for the effects of incest. Psychotherapy: Theory, Research and Practice, 20(4), 503-514.

Walker, L. E. (1980). Battered women. In A. M. Brodsky & R. T. Hare-Mustin (Eds.), Women and psychotherapy (pp. 339-363). New York: Guilford Press.

Walker, L. E. (1981). Battered women: Sex roles and clinical issues. Professional Psychology, 12(1), 81-91.

Walker, L. E. (1985). Feminist forensic psychology. In L. B. Rosewater & L. E. Walker (Eds.), A handbook of feminist therapy (pp. 274-284). New York: Springer.

Walker, L. S. (1981). Are women's groups different? Psychotherapy: Theory, Research and Practice, 18(2), 240-245.

Wallis, L. A., & Frings, J. (1984). National Institutes of Health gender staffing patterns. New York: Regional Council for Women in Medicine, Inc.

Weick, A., & Vandiver, S. (Eds.). (1980). Women, power, and change. New York: Springer.

Weissman, M. M., & Klerman, G. L. (1973). Psychotherapy with depressed women: An empirical study of content, themes and reflection. The British Journal of Psychiatry, 123(572), 55-61.

Whitley, B. E. (1979). Sex roles and psychotherapy: A current appraisal. Psychological Bulletin, 86(6), 1309-1321.

Whitman, J. R., & Duffy, R. (1961). The relationship between type of therapy received and a patient's perception of his illness. Journal of Nervous and Mental Disorders, 133, 288-292.

Wiesmeier, E., & Forsythe, A. B. (1982). Sexual concerns and counseling needs of "normal" women attending a student health service women's clinic. Journal of American College Health, 30(5), 212-215.

Wilkinson, D. Y. (1980). Minority women: Social-cultural issues. In A. M. Brodsky & R. T. Hare-Mustin (Eds.), Women and psychotherapy (pp. 285-304). New York: Guilford Press.

Williams, E. F. (1976). Notes of a feminist therapist. New York: Praeger.

Williams, J. B., & Spitzer, R. L. (1983). The issue of sex bias in DSM-III: A critique of "A woman's view of DSM-III" by Marcie Kaplan. American Psychologist, 38(7), 793-797.

Wolfman, B. (1984). Women and their many roles. (Work in Progress, Working Paper No. 7). Wellesley, MA: The Stone Center for Developmental Studies at Wellesley College.

Woodman, N. J., & Lenna, H. R. (1980). Counseling with gay men and women: A guide for facilitating positive life styles. San Francisco: Jossey-Bass.

Wright, C. T., Meadow, A., Abramowitz, S. I., & Davidson, C. V. (1980). Psychiatric diagnosis as a function of assessor profession and sex. Psychology of Women Quarterly, 5(2), 240-254.

Wright, R. W. (1981). Psychologists and professional liability (malpractice) insurance: A retrospective review. American Psychologist, 36, 1485-1493.

Wycoff, H. (1977a). Radical psychiatry for women. In E. I. Rawlings & D. K. Carter (Eds.), Psychotherapy for women (pp. 370-391). Springfield, IL: Charles C. Thomas.

Wycoff, H. (1977b). Solving women's problems. New York: Grove Press.

Zilbergeld, B., & Kilmann, P. R. (1984). The scope and effectiveness of sex therapy. Psychotherapy, 21(3), 319-326.

Zuckerman, E. (1979). Changing directions in the treatment of women: A mental health bibliography (DHEW Publication N. ADM 79-749). Washington, DC: ADAMHA.

B. Sex Role Issues in Supervision

Abramowitz, S. I., & Abramowitz, C. V. (1976). Sex role
    psychodynamics in psychotherapy supervision. American
    Journal of Psychotherapy, 30(4), 583-592.

These authors have focused on the malesupervisor-
female trainee dyad. Pointing to a particular sex
role stereotyped issue to overcome in supervision,
they suggest the female trainee may hold onto a passive dependent stance and find it difficult to move
from book learning and didactic instruction from
supervision to a more active, assertive decision-
making stance. Hostile dependent strategies such as
seductive flattery may be used to serve immediate ego
protective needs, but block fuller professional
functioning.

Alonso, A., & Rutan, J. S. (1978). Cross-sex supervision
    for cross-sex therapy. American Journal of
    Psychiatry, 135(8), 928-931.

Looking at the problem of cross-sex empathy, the
authors point to serious gaps in male trainees'
tendency to present material about their female
patients' aggression, ambition, creativity and long
term goals. They conclude this tendency is the male
trainees' attempt to "overcome the threat of fusion
with a benign powerful female supervisor." The female
supervisor can provide a role model for the male
trainee and help him identify more safely with a woman
in relative power and thus deal more appropriately
with such "countertransference deafness" with his
female patients.

American Psychological Association. (1983a). Graduate
    faculty interested in the psychology of women
    1982-1983. Washington, DC: Author.

American Psychological Association. (1983b). Understanding
    the manuscript review process: Increasing the
    participation of women (2nd ed.). Washington, DC:
    Author.

Braslow, J. B., & Heins, M. (1981). Women in medical
     education--A decade of change. New England Journal
     of Medicine, 304(19), 1129-1135.

Brodsky, A. M. (1980). Sex role issues in the supervision
     of therapy. In A. Hess (Ed.), Psychotherapy
     supervision: Theory, research and practice (pp.
     509-522). New York: John Wiley.

     In this paper Brodsky has proposed remedial techniques
     to counteract gender stereotyping in supervision. One
     suggestion is that female trainees present insights to
     male supervisees on gender issues such as rape victi-
     mization and ambivalence about mothering, while female
     supervisors can also learn from male supervisees dif-
     ficulties regarding the male sex role. Brodsky also
     includes a sensitive discussion of the ethical consi-
     derations of sexual involvement of supervisor and
     supervisee and how it can interfere in the process of
     supervision.

Cypress, B. K. (1980). Characteristics of visits to female
     and male physicians (The National Ambulatory Medical
     Care Survey--United States, 1977). Hyattsville, MD:
     National Center for Health Statistics.

Davidson, V. (1984). Psychiatry's problem with no name:
     Therapist-patient sex. In P. P. Rieker & E. Carmen
     (Eds.), The gender gap in psychotherapy: Social
     realities and psychological processes (pp. 361-368).
     New York: Plenum. (Reprinted from American Journal of
     Psychoanalysis, 1977, 37, 43-50)

Friedlander, S. R., Dye, N. W., Costello, R. M., & Kobos, J.
     C. (1984). A developmental model for teaching and
     learning in psychotherapy supervision. Psychotherapy,
     21(2), 189-196.

Harway, M. (1979). Training counselors. Counseling
     Psychologist, 8(1), 8-9.

Harway, M., & Astin, H. S. (1977). Sex discrimination in
     career counseling and education. New York: Praeger.

Johnson, M. (Ed.). (1982). Teaching psychology of women [Special issue]. Psychology of Women Quarterly, 7(1).

Kaplan, A. G. (1984). Toward an analysis of sex-role-related issues in the therapeutic relationship. In P. P. Rieker & E. Carmen (Eds.), The gender gap in psychotherapy: Social realities and psychological processes (pp. 349-360). New York: Plenum. (Reprinted from Psychiatry, 1979, 42[5], 112-120)

Leighton, J. (1984). Gender stereotyping in supervisory styles. Unpublished manuscript.

Using Chodorow and Gilligan's differentiation of "feminine" and "masculine" modes of knowing and being, the author has applied this model to styles of supervision. She has pointed to the "masculine" style as aimed toward individuation and defensive ego boundaries; therefore, supervision in this mode imparts cognitive knowledge and the development of abstract thinking. Her thesis has further seen the feminine mode as allowing personal boundaries to be crossed and as helping the trainee to feel better understood and to feel less persecutory anxiety, which may aid learning. Neither style is without problems and can misfire, but Leighton has concluded that both modes are needed to most effectively help students integrate didactic teaching with empathic understanding. A good review of a limited literature has been included.

Munson, C. E. (1979). Evaluation of male and female supervisors. Social Work, 24(2), 104-110.

This study of workers' satisfaction with their supervisors found that female supervisors received significantly higher scores on most of the variables considered. The article explores a number of myths about females as supervisors that are contradicted by the findings.

National Association of Social Workers. (1983). Membership survey shows practice shifts. NASW NEWS, 28.

Newman, A. S. (1981). Ethical issues in the supervision of psychotherapy. <u>Professional Psychology: Research and Practice</u>, <u>12</u>(6), 690-695.

Phillips, G. L., & Kanter, C. N. (1984). Mutuality in psychotherapy supervision. <u>Psychotherapy</u>, <u>21</u>(2), 178-183.

Porter, N. (1985). Supervision from a feminist perspective: New perspectives on therapy supervision. In L. B. Rosewater & L. F. Walker (Eds.), <u>A handbook of feminist therapy</u> (pp. 332-343). New York: Springer.

Rickel, A. U., Forsberg, L. K., Gerrard, M., & Iscoe, I. New directions for women: Moving beyond the 1980s. In A. U. Rickel, M. Gerrard, & I. Iscoe, (Eds.), <u>Social and psychological problems of women: Prevention and crisis intervention</u> (pp. 301-312). New York: Hemisphere Publishing.

Rieker, P. P., & Carmen, E. H. (1984). Teaching value clarification: The example of gender and psychotherapy. In P. P. Rieker & E. Carmen (Eds.), <u>The gender gap in psychotherapy: Social realities and psychological processes</u> (pp. 337-348). New York: Plenum. (Reprinted from <u>American Journal of Psychiatry</u>, 1983, <u>140</u>[4], 410-415)

Russo, N. F. (1984). <u>Women in the American Psychological Association</u>. Washington, DC: American Psychological Association.

Stone, A. A. (1984). Sexual misconduct by psychiatrists: The ethical and clinical dilemma of confidentiality. In P. P. Rieker & E. Carmen (Eds.), <u>The gender gap in psychotherapy: Social realities and psychological processes</u> (pp. 369-374). New York: Plenum. (Reprinted from <u>American Journal of Psychiatry</u>, 1982, <u>140</u>[2], 195-197)

C. Psychotherapy Research

American Psychological Association. (1978). Status report on the federal budget as it affects psychology, and behavioral and social science research, training and services. Washington, DC: Author.

American Psychological Association. (1981). Division 35. Task force on nonsexist research: Guidelines for nonsexist research. Washington, DC: Author.

Brodsky, A. M. (1982). Sex, race and class issues in psychotherapy research. In J. Harvey & M. Parks (Eds.), Master lecture series: Vol. I. Psychotherapy research and behavior change (pp. 123-149). Washington, DC: American Psychological Association.

Brodsky, A. M., & Hare-Mustin, R. T. (Eds.). (1980). Women and psychotherapy: An assessment of research and practice. New York: Guilford Press.

Clarke, K. (1984). Focus: Grants for women and girls. The Foundation Grants Index Bimonthly. New York: The Foundation Center.

Cross, D. G., & Sheehan, P. (1981). Classification of variables in psychotherapy research: Therapeutic changes and the concept of artifact. Psychotherapy: Theory, Research and Practice, 18(3), 345-353.

Feminist Research [Special section]. (1981). Psychology of Women Quarterly, 5(4), 595-653.

Goldfried, M. R. (1984). Training the clinician as scientist-professional. Professional Psychology: Research and Practice, 15(4), 477-481.

Association for Women in Psychology. (1985). An international feminist mental health agenda. Washington, DC: Author.

Johnson, M., & Auerbach, A. H. (1984). Women and
    psychotherapy research. In L. E. Walker (Ed.),
    Women and mental health policy (pp. 59-78).
    Beverly Hills, CA: Sage.

Ketterer, R. F., Bader, B. C., & Levy, M. R. (1980).
    Strategies and skills for promoting mental health.
    In R. H. Price, B. C. Bader, & J. Monohan (Eds.),
    Sage annual reviews of community mental health:
    Vol. 2. Prevention and mental health: Research,
    policy, and practice. Beverly Hills, CA: Sage.

Lachman, M. E. (1984). Methods for a life-span
    developmental approach to women in the middle years.
    In G. Baruch & J. Brooks-Gunn (Eds.), Women in midlife
    (pp. 31-68). New York: Plenum.

London, P., & Klerman, G. L. (1982). Evaluating psycho-
    therapy. American Journal of Psychiatry, 139(6),
    709-717.

Maher, B. A. (Ed.). (1978). Methodology in clinical
    research [Special issue]. Journal of Consulting and
    Clinical Psychology, 46(4).

Meltzoff, J., & Kornreich, M. (Eds.). (1970). Research
    in psychotherapy. Chicago: Aldine Press.

Subpanel on the Mental Health of Women. (1978). Report to
    the President (Vol. III) (pp. 1022-1116). Washington,
    DC: U.S. Government Printing Office.

Morin, S. F. (1977). Heterosexual bias in psychological
    research on lesbianism and male homosexuality.
    American Psychologist, 32(8), 629-637.

Parloff, M. B. (1982). Psychotherapy research evidence and
    reimbursement decision: Bambi meets Godzilla.
    American Journal of Psychiatry, 139(6), 718-727.

President's Commission on Mental Health (1978). Report to
    the President (Vol. 1). Washington, DC: U.S.
    Government Printing Office.

Richardson, B. L., & Wirtenberg, J. (1983). Sex role research: Measuring social change. New York: Praeger.

Roberts, H. (Ed.). (1981). Doing feminist research. London: Routledge & Kegan Paul.

Russo, N. F. (Ed.). (1985). Developing a national agenda to address women's mental health needs. Washington, DC: American Psychological Association.

Sherman, J. A., & Denmark, F. L. (Eds.). (1978). Psychology of women: Future directions of research. New York: Psychological Dimensions.

Song, B. E. (1978). Lesbian research: A critical evaluation. In G. Vida (Ed.), Our right to love: A lesbian resource book. Englewood Cliffs, NJ: Prentice-Hall.

Stanley, L., & Wise, S. (1983). Breaking out: Feminist consciousness and feminist research. London: Routledge & Kegan Paul.

Stricker, G. (1977). Implications of research for psychotherapeutic treatment of women. American Psychologist, 32(1), 14-22.

Studying women in a changing world [Special issue]. (1982). Journal of Social Issues, 38(1).

Tangri, S. S., & Strausberg, G. L. (1979). Can research on women be more effective in shaping policy? Psychology of Women Quarterly, 3, 321-343.

Task Force on Nonsexist Research. (1981). Guidelines for nonsexist research. Washington, DC: The American Psychological Association, Division 35.

Unger, R. K. (1984). Hidden assumptions in theory and research on women. In C. M. Brody (Ed.), Women therapists working with women: New theory and process of feminist theory (pp. 119-134). New York: Springer.

Wallston, B. S.   (1981).   What are the questions in
      psychology of women?   A feminist approach to research.
      Psychology of Women Quarterly, 5(4), 595-617.

Worell, J.   (1978).   Sex roles and psychological well-being:
      Perspectives and methodology.   Journal of Consulting
      and Clinical Psychology, 46(4), 777-791.

PART VI

FEMALE PSYCHOLOGY IN A BIOLOGICAL, POLITICAL

AND SOCIOLOGICAL CONTEXT

There is a need to review the woman's inner world within the context of the social, cultural and political forces in contemporary society. (N.A.)

A. Anthropology and Sociobiology

Bleier, R. (1984). Science and gender: A critique of
    biology and its theories on women. New York:
    Pergamon Press.

Hrdy, S. B. (1981). The woman that never evolved.
    Cambridge, MA: Harvard University Press.

Kanter, R. M. (1984). Some effects of proportions on group
    life: Skewed sex ratios and responses to token women.
    In P. P. Rieker & E. Carmen (Eds.), The gender gap in
    psychotherapy: Social realities and psychological
    processes (pp. 53-78). New York: Plenum. (Reprinted
    from American Journal of Sociology, 1977, 82[5],
    965-990)

MacCormack, C., & Strathern, M. (Eds.) (1980).
    Nature, culture and gender. New York: Cambridge
    University Press.

Ortner, S. B., & Whitehead, M. (Eds.). (1981). Sexual
    meanings: The cultural construction of gender and
    sexuality. New York: Cambridge University Press.

Paige, K. E., & Paige, J. M.   (1981). The politics of
    reproductive ritual. Berkeley, CA: University of
    California Press.

Petersen, A. C. (1984, August). <u>Biology and the psychology of women: What's new and so what?</u> Paper presented at the meeting of the American Psychological Association, Toronto, Canada.

Reiter, R. R. (Ed.). (1975). <u>Toward an anthropology of women</u>. New York: Monthly Review Press.

Rubin, G. (1975). The traffic in women: Notes on the "political economy" of sex. In R. R. Reiter (Ed.), <u>Toward an anthropology of women</u>. New York: Monthly Review Press.

A very original anthropological article defining what the author calls the sex/gender system. It also connects with Levi-Strauss, Lacan and Mitchell.

Sanday, P. R. (1981). <u>Female power and male dominance: On the origins of sexual inequality</u>. New York: Cambridge University Press.

Sanjek, R. (1982). The American Anthropological Association resolution on the employment of women: Genesis, implementation, disavowal, and resurrection. <u>Signs</u>, <u>7</u>(4), 845-868.

Tanner, N. M. (1981). <u>On becoming human</u>. New York: Cambridge University Press.

Tobach, E., & Rossoff, B. (Series Editors). <u>Genes and gender</u>. Staten Island, NY: Gordian Press.

Vol. 1. Tobach, E., & Rossoff, B. (Eds.). (1978). <u>On hereditarianism and women</u>.

Vol. 2. Tobach, E., & Rossoff, B. (Eds.). (1979). <u>Pitfalls in research on sex and gender</u>.

Vol. 3. Tobach, E., & Rossoff, B. (Eds.). (1980). <u>Genetic determinism and children</u>.

Vol. 4. Fooden, M., Gordon, S., & Hughley, B. (Eds.). <u>The second sex and women's health</u>.

Selected References on Sociobiology

(Compiled by Division 35 Task Force on Sociobiology, APA)

Technical Scientific Writings

Alexander, R. D. (1974). The evolution of social behavior. Annual Review of Ecology and Systematics, 5, 325-383.

Darwin, C. (1859). On the origin of species by means of natural selection. London, England: J. Murray.

Darwin, C. (1871). The descent of man and selection in relation to sex. London, England: J. Murray.

Hamilton, W. D. (1964a). The genetical evolution of social behavior: I. Journal of Theoretical Biology, 7, 1-16.

Hamilton, W. D. (1964b). The genetical evolution of social behavior: II. Journal of Theoretical Biology, 7, 17-52.

Hamilton, W. D. (1971). Geometry of the selfish herd. Journal of Theoretical Biology, 31, 295-311.

These three articles form part of the original literature defining the field of sociobiology.

Lumsden, C. J., & Wilson, E. O. (1981). Genes, mind, and culture. Cambridge, MA: Harvard University Press.

Mackey, W. C. (1979). Parameters of the adult-male-child bond. Ethology and Sociobiology, 1(1), 59-76.

Ralls, K. (1976). Mammals in which females are larger than males. Quarterly Review of Biology, 51(2), 245-276.

Ralls, K. (1977). Sexual dimorphism in mammals: Avian models and some unanswered questions. American Naturalist, 111, 917-981.

This writer is a woman.

Strayer, F. F., & Freedman, D. G. (1980). <u>Dominance relations: An ethological view of human conflict and social interactions</u>. New York: Garland STPM Press.

Trivers, R. L. (1971). The evolution of reciprocal altruism. <u>Quarterly Review of Biology</u>, <u>46</u>(1), 35-57.

Trivers, R. L. (1972). Parental investment and sexual selection. In B. Campbell (Ed.), <u>Sexual selection and descent of man 1871-1971</u> (pp. 136-179). Chicago: Aldine.

Trivers, R. L. (1974). Parent-offspring conflict. <u>American Zoologist</u>, <u>14</u>(1), 249-264.

Trivers, R. L., & Willard, D. E. (1973). Natural selection of parental ability to vary the sex ratio of offspring. <u>Science</u>, <u>179</u>(4068), 90-92.

Four articles which are important to the original definition of the field of sociobiology.

Wade, M. J. (1980). Kin selection: Its components. <u>Science</u>, <u>210</u>(4470), 665-667.

West-Eberhard, M. J. (1975). The evolution of social behavior by kin selection. <u>Quarterly Review of Biology</u>, <u>50</u>, 1-33.

Williams, G. C. (1975). <u>Sex and evolution</u>. Princeton, NJ: Princeton University Press.

Wilson, E. O. (1975). <u>Sociobiology: The new synthesis</u>. Cambridge, MA: Harvard University Press.

The most well-known work; in fact, some people equate sociobiology and Wilson.

Edited Books on Sociobiology (Non-popular)

Campbell, B. (Ed.). (1972). Sexual selection and the descent of man, 1871-1971. Chicago: Aldine.

Chagnon, N. A., & Irons, W. G. (Eds.). (1979). Evolutionary biology and human social behavior: An anthropological perspective. North Scituate, MA: Duxbury Press.

Crook, J. H. (Ed.). (1970). Social behavior in birds and mammals: Essays on the social ethology of animals and man. New York: Academic Press.

Eisenberg, J. F., & Dillon, W. S. (Eds.). (1971). Man and beast: Comparative social behavior. Washington, DC: Smithsonian Institution Press.

Hunt, J. H. (Ed.). (1980). Selected readings in sociobiology. New York: McGraw-Hill.

Lockard, J. S. (Ed.). (1980). Evolution of human social behavior. New York: Elsevier.

The editor is a woman.

Marler, P., & Vandenberg, J. (Eds.). (1979). Handbook of behavior: Vol. 3, Social behavior and communication. New York: Plenum.

Williams, G. C. (Ed.) (1971). Group selection. Chicago: Lieber-Atherton.

Less Technical Works (for the Scientist-in-general or College Students)

Alexander, R. D. (1979). Darwinism and human affairs. Seattle, WA: University of Washington Press.

Barash, D. P. (1977). Sociobiology and behavior. New York: Elsevier.

Bonner, J. T. (1980). <u>The evolution of culture in animals</u>.
    Princeton, NJ: Princeton University Press.

Daly, M., & Wilson, M. (1978). <u>Sex, evolution and
    behavior: Adaptations for reproduction</u>. North
    Scituate, MA: Duxbury Press.

Dawkins, R. (1976). <u>The selfish gene</u>. New York: Oxford
    University Press.

Symmons, D. (1979). <u>The evolution of human sexuality</u>. New
    York: Oxford University Press.

<u>Popular Books on Sociobiology</u>

Barash, D. (1979). <u>The whisperings within</u>. New York:
    Harper & Row.

    This book has significant problems in its analysis.
    For example, the author cites concept of "Rape in
    ducks" to support the viewpoint of genetically
    determined violence against women. Read with caution.
    (L.S.B.)

Hapgood, R. (1979). <u>Why males exist: An inquiry into the
    evolution of sex</u>. New York: Mentor.

Wilson, E. O. (1978). <u>On human nature</u>. Cambridge, MA:
    Harvard University Press.

<u>Older Popular Works</u> (Prior to the invention of the term
sociobilogy)

Ardrey, R. (1961). <u>African genesis</u>. New York: Atheneum.

Ardrey, R. (1966). <u>The territorial imperative</u>. New York:
    Atheneum.

    Written by a non-scientist; but highly influential.

Lorenz, K.   (1966).   On aggression. New York: Harcourt,
    Brace, and World.

Reviews Critiques, and Commentary on Sociobiology

Barlow, G. W., & Silverberg, J. (Eds.).   (1980).
    Sociobiology: Beyond Nature/Nurture: Reports,
    definitions, debate. Boulder, CO: Westview Press.

Bock, K.   (1980).   Human nature and history: A response to
    sociobiology. New York: Columbia University Press.

Campbell, D.   (1975, December). Presidential address to APA
    annual meeting. American Psychologist,   1103-1126.

    Discusses sociobiology at length.

Caplan, A. L. (Ed.).   (1978). The sociobiology debate:
    Readings on ethical and scientific issues. New York:
    Harper & Row.

Corning, P. A. (1980). What (could be) (is not) wrong
    with human ethology (choose one). Human Ethology
    Newsletter, Summer, (30), 11-13.

Gould, S. J. (1980). The panda's thumb: More reflections
    in natural history. New York: Norton.

Hailman, J., & Dawkins, R. (Eds.).   (1976). Multiple
    reviews of Sociobiology. Animal Behavior, 24,
    698-714.

Hardy, S. (1979). Review of The evolution of human
    sexuality. Quarterly Review of Biology, 54, 309-314.

A critique of human ethology [Special issue]. (1980,
    Spring). Human Ethology Newsletter.

    Contributions by S. A. Barnett, W. C. Mackey, I. Eibl-
    Eibesfeldt, G. Y. Larsen, and G. F. McCracken.

Montagu, A. (1980). Sociobiology examined. Oxford,
     England: Oxford University Press.

Ruse, M. (1979). Sociobiology: Sense or nonsense? Boston:
     D. Reidel.

Sahlins, M. D. (1976). The use and abuse of biology:
     An anthropological critique of sociobiology.
     Ann Arbor, MI: University of Michigan Press.

Reviews and discussion of The evolution of human sexuality
     by 25 sexologists. (1980). Behavioral and Brain
     Sciences, 3, 171-124.

Sociobiology [Special issue]. (1979). Behavioral Science,
     24(1).

Sociobiology Study Group. (1977). Sociobiology: A new
     biological determinism. In Ann Arbor Science for the
     People Editorial Collective (Eds.), Biology as a
     social weapon (pp. 139-149). Minneapolis, MI:
     Burgess.

Sociobiology and Women's Issues

Fedigan, L. M. (1980). Monkey business: The social life of
     primates. Eden Press Women's Publications.

Kleiman, D. G. (1977). [Review of Sociobiology: The new
     synthesis]. Signs, 3, 493-495.

Lowe, M. (1978). Sociobiology and sex differences. Signs,
     4, 118-125.

Lowe, M. (1980). Reply to Ralls. Signs, 5, 546-47.

Ralls, K. (1980). Comment on Lowe's "Sociobiology and sex
     differences." Signs, 5, 544-546.

Shaw, E., & Darling, J. (1984). Female strategies.
     New York: Walker & Co.

Small, M. (Ed.). (1984). Female primates: Studies by woman primatologists. New York: A. R. Liss.

Sunday, S. R., & Tobach, E. (Eds.). (in press). Genes and gender, Vol. 1. Violence against women: A critique of the sociobiology of rape. New York: Gordian Press.

Wasser, S. K. (Ed.). (1983). The social behavior of female vertebrates. New York: Academic press.

B. Ethnicity and Women

Ethnicity and Women is an area of growing information. Much work in this important area is being done at the dissertation level and bibliographies can be obtained from APA's program on Women. (N.A.)

Acosta, F. (1980). Self-described reasons for premature termination of psychotherapy by Mexican American, Black American, and Anglo-American patients. Psychological Reports, 47, 435-443.

Allen, L., & Britt, D. W. (1984). Black women in American society: A resource development perspective. In A. U. Rickel, M. Gerrard, & I. Iscoe, (Eds.), Social and psychological problems of women: Prevention and crisis intervention (pp. 61-84). New York: Hemisphere Publishing.

Belle, D. (1984). Inequality and mental health: Low income and minority women. In L. E. Walker (Ed.), Women and mental health policy (pp. 135-150). Beverly Hills, CA: Sage.

Black women [Special issue]. (1982). Psychology of Women Quarterly, 6(3).

Block, C. B. (1984). Diagnostic and treatment issues for black patients. The Clinical Psychologist, 37(2), 51-54.

Block, C. B. (1984). Psychotherapy and the black patient. The Clinical Psychologist, 37(2).

Boyd, N. (1979). Black families in therapy: A study of clinician's perceptions. Sandoz Psychiatric Spectator, 11(7), 21-25.

Boyd-Franklin, N. (1984). Issues in family therapy with black families. The Clinical Psychologist, 37(2), 54-58.

Copeland, E. J. (1982). Oppressed conditions and the
     mental health needs of low-income black women:
     Barriers to services, strategies for change. Women
     and therapy, 1(1), 13-26.

Davis, L. (1975). The black woman in American society:
     A selected annotated bibliography. Boston: G. K.
     Hall.

Dudley, G. R., & Rawlins, M. (Eds.). Psychotherapy with
     ethnic minorities [Special issue]. Psychotherapy:
     Theory, Research, Practice, 22.

Heschel, S. (1983). On being a Jewish feminist: A reader.
     New York: Schocken Books.

Jones, E. E. (1984). Some reflections on the black patient
     and psychotherapy. The Clinical Psychologist, 37(2),
     62-65.

Jones, J. M., & Block, C. B. (1984). Black cultural
     perspectives. The Clinical Psychologist, 37(2),
     58-62.

Jones, A., & Seagull, A. (1977). Dimensions of the rela-
     tionship between the black client and the white thera-
     pist: A theoretical overview. American Psychologist,
     32(10), 850-856.

Joseph, G. I., & Lewis, J. (1981). Common differences:
     Conflicts in black and white feminist perspectives.
     New York: Anchor Books.

Mays, V. M. (1983). The black woman: A bibliographic
     guide to social science and mental health research
     on black females. Washington, DC: Division of
     Psychology of Women, American Psychological
     Association.

McGoldrick, M., et al. (1982). Ethnicity and family therapy.
     New York: Guilford Press.

     (See Chapters 1, 2, 4, 5, 8, 9, 16, 17, and 26).

Murray, S. R., & Mednick, M. T. S. (1977). Black women's achievement orientation: Motivational and cognitive factors. Psychology of Women Quarterly, 1(3), 247-259.

Murray, S. R., & Scott, P. B. (Eds.). (1982). Black women [Special issue]. Psychology of Women Quarterly, 6(3).

Olmeda, E. L., & Parron, D. L. (1981). Mental health of minority women: Some special issues. Professional Psychology, 12(1), 103-111.

Racism and sexism in black women's lives [Special issue]. (1983). Journal of Social Issues, 39(3).

Rodgers-Rose, La F. (Ed.). (1980). The Black woman. Beverly Hills, CA: Sage Publications.

    An examination, by Black women contributors, of the relationship of the Black woman to the Black man, family, community, the political and educational systems, and the economy.

Russo, N. F., Olmedo, E., Stapp, J., & Fulcher, R. (1981). Women and minorities in psychology. American Psychologist, 36(11), 1323-1371.

Seligman, M. (1975). Helplessness: On depression, development and death. San Francisco: W. H. Freeman.

Smith, B. (Ed.). (1983). Home girls: A black feminist anthology. New York: Kitchen Table, Women of Color Press.

Smith, E. H. (1981). Mental health and service delivery systems for black women. Journal of Black Studies, 12(2), 126-141.

Solo, E., & Shaver, P. (1982). Sex-role traditionalism, assertiveness and symptoms of Puerto Rican women living in the United States. Hispanic Journal of Behavioral Sciences, 4(1), 1-19.

Spurlock, J. (1984). Black women in the middle years. In
     G. Baruch & J. Brooks-Gunn (Eds.), <u>Women in midlife</u>
     (pp. 11-30). New York: Plenum.

Trotman, F. K. (1984). Psychotherapy with black women and
     the dual effects of racism and sexism. In C. M.
     Brody (Ed.), <u>Women therapists working with women: New
     theory and process of feminist theory</u> (pp. 96-108).
     New York: Springer.

True, R. H. (1981). The profile of Asian American women.
     In S. Cox (Ed.), <u>Female psychology</u> (pp. 124-135).
     New York: St. Martin's.

Westmoreland, G. (1974). <u>An annotated guide to the basic
     reference books on the Black American</u>. Wilmington,
     DE: Scholarly Resources, Inc.

Women's Task Force. (1983). <u>Special populations: Problems
     and perspectives</u>. Lansing, MI: Michigan Department
     of Mental Health.

Wortman, R. (1981). Depression, danger, dependency,
     denial: Work with poor, black, single parents.
     <u>American Journal of Orthopsychiatry</u>, <u>51</u>(4), 662-671.

Yamauchi, J. S. (1981). <u>The cultural integration of Asian
     American professional women: Issues of identity and
     communication behavior</u> (Final Report). Washington,
     DC: National Institute of Education. (ERIC Document
     Reproduction Service No. ED 212 545)

C. Feminist Theory

Bernard, J. (1981). The female world. New York: Free
    Press/MacMillan.

    A study of the female world in itself, apart from its
    impact on the male world. Included are conceptualiza-
    tions of the female world, the social and group struc-
    ture and the culture of the female world, and the
    economic and political aspects of women's status.

Bleier, R. (1984). Science and gender: A critique of
    biology and its theories on women. Elmsford, NY:
    Pergamon Press.

Bond, M. A., & Kelly, J. G. (1984). Social support and
    efficacy in advocacy roles: A case study of two
    women's organizations. In A. U. Rickel, M. Gerrard,
    & I. Iscoe, (Eds.), Social and psychological problems
    of women: Prevention and crisis intervention (pp.
    173-196). New York: Hemisphere Publishing.

Bowles, G., & Duelli Klein, R. (Eds.). (1983). Theories
    of women's studies. London: Routledge & Kegan Paul.

Brownmiller, S. (1984). Femininity. New York: Simon and
    Schuster.

Chesler, P. (1972). Women and madness. Garden City, NY:
    Doubleday.

Cott, N. F., & Pleck, E. H. (Eds.). (1979). A heritage
    of her own: Toward a new social history of American
    women. New York: Simon & Schuster.

Cox, S. (1981). Female psychology: The emerging self.
    New York: St. Martin's Press.

    This book provides a collection of empirical and theo-
    retical papers from the feminist psychological litera-
    ture. It emphasizes the social and political rather
    than biological bases of women's behavior. Areas
    include: biological and cultural perspective; survey

of sex-difference research; ethnic diversity of Black, Asian, Chicano and Native American women; a sociopolitical analysis of the psychology of women at intrapsychic and interpersonal levels; experience of sexuality and intimacy.   References at the end of each section will help reader pursue various topics.

Daly, M. (1978). Gyn/ecology: The metaethics of radical feminism. Boston: Beacon Press.

Daly, M. (1984). Pure lust. Boston: Beacon Press.

de Beauvoir, S. (1953). The second sex. New York: Knopf.

De Riencourt, A. (1974). Sex and power in history. New York: D. Mckay Co.

Dinnerstein, D. (1977). The mermaid and the minotaur. New York: Harper Colophone.

Eichenbaum, L., & Orbach, S. (1982). Outside in and inside out--Women's psychology: A feminist psychoanalytic approach. London, England: Penguin Books.

Feminist theory [Special issue]. (1982). Signs, 7(3).

Friedan, B. (1976). It changed my life: Writings on the women's movement. New York: Random House.

Friedan, B. (1963). The feminine mystique. New York: Norton.

Gallop, J. (1982). The daughter's seduction: Feminism and psychoanalysis. Ithaca, NY: Cornell University Press.

Goffman, E. (1979). Gender advertisements. New York: Harper & Row.

Gornick, V., & Moran, B. (1971). Women in sexist society. New York: Basic Books.

Greer, G. (1971). The female eunuch. New York: McGraw.

Harding, S., & Hintikka, M. B. (1983). _Discovering reality: Feminist perspectives on epistemology, metaphysics, methodology and philosophy of science._ Boston: D. Reidel.

Henley, N. M. (1977). _Body politics: Sex and nonverbal communication._ Englewood Cliffs, NJ: Prentice-Hall.

Henley, N. M. (in press). Review essay: Psychology and gender. _Signs._

Hier, D. B. (1981). Sex differences in brain structure. In A. Ansara, N. Geschwind, A. Galaburda, M. Albert, & N. Gartrell (Eds.), _Sex differences in dyslexia._ Towson, MD: Orton Dyslexia Society.

Hinton, A. P., Sherby, L. B., & Tenbusch, L. G. (1982). _Getting free._ New York: Grove Press.

Hole, J., & Levine, E. (1971). _Rebirth of feminism._ New York: Quadrangle Books.

Janeway, E. (1971). _Man's world woman's place: A study in social mythology._ New York: Morrow, William & Co.

Joseph, G. I., & Lewis, J. (1981). _Common differences: Conflicts in black and white feminist perspectives._ New York: Anchor Press.

Kaufman, D. R. (1984). Some feminist concerns in an age of networking. In C. M. Brody (Ed.), _Women therapists working with women: New theory and process of feminist therapy_ (pp. 157-164). New York: Springer.

Koedt, A., Levine, E., & Rapone (1973). _Radical feminism._ New York: Quadrangle Books.

Kramarae, C. (1981). _Women and men speaking._ Rowley, MA: Newbury House Publication.

Lerman, H. (1985). Some barriers to the development of a feminist theory of personality. In L. B. Rosewater, & L. E. Walker (Eds.), _A handbook of feminist therapy_ (pp. 5-12). New York: Springer.

Lewin, M. (Ed.). (1984). In the shadow of the past:
    Psychology portrays the sexes--A social and
    intellectual history. New York: Columbia University
    Press.

Lowe, M., & Hubbard, R. (Eds). ((1983). Woman's nature:
    Rationalizations of inequality. New York: Pergamon.

Mander, A. V., & Rush, A. K. (1974). Feminism as therapy.
    New York: Random House.

Mayes, S. S. (1984). Women in positions of authority:
    A case study of changing sex roles. In P. P. Rieker &
    E. Carmen (Eds.), The gender gap in psychotherapy:
    Social realities and psychological processes (pp.
    91-103). New York: Plenum. (Reprinted from Signs,
    1979, 4[3], 556-568)

Millett, K. (1971). Sexual politics. New York: Doubleday.

Mitchell, J. (1971). Women's estate. London, England:
    Penguin Books.

Morgan, R. (Ed.). (1984). Sisterhood is global: The
    international women's movement. Garden City, NY:
    Anchor/Doubleday.

Oakley, A. (1972). Sex, gender and society. New York:
    Harper & Row.

Oakley, A. (1976). Woman's work. New York: Vintage Books/
    Random House.

Oakley, A. (1981). Subject women. New York: Pantheon
    Books.

Pleck, J. H. (1984). Men's power with women, other men,
    and society: A men's movement analysis. In P. P.
    Rieker & E. Carmen (Eds.), The gender gap in
    psychotherapy: Social realities and psychological
    processes (pp. 79-90). New York: Plenum. (Reprinted
    from R. A. Lewis [Ed.], [1981], Men in difficult
    times. Englewood Cliffs, NJ: Prentice-Hall)

Reinharz, S., Bombyk, M., & Wright, J. (1983). Methodological issues in feminist research: A bibliography of literature in women's studies, sociology and psychology. _Women's Studies International Forum_, _6_(4), 437-454.

Roberts, H. (Ed.). (1981). _Doing feminist research_. London: Routledge & Kegan Paul.

Roszak, B., & Roszak, T. (1969). _Masculine/Feminine: Readings in sexual mythology and the liberation of women_. New York: Harper & Row.

Rowland, R. (1984). _Women who do and women who don't join the women's movement_. London: Routledge & Kegan Paul.

Rubin, L. (1979). _Women of a certain age: The midlife search for self_. New York: Harper & Row.

Sanday, P. R. (1981). _Female power and male dominance: On the origins of sexual inequality_. Cambridge, England: Cambridge University Press.

Sayers, J. (1982). _Biological politics: Feminist and anti-feminist perspectives_. London: Tavistock.

Schwarzer, A. (1984). _After the second sex: Conversation with Simone de Beauvoir_. New York: Pantheon Books.

Stanley, L., & Wise, S. (1983). _Breaking out: Feminist consciousness and feminist research_. London: Routledge & Kegan Paul.

Theory issues [Special issues]. (1979). _Sex Roles_, _5_(2).

Thorne, B., Kramarae, C., & Henley, N. M. (Eds.).)1983). _Language, gender and society_. Rowley, MA: Newbury House Publishers.

Treblicot, J. (Ed.). (1983). _Mothering: Essays in feminist theory_. Totowa, NJ: Rowman & Allanheld.

Unger, R. K. (1983). Through the looking glass: No
     wonderland yet (The reciprocal relationship between
     methodology and models of reality). <u>Psychology of
     Women Quarterly</u>, <u>8</u>, 9-32.

Van Herck, J. (1982). <u>Freud on femininity and faith</u>.
     Berkeley, CA: University of California Press.

Weisstein, N. (1971). Psychology constructs the female.
     In V. Gornick & B. Moran (Eds.), <u>Women in sexist
     society: Studies in power and powerlessness</u> (pp.
     133-146). New York: Basic Books.

     This article is important for its early date in the
     new wave of feminist criticism, but more important for
     its methodological sophistication and its epistemolo-
     gical rigor in introducing the idea of context--here
     the social and political context--into research.

Wirtenberg, J., & Tangri, S. S. (1981). Women and the
     future [Special issue]. <u>Psychology of Women</u>, <u>6</u>(1).

APPENDIX

Sources and Other Bibliographies

Baer, H. R., & Sherif, C. W. (1974). A topical bibliography (selectively annotated) on psychology of women. Washington, DC: American Psychological Association.

Carey, E. A. (1976). Issues in the psychology and counseling of women. Boston, MA: Womanspace, Feminist Therapy Collective.

Carey, E. A., Murphy, B., & Wasserman, C. (1975). Counseling women: A bibliography. Boston, MA: Womanspace, Feminist Therapy Collective.

Cromwell, P. E. (1974). Women and mental health, selected annotated references 1970-1973. Rockville, MD: National Institute of Mental Health, Division of Scientific and Technical Information.

Center for the Study of Anorexia and Bulimia
        1 West 91st. Street
        New York, N.Y. 10024
        (212) 595-3449.

CSWE Commission on the Role and Status of Women in Social Work Education
        Council on Social Work Education
        111 Eighth Avenue, Suite 501
        New York 10011
        (212) 242-3800

Gottlieb, N. with the assistance of Pettersen, M., & Carr, P. (1981). New knowledge about women--A selected annotated bibliography. New York: Council on Social Work Education.

Grady, K. E., Brannon, R., & Pleck, J. H. (1979). The male
    sex role: A selected and annotated bibliography.
    Rockville, MD: U.S. Department of Health, Education, &
    Welfare, Public Health Service.

Henley, N. M. (1974). Resources for the study of
    psychology and women. R. T.: Journal of Radical
    Therapy, 4, 20-21.

Jovanovich, J. et al. (1972). Women and psychology.
    Cambridge, MA: Cambridge-Goddard Graduate School
    for Social Change.

Mays, V. M. (Ed.). (1983). The black woman: A
    bibliographic guide to social science and mental health
    research on black females. Washington, DC: Division
    of Psychology of Women, American Psychological
    Association.

Midlarsky, E. (1977). Women, psychopathology, and
    psychotherapy: A partially annotated bibliography.
    Washington, DC: Journal Supplement Abstract Service
    (JSAS), American Psychological Association.

National Center on Women and Family Law
    799 Broadway, Room 402,
    New York, NY 10003
    (212) 674-8200

Parlee, M. B. (1975). Review essay: Psychology. Signs,
    1(1), 119-138.

Project on the Status and Education of Women
    Association of American Colleges
    1818 R Street, N.W.
    Washington, DC 20009
    (202) 387-1300

Reinharz, S., Bombyk, M., & Wright, J. (1983).
    Methodological issues in feminist research: A
    bibliography of literature in women's studies,
    sociology and psychology. Women's Studies
    International Forum, 6(4), 437-454.

Sherman, J. A. (1971). <u>On the psychology of women: A</u>
     <u>survey of empirical studies</u>. Springfield, IL: Charles
     C. Thomas.

Vaughter, R. M. (1976). Review essay: Psychology.
     <u>Signs</u>, <u>2</u>(1), 120-146.

Walstedt, J. J. (1973). <u>The psychology of women</u>:
     <u>A partially annotated bibliography</u>. Pittsburgh,
     PA: Know.

Walton, J. B. <u>Traditions and transitions: Women's</u>
     <u>studies and a balanced curriculum--A bibliography</u>.
     Claremont, CA: Scripps College.

Wasmuth, M. (1979). <u>Counseling older women: An annotated</u>
     <u>bibliography</u>. Boston: Womanspace.

Womanspace
     636 Beacon Street
     Boston, MA 02215

INDEX

Abel, G., 121
Abel, G. G., 194
Abelin, E. L., 50, 66
Abraham, G. E., 145
Abraham, S., 125
Abrahamsen, P., 120
Abramowitz, C. V., 274
Abramowitz, S. I., 250,
    273, 274
Abramson, P., 262
Acosta, F., 244, 291
Adams, M., 218
Adams, P. L., 179
Adler, N., 203
Adler, T. F., 97
Ageton, S. S., 75
Agras, W. S., 121
Alagna, S. W., 107, 146
Albino, J. E., 145
Albro, J., 154
Alderaran, 132
Alexander, J., 179
Alexander, L. B., 96
Alexander, R. D., 284, 286
Al-Issa, I., 80, 227
Allen, L., 291
Allington, D. E., 219
Allison, J. R., 203
Alonso, A., 274
Alpert, J. L., 179, 183
Alyn, J. H., 244
Ambert, A., 161
Ament, A. J., 209
Amir, M., 194
Anderson, B. L., 210
Anderson, S. C., 112
Ansley, M. Y., 109
Antonovsky, A., 165

Aponte, H., 120
Applegarth, A., 92, 219
Arcana, J., 179
Ardrey, R., 287
Arkway, C., 237
Armitage, K. J., 245
Arms, S., 203
Armstrong, L., 245
Arney, W. R., 203
Arnoff, M. S., 146
Arons, E., 262
Asch, A., 252
Ashford, J., 179
Aslin, A. L., 161
Asnis, G., 254
Astin, H. S., 219, 275
Atkeson, B. M., 194, 195,
    196
Atkinson, A. K., 106, 203
Auerbach, A. H., 279
Austin, N., 37
Axelrod, R., 194

Babcock, M. L., 112
Bachrach, L., 227
Bader, B. C., 233, 279
Baer, H. R., 301
Baker, D. P., 93
Baker, L., 136
Baker, S. W., 41, 80
Bannon, J. A., 66
Baran, A., 99
Barash, D., 287
Barash, D. P., 286
Barbach, L. G., 210
Barcai, A., 120

Bardwick, J. M., 80, 203
Barglow, P., 80
Barker, G. H., 204
Barlow, D. H., 121, 122
Barlow, G. W., 288
Barnett, M., 41
Barnett, R. C., 66, 80,
    81, 179, 190, 219, 245
Barnewott, D., 85
Barr, W. E., 148
Barrett, C. J., 218, 245
Barrett, R. C., 190
Bart, P. B., 106, 179,
    194, 201, 209
Baruch, G. K., 66, 80, 81,
    87, 179, 190, 219
Baskin, D., 170
Bass, D., 138
Bass, E., 138
Bass, R. A., 245
Bassin, D., 59
Bassuk, E. L., 227
Bateman, N., 112
Baxter, E., 227
Bayes, M., 92
Bayles, M., 232
Beavers, R. W., 245
Beck, E., 88, 170
Becker, J. V., 194
Becker, L. A., 244
Beckman, L. J., 112
Behling, J., 235
Beiger, R., 154
Beinart, H., 131
Belfer, M. L., 112
Bell, A., 154
Bell, N., 180, 209
Bell, R. Q., 41, 48
Belle, D., 106, 180,
    227, 228, 232, 291
Belle, J. C., 229
Belsky, J., 102
Belzer, E. G., 210
Bem, S. L., 100, 164

Bemis, K. M., 119, 122
Ben-Tovim, D. I., 126
Benedek, T., 66, 180
Benet, M. K., 99
Benjamin, J., 246
Benson, A., 119
Berenbaum, S., 92
Berg, P. I., 245
Berger, C. R., 165
Berger, G. S., 206
Berger, J., 113
Berger, M., 117, 246
Bergman, A., 51
Bergmann, M., 55
Berlin, I. N., 180
Berlin, S. B., 239
Berliner, B., 172
Berliner, L., 246
Berman, P. W., 81
Bern, L., 158
Bernard, J., 81, 85, 106,
    161, 180, 184, 228, 295
Bernardez, T., 100, 228,
    246
Bernay, T., 104
Berndt, D. J., 106
Berndt, S. M., 106
Bernstein, A. E., 246
Bernstein, B. E., 161
Bernstein, D., 64, 180
Bernstein, I., 172
Bernstein, M., 188
Bernstein, S., 168
Best, C. L., 202
Best, R., 71
Beumont, P. J. V., 123,
    125, 126, 129
Beutler, L. E., 246
Bhanji, S., 121
Bibring, G. L., 204
Bieker, P. P., 246
Biller, H. B., 67
Billingsley, D., 246
Binswanger, L., 40

Birnbaum, J. A., 92
Birns, B., 41
Blakeney, P. E., 210
Blazer, D., 120
Blechman, E. A., 37, 246, 247
Bleier, R., 282, 295
Blinder, B. J., 121
Block, C. B., 291, 292
Block, M. R., 81, 190
Bloom, B. L., 218
Bloom, L., 100
Blum, B. L., 204
Blum, H. P., 81, 138, 172
Blumstein, P., 220
Bock, K., 288
Bohen, H. H., 117
Bolen, J. S., 38
Bolitho, F., 238
Bombyk, M., 299, 302
Bonaparte, M., 20
Bond, M. A., 295
Bonner, J. T., 287
Boon, C., 201
Bordin, E. S., 265
Borman, L. D., 247, 259
Bornstein, M. T., 247
Bornstein, P. H., 247
Boskind-Lodahl, M., 125, 132
Boskind-White, M., 130, 131
Bosma, B. J., 247
Boswell, J., 154
Bouhoutsos, J. C., 247, 253, 256, 264
Bowker, L. H., 138
Bowles, G., 295
Boyd, N., 291
Boyd-Franklin, N., 291
Brackney, B. E., 77
Braen, G. R., 202
Braiker, H., 161
Brandenburg, J. B., 228

Brandwein, R. A., 228
Brannon, R., 67, 68, 69, 302
Braslow, J. B., 275
Breines, W., 138, 194
Bremer, T. H., 92
Brenner, D., 130
Bresnick, E., 204
Brewin, R., 115
Brickman, J., 138
Britt, D. W., 291
Brittain, J. R., 206
Broderick, P. C., 184
Brodsky, A. M., 244, 247, 248, 251, 256, 275, 278
Brody, C. M., 248
Brody, E. M., 190, 196
Brody, L., 93
Bromet, E., 238
Bronfenbrenner, U., 102
Bronson, S. K., 68
Brooks, V. R., 248
Brooks-Gunn, J., 51, 75, 81, 87, 165
Broughan, K. G., 260
Broverman, D., 248
Broverman, I., 248
Brown, C. R., 249
Brown, G. W., 106
Brown, L. S., 228, 249
Brown, R., 154
Browning, C., 96
Brownmiller, S., 194, 295
Bruch, H., 119, 121, 129, 132, 133
Brunswick, R. M., 20
Bry, B. H., 112
Bryson, J. B., 117
Bryson, R., 117
Burgess, A. W., 138, 195, 201
Burgner, M., 55
Burke, C., 34
Burns, C., 180

Burstow, B., 40
Burt, M. R., 112
Burtle, V., 112, 252, 263
Buscher, M., 116, 240
Butler, B., 122
Butler, C., 210, 249
Butler, M., 165
Butler, S. E., 249
Byrne, P., 209

Caille, P., 120
Caldwell, M. A., 154
Caldwell, R. A., 218
Calhoun, K. S., 194, 195,
    196, 200
Calhoun, L. G., 196
Cammaert, L. P., 249
Campbell, B., 286
Campbell, D., 288
Campbell, L., 99
Cann, A., 196
Cano, L., 92
Canter, R. J., 75
Cantor, D. W., 161
Caplan, A. L., 288
Caplan, P. J., 173, 175
Carey, E. A., 301
Carey, G., 190
Carlson, B., 139
Carlson, R., 81
Carmen, E. H., 138, 139,
    228, 249, 265, 277
Carr, P., 301
Carroll, M., 112
Carter, D. K., 264
Carver, W., 180
Casper, R. C., 127, 133
Cass, V., 155
Cassidy-Brinn, 180
Cauwels, J., 133
Ceaser, M., 133
Chafetz, J., 155

Chagnon, N. A., 286
Chamberlain, P., 235
Chamberlin, J., 218
Chambless, D. L., 193
Chan, F. A., 210
Chapin, H., 121
Charles, A. O., 230
Chasseguet-Smirgel, J.,
    27, 62
Chernesky, R. H., 220
Chernin, K., 134
Cherry, F., 220
Chesler, P., 249, 295
Chesney, A. P., 210
Chiauzzi, E. J., 217
Chico, N. P., 181
Chiriboga, D. A., 161
Chodoff, P., 149
Chodorow, N., 42, 181, 185
Ciali, S. D., 165
Cicchinelli, L. F., 229
Cichon, J., 194
Clance, P. R., 92, 256
Clark, D., 155
Clarke, K., 278
Clarke, S. K., 113
Clarkin, J., 146
Clarkson, F., 248
Clement, P., 135
Clower, V. L., 71, 211
Coates, D., 196
Coburn, K., 100
Cochran, S., 158
Cohen, L. H., 263
Cohen, M. B., 28, 90
Cohen, S., 220
Colao, F., 196
Cole, C. F., 202, 271
Cole, C. M., 210
Cole, N. S., 249
Coleman, A., 204
Coleman, L., 204
Collier, H., 249
Collins, S., 161

Colten, M. E., 115
Comstock, B. S., 90
Condry, J. C., 165
Connell, D. M., 75
Connor, B., 112
Connors, M., 130
Conrad, C., 232
Conrad, D., 120, 134
Constantino, C., 139
Cook, A. S., 42
Cooke, C. W., 145
Cooper, P. J., 130, 204
Cooperstock, R., 113, 250
Copeland, E. J., 292
Corning, P. A., 288
Corrigan, E., 113
Coser, R. L., 185
Costello, C. G., 106
Costello, R. M., 275
Cott, N. F., 295
Cottler, L. B., 250
Courtois, C. A., 196
Covi, L., 127
Cowan, G., 250
Cox, S., 109, 295
Crane, M., 168
Crisp, A. H., 122, 123,
    125, 126, 127, 129, 134
Crits-Cristoph, P., 118
Crockett, L. J., 93
Cromwell, P. E., 229, 301
Crook, J. H., 286
Crosby, F. J., 220
Cross, D. G., 278
Crouter, A. C., 102
Cruikshank, M., 155
Crull, P., 220
Cugliani, A., 236
Cullari, S., 134
Culp, R. E., 42
Cummings, N. A., 229, 251,
    268
Cummings, T., 244

Cunningham, J. D., 156,
    161
Cunningham, S., 122
Curlee, J., 113
Curlee, M., 220
Curtis, C., 235
Cushey, W., 113
Cutler, L., 161
Cypress, B. K., 229, 275

Dahlberg, C. C., 250
Dailey, D. M., 229
Daly, M., 287, 296
Dan, A., 145
Daniels, P., 182
Dann, A. J., 184
Darling, J., 289
Darling, J. F., 41
Darwin, C., 284
Datan, N., 165, 190
Davenport, J., 250
Davenport, Y., 233
David, D., 67
David, H. P., 91
David, M., 112
Davidson, C. V., 250, 273
Davidson, J. L., 81, 190
Davidson, V., 250, 275
Davidson, W., 173
Davis, J. M., 127, 133
Davis, K. L., 131
Davis, L., 139, 292
Davis, L. J., 190, 196
Dawkins, R., 287, 288
De Beauvoir, S., 28, 296
De Castillejo, I. C., 38
De Riencourt, A., 296
De Rosis, H., 82
Deal, T., 220
Dean, C., 207
Deaux, K., 165, 171, 220

Debrovner, C. H., 145, 204
DeBruijn, G., 211
Deitch, I., 93
Dekker, J., 211
DeKraai, M. B., 250
Del Gaudio, A. C., 109
Delaney, J., 145, 204
DeLeon, P., 251
Delk, J. L., 251
Delorey, C., 145
Denmark, F. L., 88, 165, 171, 237, 280
Densen-Gerber, J., 113
Derogatis, L., 127
DeRosis, H., 82
Dervin, D., 55
Desimone, D., 73
Deutsch, C. J., 253
Deutsch, F., 124
Deutsch, H., 20
Devinis, L., 136
Devins, R., 218, 221
Deykin, E. Y., 99, 107
Dillon, W. S., 286
Dimidjian, V. J., 251
Dinnerstein, D., 42, 182, 296
Distler, B., 51
Dittmar, N. D., 229
Doat, A., 156
Dobash, R., 139
Dobash, R. E., 139
Dohrenwend, B., 108, 230
Dohrenwend, B. S., 230, 262
Don, D., 182
Donnerstein, E., 139
Dorr, D., 82
Douvan, E., 75, 80, 221
Dowling, C., 104
Downer, C., 180
Doyle, J. A., 67, 165
Duddle, M., 127
Dudley, G. R., 251, 292

Duelli Klein, R., 295
Duffy, M., 190
Duffy, R., 272
Duke, M., 122
Dunlop, K. H., 102
Dunn, D., 225
Dupkin, C., 175
Durand, D. E., 113
Durden-Smith, J., 73
Dutton, D., 140
Dweck, C. S., 93, 173
Dworkin, S., 145
Dye, N. W., 275

Eagan, A., 145
Eagly, A. H., 165
Eaton, M., 245
Eccles, J. S., 221
Eckenrode, J., 82
Eckert, E. D., 127, 131, 133
Edelwich, J., 251
Edgucumbe, R., 55, 62
Ehrenreich, B., 204
Ehrhardt, A., 47
Eichenbaum, L., 43, 82, 104, 251, 296
Eichler, L. S., 205
Eidskess, P., 116, 240
Eiduson, B. T., 183
Eisenberg, J. F., 286
Eisenbud, R. J., 155
Eldred, C. A., 113
Ellinwood, E. H., 114
Ellis, E. M., 195, 196
Ellison, C. R., 251
Englander, S. W., 76
English, D., 204
Enna, B., 173
Entwisle, D. R., 93
Epstein, R., 37
Erikson, E. H., 71, 82, 88

Escamilla-Mondanaro, J., 251
Etaugh, C., 93
Ettorre, E. M., 155
Evans, S. L., 94
Everaerd, W., 211
Everhart, D., 256
Ezell, H. F., 230

Fabrikant, B., 251
Fairburn, C. G., 130, 134
Fairchild, B., 155
Falk, J. R., 135
Falstein, E., 129
Farber, L., 150
Fast, I., 28, 52
Fedigan, L. M., 289
Fee, E., 145
Feighner, J. P., 126
Feinstein, S., 129
Feldman, J., 262
Feldman, S. S., 183
Feldman-Summer, J., 252
Feldman-Toledano, Z., 121
Fennimore, D, 254
Ferber, M. A., 93, 221
Fernandez, V., 260
Ferrell, R. B., 122
Ferrerya, S., 252
Fidell, L. S., 84, 114,
    167, 230
Filer, R. K., 221
Fine, M., 197, 252
Finkelhor, D., 140
Finn, S. E., 258
Fisher, S., 205
Fishman, C. H., 121
Fishman, P., 221
Flaherty, M., 210
Flax, J., 183
Fleishman, E. G., 52, 165,
    166

Fleming, J. B., 140
Fliegel, Z. O., 28
Florin, I., 131
Fodor, I. G., 37, 121,
    134, 193, 252
Fogel, R., 93
Fooden, M., 283
Forer, B., 247
Forman, B. D., 197
Formanek, R., 43, 107
Forrest, T., 67
Forsberg, L. K., 277
Forsythe, A. B., 272
Fortune, M. M., 140
Foster, M. A., 117
Foster, S. A., 235
Fowlkes, M. R., 214
Fox, L. H., 93
Fox, M. L., 183
Fraiberg, S., 72
Frank, E., 197
Frankel, S., 56
Frankfort, E., 146
Franks, V., 230, 231, 252,
    253, 263
Freedman, D. G., 285
Freedman, J., 156
Freeman, D., 121
Freeman, L., 22
Fremouw, W. J., 131, 135
Freud, S., 17, 18, 19
Friday, N., 183
Fried, E., 82, 173
Friedan, B., 296
Friedenberg, L., 82, 182
Friedlander, S. R., 275
Friedman, M., 93
Friedman, R. C., 146, 204
Friedman, S. S., 253
Friedrich, P., 38
Frieze, I. H., 82, 140,
    197, 224
Frings, J., 240, 271
Frodi, A., 100

Fu, V. R., 62, 76
Fuentes, M., 191, 198
Fulcher, R., 237, 293
Furstenberg, F., 162
Futterman, L., 119
Fyans, L. J., 93

Gager, N., 197
Galdston, R., 122
Galenson, E., 43
Galinsky, E., 221
Gallessich, J. M., 94
Galligan, P., 224
Gallop, J., 34, 296
Gans, L., 253
Gardiner, M., 174
Garfinkel, P. E., 119,
    125, 126, 127, 128,
    134, 135
Garner, D. M., 119, 122,
    125, 126, 127, 134, 135
Garnets, L., 166
Garrison, D., 23
Gartrell, N., 156, 253
Gath, D., 204
Gatrell, N., 253
Gatz, M., 191, 198
Gechtman, L., 253
Gee, P. W., 140
Geis, B. D., 205
Gelb, L., 166
Gelder, M. G., 193
Geller, J. L., 119
Gelles, R. J., 140, 143
Gelpi, B. C., 38
George, G. C. W., 123, 126
Gerner, D. M., 128
Gerrard, M., 205, 265, 277
Gerson, M., 183
Gibbs, M. S., 253
Giele, J. Z., 82, 191
Gigy, L. L., 218

Giholami, C., 120
Gilbert, L. A., 83, 94,
    117, 158, 253
Gillespie, W. H., 29, 211
Gilliard, D., 93
Gilligan, C., 29, 30, 64,
    83
Gladieux, J. D., 183
Gleicher, N., 208
Glenn, J., 211
Glover, L., 56, 63
Glover, N., 184
Glynn, T. S., 112, 115
Goff, G., 131
Goffman, E., 296
Goffman, J. M., 141
Gold, J., 96
Gold, J. A., 115, 233
Gold, M. E., 221
Gold, P., 233
Goldberg, A. S., 221
Goldberg, S. C., 133
Goldenberg, I., 126
Goldenberg, S. G., 127
Goldfried, M. R., 278
Goldman, G. P., 83
Goldman, J., 228
Goldstein, A. J., 193
Goldstein, S., 254
Golub, S., 76, 146, 205
Gomberg, E. S., 114, 115,
    231
Gongla, P., 184
Gonsiorek, J., 156, 253,
    266
Gonzalez, E. R., 146
Goodman, B., 156
Goodman, M., 205
Goodsit, A., 123
Goodwin, D. W., 153
Gordon, E. W., 103
Gordon, L., 138, 194
Gordon, M. T., 200
Gordon, S., 283

Gore, S., 82

Gorham, D., 83

Gornick, V., 296

Gottlieb, N., 253, 301

Gould, K. H., 90

Gould, L., 166

Gould, S. J., 288

Gove, W. R., 162, 231

Grady, K. E., 68, 166, 302

Grambs, J. D., 81, 190

Gray, J. D., 117

Green, A., 100

Green, J., 126

Green, R. S., 130

Greenacre, P., 23, 198

Greenberg, M., 247

Greenberg, R., 205

Greenberg, S., 184

Greene, L. R., 254

Greenfeld, S., 221

Greenglass, E. R., 166,
    218, 221, 231

Greenspan, M., 254

Greenwood, S., 205

Greer, G., 296

Greiner, L., 221

Grisius, R., 130

Groen, J. J., 121

Gross, H. E., 184

Grossman, F. K., 205

Grossman, W., 59

Groth, N., 138

Gullahorn, J., 83

Gump, J. P., 166

Gundlach, R. H., 156

Gurman, A. S., 254

Gutek, B. A., 223

Gutmann, D., 80

Guttentag, M., 231, 232

Guze, S. B., 126, 153

Haas, L. J., 254

Haber, B., 83

Hafner, R. J., 193

Hailman, J., 288

Haire, D., 206

Halbreich, U., 254

Hall, J., 171, 254, 255

Hall, K. P., 222

Hall, N., 184

Hall, S. M., 135

Halleck, S. L., 232

Halmi, K. A., 122, 125,
    127, 133, 135

Halpern, S., 198

Halversen, P. A., 131

Hamilton, J. A., 107, 146,
    232, 254

Hamilton, W. D., 284

Hammer, S., 68, 184

Hammersmith, S. K., 154

Hanckel, F., 156

Hand, D., 128

Hapgood, R., 287

Harding, B., 125, 126

Harding, S., 297

Hardy, S., 288

Hare-Mustin, R. T., 184,
    247, 248, 254, 255, 278

Harmatz, J. S., 112

Harragan, B. L., 222

Harris, B., 224, 232

Harris, H., 212

Harris, T., 106

Harrison, M., 146, 147, 206

Hart, H. H., 174

Hartley S. F., 181

Harvey, J., 255

Harway, M., 275

Hauser, B. B., 264

Havassy, B., 135

Hawkey, L., 76

Hawkins, R., 135

Hawkins, R. O., Jr., 261

Hay, J., 187

Hayes, C. D., 102

Hayward, N., 155
Heckerman, C. L., 84
Heffner, E., 184
Heilbrun, A., 94
Heilbrun, A. B., Jr., 68,
    76, 167
Heilbrun, C. G., 84, 167
Heiman, J. R., 212
Heiman, M., 212
Heins, M., 275
Hellinger, M. L., 249
Helmreich, R. L., 170, 171
Henderson, J., 68
Hendricks, M. C., 84
Henley, N. M., 84, 85,
    167, 168, 239, 297,
    299, 302
Herman, C. P., 123, 130
Herman, J., 141, 198
Herold, J., 225
Herrington, L. H., 141,
    198
Herzog, D. B., 128, 130
Heschel, S., 292
Hess, B. B., 162
Hidalgo, H., 156
Hier, D. B., 297
Hilberman, E., 141, 232
Hinkle, B., 167
Hinkle, D. E., 62, 76
Hintikka, M. B., 297
Hinton, A. P., 297
Hirsch, M., 185
Hirschman, L., 141, 198
Hite, S., 212
Hodges, W. F., 218
Hoffman, D. M., 84, 167
Hoffman, L., 120
Hoffman, L. W., 96, 102,
    221
Hole, J., 297
Hollender, M., 150
Hollister, L. E., 131
Holmes, D. S., 92

Holmes, K., 198
Holmstrom, L. H., 138, 195
Holroyd, J. C., 244, 247,
    255, 256
Honas, J. M., 131
Hopkins, T. J., 256
Hoppe, R. B., 256
Hopper, K., 227
Horner, M. S., 80, 86, 94,
    95
Horney, K., 23, 24
Hornstein, F., 180
Horowitz, M. J., 151
Hotaling, G., 140
Houben, M., 120
House, R. C., 130
Housley, P. C., 42
Howard, D. R., 199
Howard, K. I., 263
Howell, E., 232
Howell, N., 201
Hrdy, S. B., 282
Hsu, L. K. G., 127
Hubbard, R., 85, 167, 234,
    298
Hudson, J. I., 125, 131
Huesmann, L. R., 108, 174
Hughes, K., 252
Hughes, M., 162
Hughes, R., 115
Hughley, B., 283
Hulce, M., 136, 152, 193,
    223, 235, 261
Hulka, B. S., 226
Hungerford, L., 266
Hunt, J. H., 286
Hunt, M., 196
Hunter, D., 151
Hurt, S. W., 146
Hustin-Stein, A. E., 95

Imes, S., 256

Insler, V., 207
Irigaray, L., 34
Irons, W. G., 286
Iscoe, I., 265, 277
Israel, D., 85
Israel, J., 256

Jaccoby, E. E., 47
Jacklin, C. N., 46, 73
Jackson, C. N., 168
Jacobson, E., 64
Jacobson, S., 107
Jakubowski, P., 256
Jakubowski-Spector, P., 37
James, J, 198
Janeway, E., 297
Janoff-Bulman, R., 198
Jansen, M. A., 141
Jarett, L. R., 256
Jayne, C., 213
Joffe, C., 91
Johnson, A. G., 199
Johnson, C., 130
Johnson, J. E., 75
Johnson, M., 233, 257,
    260, 265, 276, 279
Johnson, P. B., 82
Johnson, R., 38
Johnson, S. M., 163
Johnston, D. W., 193
Jonas, J. M., 125
Jones, A., 257, 292
Jones, A. R., 34
Jones, D., 127
Jones, E., 24
Jones, E. E., 292
Jones, G., 252
Jones, J. M., 292
Jordan, B. T., 151
Jordan, H., 257
Jordan, J., 270
Josefowitz, N., 222

Joseph, G. I., 292, 297
Jovanovich, J., 302
Judas, I., 129
Jung, C. G., 185

Kaczala, C. M., 97
Kafka, M. S., 233
Kahn, A. J., 102, 222
Kahn, S. E., 257
Kalant, O., 115
Kalucy, R. S., 126, 127
Kamarek, T., 220
Kamerman, S. B., 102, 222
Kanter, C. N., 277
Kanter, R. M., 282
Kaplan, A. G., 30, 84,
    168, 257, 270, 276
Kaplan, E., 211
Kaplan, J., 51
Kaplan, M., 233, 257, 258
Kaschak, E., 234
Kass, F., 258
Katan, A., 199
Katz, J., 123
Kaufman, D. R., 95, 297
Kaufman, M. R., 124
Keith, L. G., 206
Kelley, H. H., 161
Kelly, J. G., 295
Kempler, S., 151
Kendell, R. E., 151
Kennedy, A., 220
Kent, D. R., 206
Kenworthy, J. A., 268
Kerson, T. S., 96
Kessler, D., 168
Kessler, R., 233
Kessler, S., 233
Kestenbaum, C. J., 68
Kestenberg, J. S., 56, 57,
    76, 156, 174, 206
Kettere, R. F., 233

Ketterer, R. F., 279
Kilmann, P. R., 273
Kilpatrick, D. G., 199
Kimmel, E., 269
King, L. S., 142
Kingston, P. W., 102, 222
Kinney, E. L., 115, 233
Kinsey, B. A., 115
Kipper, D. A., 207
Kirk, R. J., 222
Kirkpatrick, M., 86, 156, 157, 213
Kirsch, B., 258
Kirsh, B., 81
Kirshner, L. A., 258
Kleeman, J., 30, 44
Kleiman, D. G., 289
Klein, M. H., 254
Kleinke, C. L., 108
Klerman, G. L., 107, 108, 110, 111, 234, 258, 272, 279
Klykylo, 135
Kobos, J. C., 275
Koedt, A., 297
Koeske, R., 207
Kohlberg, L., 44
Kohut, H., 213
Kolbenschlag, M., 35
Konopka, G., 76, 77
Kopp, C. B., 86
Korner, A. F., 44
Kornfein, M., 179
Kornhaber, A., 131
Kornreich, M., 279
Korslund, M. K., 62, 76
Koss, M. P., 200
Koufacos, C., 268
Kraft, A. D., 207
Kraines, R., 191
Kramarae, C., 239, 297, 299
Kramare, C., 299
Kramer, S., 63

Kravetz, D., 258, 260
Krieger, S., 157
Krohn, A., 151
Krohn, J., 151
Krueger, D. W., 96
Krulewitz, J. E., 199
Kurash, C., 131
Kuriansky, J. B., 213
Kushner, R., 147
Kutner, N. G., 147
Kutza, E., 258
Kwower, J., 258

LaBarbera, J. D., 168
Lacan, J., 35, 151
Lachman, M. E., 84, 279
Lachmann, F., 189
Ladd, F., 259
Laiderman, P. H., 48
Laing, M., 259
Lamb, M. E., 68, 185
Lampl-de Groot, J., 63, 213
Lang, J. A., 30, 44
Lanir, S., 136, 152, 193, 223, 235, 261
LaPointe, K. A., 259
Lark, S., 147
Larson, R., 130
Lasagna, L., 135
Lauersen, N., 147
Lauriat, A., 227
Lawrence, R., 111
Laws, J. L., 162, 168, 214
Laws, S., 147
Lear, J. G., 234
Lee, E. S., 225
Leifer, M., 207
Leighton, J., 276
Leitenberg, H., 121
Lenna, H. R., 160, 272
Lennane, K. J., 234

Lennane, R. J., 234
Lenney, E., 96
Lenny, E., 164
Lenzer, G., 174
Leonard, L. S., 35
Leonard, M., 68, 77
Lerman, H., 247, 259, 297
Lerner, H. E., 60, 84,
    100, 105, 152, 168, 259
Lerner, L., 30, 53, 84,
    174, 185
Lerner, R. M., 77
Lesnoff-Caravaglia, G.,
    191
Lessing, D., 162
Lester, E., 63
Levenkron, S. A., 119
Levenson, H., 264
Levine, E., 297
Levine, I. S., 234
Levy, M. R., 233, 279
Lewin, M., 85, 298
Lewis, C., 130
Lewis, H. B., 31, 45, 64,
    65
Lewis, J., 292, 297
Lewis, M., 45
Lewis, R. A., 68
Lewis, S., 157
Lewittes, H. J., 100
Lichtenberg, J., 45
Lieberman, F., 77
Lieberman, M., 259
Lief, H. I., 162
Lifton, B. J., 99
Lightner, J., 232
Lindner, R., 135
Linn, M., 96
Lipman, R., 127
Lipton, M. J., 145, 204
Lloyd, C., 107
Lockard, J. S., 286
Lockheed, M. E., 222
Lodahl, M. R., 135

Loe, H., 225
Logan, D. D., 234
London, P., 234, 279
Loney, J., 125
Long, J., 85
Longfellow, C., 185, 228
Lopata, H. A., 85
LoPiccolo, J., 212, 266
Lorber, J., 184, 185
Lorenz, K., 288
Lorion, R. P., 260
Lott, B., 199
Loulan, J., 157, 214
Lowe, M., 85, 167, 234,
    289, 298
Luker, K., 91
Lumsden, C. J., 284
Luria, Z., 214
Lyon, P., 157
Lyons, H., 149

Macaulay, J., 100
Maccoby, E. E., 46, 73, 168
MacCormack, C., 282
Mackey, W. C., 284
Macklin, E., 185
Maffeo, P. A., 260
Magnus, E. M., 207
Maher, B. A., 279
Makosky, V., 228
Malamuth, N., 199
Maloney, M. J., 135
Manalis, S. A., 174
Mandel, T., 157
Mander, A. V., 298
Manley, R. O., 96
Manzanares, D. L., 229
Maoz, B., 165
March, V., 126
Marciniak, D., 260
Marcus, I., 214
Marcus, M., 174

Marecek, J., 258, 260

Margolin, G., 260

Marilov, V., 126

Markus, H., 168

Marler, P., 286

Marmor, J., 152, 157

Marsh, J. C., 115

Martin, D., 142, 143, 157

Masnick, B. R., 264

Mason, J. K., 108

Masson, J. M., 31

Mathew, R. J., 108

Mathews, A. M., 193

Mathews, W. S., 51

Matza, D., 157

Maxmen, J. S., 122

Mayes, S. S., 298

Mayo, C., 85, 168

Mays, V. M., 292, 302

Mazor, M. D., 207

Mazur, D., 136

McAdoo, H., 218

McCann, L., 205

McCarthy, S. J., 186

McCartney, J., 117

McClintock, M., 184

McCrady, B. S., 122

McDougall, J., 31, 157

McGoldrick, M., 292

McGuin, D. G., 85

McGuinness, B., 125

McGuire, J. M., 110

McKeever, P., 207

McKenna, W., 168, 233

McMahon, S. L., 260

McRae, J., 233

Meade, R. G., 214

Meadow, A., 273

Mednick, M. T. S., 85, 96, 97, 293

Meltzoff, J., 279

Menaker, E., 174, 222

Mendell, D., 31, 56, 63

Mendels, J., 126

Menning, B. E., 207

Mermelstein, R., 220

Meyer, J., 175

Meyer, J. K., 158

Meyers, S., 207

Meyers-Abell, J., 141

Michels, R., 234

Midlarsky, E., 261, 302

Milgrom, J. H., 266

Miller, A., 31, 85, 199

Miller, J. B., 25, 31, 85, 86, 101, 228, 234, 261

Miller, P. Y., 214

Miller, S., 122

Millett, K., 32, 298

Millman, M., 136

Mills, T., 139

Milman, D. S., 83

Milner, E., 77

Milner, J. R., 179

Mintz, I., 131

Minuchin, S., 136

Mischel, W., 46

Mitchell, D., 207

Mitchell, J., 35, 131, 298

Mogul, K. M., 222, 261

Moldofsky, H., 127, 135

Money, J., 47

Montagu, A., 289

Montgrain, N., 35, 214

Monti, P. M., 122

Moore, B., 214, 215

Moore, E. C., 147

Moran, B., 296

Morgan, R., 298

Morgan, S., 207

Morin, S. F., 158, 279

Morrissey, E., 115

Moses, A. E., 158, 261

Moss, H. A., 47

Mott, F. L., 223

Moulton, R., 25, 60, 86, 215

Mowbray, C. T., 136, 152,
    193, 223, 235, 261
Mulvey, A., 108, 262
Mundy, J., 262
Munoz, R., 126
Munson, C. E., 276
Muroff, M., 32
Murphy, B., 301
Murray, J., 262
Murray, S. R., 97, 293
Myers, M. F., 262

Nadelson, C. C., 86, 87,
    101, 105, 162, 199,
    208, 262
Nagera, H., 32
Naierman, N., 235
Nakamura, C. Y., 186
Napoli, M., 147
Nash, S. C., 183
Nathans, J., 262
Nelson, B., 142
Nelson, S., 173
Nesselson, C., 253
Neugarten, B. L., 191
Neuhaus, M., 131
Neuhring, E. M., 148
Neuman, P. A., 131
Neumann, E., 38
Newcombe, N., 96
Newman, A. S., 277
Newman, F., 175
Newton, N., 184
Newton, P., 92
Nieva, V. F., 223
Nollen, S. D, 223
Norman, D. K., 128
Norwood, R., 175
Notman, M. T., 86, 87,
    101, 162, 199, 208, 262
Novara, R., 262

Nye, F. I., 102

O'Brien, P. H., 194
O'Connell, A. N., 97
O'Conner, D., 213
O'Donnell, L., 88, 225
O'Farrell, B., 223
O'Hare, J., 199
O'Leary, V. E., 87, 169,
    223
O'Toole, A., 237
Oakland, T., 69
Oakley, A., 208, 298
Odent, M., 186
Oline, P., 157
Oliner, M., 53
Olmeda, E. L., 235, 237,
    293
Olson, J. P., 48
Onorato, R., 260
Orbach, S., 43, 82, 104,
    125, 136, 251, 296
Orlando, J. A., 200
Orlinsky, D. E., 263
Ortner, S. B., 36, 282
Osmond, H., 263
Otto, W. F., 38
Ovesey, L., 47, 169
Oyster-Nelson, C. K., 263

Padesky, C., 158
Paige, J. M., 282
Paige, K. E., 282
Painter, S. L., 140
Paisley, W., 165
Palazzoli, M. S., 121, 123
Palmer, R. L., 127
Palombo, J., 207
Paludi, M. A., 93
Panken, S., 175

Pannor, R., 99
Parens, H., 54, 63
Parker, F. B., 116
Parker, J., 120
Parkin, A., 175
Parks, M., 255
Parlee, M. B., 148, 208,
    302
Parloff, M. B., 264, 279
Parron, D. L., 235, 293
Parry, B., 254
Parry, J., 90
Parsons, J. E., 47, 82,
    87, 97, 169
Pasquella, M. J., 97
Patti, P., 99
Paul, W., 158
Paykel, E. S., 110, 111
Payn, N., 264
Payton, C. R., 244
Pearce, D., 218
Pearlin, L., 108
Pearlman, J., 100
Pearlstein, A. V., 237
Pearson, C., 191, 198
Pearson, H. W., 115
Pedersen, F. A., 209
Penner, L., 269
Pepitone-Rockwell, F., 117
Peplau, L. A., 154, 158
Perera, S. B., 38
Perry, S., 235
Person, E. S., 32, 47, 88,
    97, 169, 216, 223, 264
Petersen, A. C., 74, 75,
    77, 78, 93, 96, 169,
    283
Peterson, C., 108
Peterson, I., 112
Peterson, T., 156
Pettersen, M., 301
Phelps, S., 37
Phillips, G. L., 277
Phillips, R. N., 208

Piazza, E., 120
Piazza, N., 120
Pierloot, R., 120
Pillay, M., 123
Pincus, C., 111
Piotrkowski, C. S., 103,
    118
Pittcatsouphes, M., 237
Pleck, E. H., 295
Pleck, J. H., 68, 69, 166,
    169, 264, 298, 302
Pogebrin, L. C., 186
Polivy, J., 123, 130
Polonsky, D. C., 105
Pomeroy, E., 245
Pope, H. G., 125, 131
Pope, K. S., 253, 264
Porcino, J., 87, 192
Porter, K. L., 85
Porter, N., 277
Post, R. D., 105
Powers, P. A., 122
Price, R. P., 235
Pyle, R. L., 131

Quinlan, P., 136
Quinn, K., 236

Rada, R., 200
Radding, N., 111
Radloff, L. S., 108, 109
Radov, C. G., 264
Ralls, K., 284, 289
Ramas, M., 152
Ramey, E. R., 81
Rampling, D., 126
Rapone, 297
Rapoport, R., 103, 118
Rau, J. H., 130
Rawlings, E. I., 264

Rawlins, M., 251, 292

Raymond, F., 220

Redgrove, P., 38, 148

Redmon, W. K., 134

Reese, M., 87

Reilly, M. E., 199

Reims, N., 250

Reinharz, S., 97, 299, 302

Reiss, B. F., 156, 158

Reiter, R. R., 283

Reitz, R., 208

Resick, P. A., 195, 200

Resnick, P. A., 199

Resnick, S., 92

Reubens, P., 152

Rexford, M. T., 186

Rice, D., 236

Rice, J., 138

Rich, A., 186

Richardson, B. L., 95,
    169, 280

Richardson, M. S., 179,
    183, 257, 265

Rickel, A. U., 106, 203,
    265, 277

Rickles, N. K., 101, 127

Riddle, D., 265

Rieker, P. P., 139, 246,
    265, 277

Rieker, P. R., 249

Riger, S., 200, 224

Riley, S., 93

Rimm, D. C., 259

Rivero, E. M., 265

Rivers, C., 219

Rix, S. E., 192

Rizzuto, A., 123

Robbins, E., 126

Robbins, J. H., 265

Roberts, A. R., 142

Roberts, H., 280, 299

Robertson, J., 109, 208

Robins, L., 250

Robson, K. S., 47

Rochlin, M., 266

Rodgers-Rose, La F., 293

Rodino, P., 142, 200

Rodolfa, E., 266

Rohrlich, J., 224

Roiphe, H., 43

Roland, A., 224

Rollins, J. C., 169, 202

Rollins, N., 120

Romer, N., 97

Rook, K., 158

Rose, J., 152

Rosenbaum, M., 32

Rosenberg, F. R., 78

Rosenfield, S., 236

Rosenkrantz, P., 248

Rosenkranz, P., 244

Rosenman, L., 236

Rosewater, L. B., 142, 266

Rosman, B. L., 136

Rosoff, B., 171

Ross, C. L., 186

Ross, J. M., 69

Ross, M. E., 186

Rossi, A. S., 87, 184,
    185, 186, 187

Rossoff, B., 283

Rost, W., 131

Roszak, B., 299

Roszak, T., 299

Roth, G., 136

Rothbart, M. K., 47

Rothblum, E. D., 230, 252,
    253

Rothman, B. K., 208

Rothstein-Fisch, C., 186

Rowland, R., 299

Roy, A., 153

Roy, R., 156, 157

Roy-Byrne, P., 148

Rubenstein, H., 236

Rubin, C., 266

Rubin, G., 36, 283

Rubin, J., 25

Rubin, L., 227
Rubin, L. B., 87, 169,
    192, 299
Rubin, R., 185
Rubinow, D. R., 148, 209
Rubinstein, E. A., 244
Ruble, D. N., 75, 82
Ruble, T. L., 169
Ruckdeschel, R., 236
Ruse, M., 289
Rush, A. K., 298
Rush, F., 200
Rushford, K. B., 237
Russell, D. E. H., 142,
    201, 224
Russell, M. S., 87
Russianoff, P., 87, 105
Russo, N. F., 91, 97, 109,
    169, 187, 209, 228,
    232, 237, 238, 277,
    280, 293
Rutan, J. S., 274
Rynearson, E. K., 99

Sachs, H., 65
Sackette, K. L., 229
Safilios-Rothschild, C.,
    87
Safir, M., 85
Sahlins, M. D., 289
Salasin, S., 231, 232
Sales, B. D., 250
Sales, E., 224, 238
Sallston, B. S., 117
Salt, P., 110
Sametz, L., 143
Samois, 58, 176
Sample, K., 116, 240
Sanday, P. R., 201, 283,
    299
Sandiford, K., 201
Sandmaier, M., 116

Sanjek, R., 283
Sarlin, C., 54
Satow, R., 153
Saunders, E., 185, 228
Savage, M., 109
Sawyer, J., 69
Saxon, J., 126
Sayers, J., 299
Sayers, M., 115
Scarato, A. M., 257
Scarf, M., 109
Schad-Somers, S., 176
Schaefer, L. C., 216
Schaefer, M., 80
Schafer, R., 32, 33, 176,
    224
Schafer, S., 158
Schecter, D., 98, 177
Scheppele, K. L., 201
Scherl, D. S., 202
Schlachet, B. C., 266
Schlesier-Stropp, B., 136
Schlesinger, B., 187
Schlossberg, N. K., 98
Schmidt, A. W., 207
Schneiderman, L. J., 245
Schnitzer, P. K., 98
Schoener, G., 266
Schover, L. R., 264, 266
Schrepf, N. A., 179
Schuckit, M., 115, 116
Schuker, E., 201
Schurr, C., 197
Schwartz, D., 135
Schwartz, E., 135
Schwartz, M. C., 267
Schwartz, P., 220
Schwarzer, A., 299
Scott, P. B., 293
Scully, D., 209
Seagull, A., 257, 292
Seaman, B., 148, 209
Seaman, G., 148, 209
Secord, P. F., 232

Seibel, M. M., 209

Seiden, A. M., 87, 209, 267

Seidler, S., 192

Seidler-Feller, D., 267

Selby, J. W., 196

Seligmann, M. E., 109, 293

Serban, G., 267

Serr, D. M., 207

Sgroi, S. M., 138

Shachar, S. A., 158

Shader, R. I., 112

Shainess, N., 105, 177

Shannon, R., 116, 240

Sharfstein, S., 234

Sharpe, K., 107, 146

Sharpe, L., 213

Sharratt, S., 158

Shaver, P., 293

Shaw, E., 289

Shaw, J. S., 165

Sheehan, P., 278

Sherby, L. B., 297

Sherfey, M. J., 216

Sherick, I., 56

Sheridan, K., 267

Sherif, C. W., 57, 88, 169, 301

Sherman, D., 129

Sherman, J. A., 33, 88, 98, 170, 244, 267, 268, 280, 303

Sherman, S. N., 268

Shields, S. A., 170

Shiflett, S., 221

Shore, B. K., 238

Shure, M. B., 187

Shuttle, P., 38, 148

Siegel, B., 60

Siegel, R., 111, 268

Siegel, R. J., 265, 268

Signorella, M. L., 170

Siladi, M., 168

Silberfarb, P. M., 122

Silver, R. L., 201

Silverberg, J., 288

Silverman, D. K., 48, 58

Silverman, M., 72

Silverman, P. R., 99, 218

Silverstein, C., 158

Simari, C. G., 170

Simmons, R. G., 78

Simons, H. F., 207

Singer, J., 38, 170

Skinner, L. J., 194

Slater, E., 153

Slevin, K. F., 170

Small, M., 290

Smart, D. E., 123, 126

Smelser, N. J., 88

Smith, A., 268

Smith, B., 293

Smith, C. A., 177, 238

Smith, C. J., 177, 238

Smith, E. H., 293

Smith, G., 229

Smith, K., 156, 157

Smith, M., 268

Smith, S., 268

Smith, W. G., 114

Sobel, S. B., 109, 237, 238, 268

Socarides, C., 159

Solo, E., 293

Solomon, L. J., 224

Solomon, M., 107

Solomon, S., 92

Solomon, Z., 238

Song, B., 265

Song, B. E., 280

Sonkin, D., 143

Sorbye, B., 120

Sorell, G. T., 77

Sorosky, A. D., 99

Sours, J. A., 123, 124

Southern, M. L., 66

Sowder, B. J., 112

Spanier, G., 162

Spence, J. T., 170, 171
Spencer, J. A., 131
Spender, D., 69, 171
Spiegel, R., 22, 109
Spieler, S., 69
Spitzer, R. L., 258, 272
Spurlock, J., 294
Stake, J. E., 98
Standish, C., 109
Staneski, R. A., 108
Stanley, L., 280, 299
Stapp, J., 237, 293
Staum, R., 225
Stearns, B., 269
Stein, L., 109
Steinberg, L. D., 102
Steinhorn, A., 78, 159, 160, 269
Steinmann, A., 269
Steinmetz, S. K., 143
Stephenson, P. S., 269
Stephenson, S., 238
Stern, J., 63
Stern, S., 124
Steuer, J. L., 192, 269
Stewart, A., 110
Stewart, B. D., 197
Stewart, W., 59
Stimmel, B., 116
Stimpson, C. R., 88, 216
Stiver, I., 105, 224
Stoekle, J. D., 240
Stoller, R., 33, 48
Stone, A. A., 239, 269, 277
Stone, G., 237
Stone, M., 153
Stonehill, E., 127
Stones, M. H., 201
Stovel, T., 122
Strathern, M., 282
Straus, M., 140
Strausberg, G. L., 280
Strauss, M. A., 143

Strayer, F. F., 285
Strean, H. S., 22
Stricker, G., 269, 280
Stringer, D. M., 143, 239
Strober, M., 126
Strouse, J., 25, 269
Stuckey, M., 130
Stueve, A., 88, 225
Stunhard, A. J., 131
Stunkard, A. J., 121
Sturdivant, S., 270
Style, C. B., 162
Suber, C. J., 244
Sugar, M., 78
Sugarman, A., 131, 136
Sullivan-Guest, S., 110
Sunday, S. S., 201, 290
Surrey, J. L., 84, 136, 257, 270
Susman, E., 233
Sussman, M. B., 162
Sutherland, S., 202
Swallow, J., 116
Swift, W. J., 124
Symmons, D., 287
Symonds, A., 143, 163, 193, 225
Szinovacz, M., 192

Tabin, D., 93
Tacts-Van Amerongen, S., 78
Talbot, E., 122
Tallman, J., 233
Talovic, S., 260
Tamerin, J., 116
Tangri, S. S., 96, 280, 300
Tanner, N. M., 283
Tarnopolsky, A., 128
Taylor, K., 199
Taylor, M. C., 171

Taymor, M. L., 204, 209
Tebbets, R., 225
Tedesco, L. A., 145
Tenbusch, L. G., 297
Tennov, D., 270
Tessman, L. H., 70
Test, M. A., 239
Thal, J., 121
Theurer, G., 257
Thoma, H., 120, 124
Thomas, E. B., 48
Thome, P. R., 100
Thompson, C., 25, 26, 61, 177
Thompson, E. G., 239
Thompson, L., 162
Thompson, M., 135
Thompson, T., 121
Thorman, G., 143
Thorne, B., 239, 270, 299
Thornton, J., 208
Thornton, L., 138
Thurer, S., 239
Tinsley, E. G., 110
Tittle, C. K., 225
Tobach, E., 171, 201, 283, 290
Todres, R., 270
Tolstrup, K., 120
Toms, D., 129
Torok, M., 58
Toth, E., 145, 204
Traupmann, J., 187
Trautmann, J., 115, 233
Travis, C., 101
Treblicot, J., 187, 299
Tresemer, D., 98, 225
Trivers, R. L., 285
Troll, L. E., 219, 271
Trotman, F. K., 270, 294
True, R. H., 294
Tucker, J., 148
Tucker, M. B., 115
Tudor, J., 231

Tully, C., 154
Turkel, A. R., 88, 271
Turner, B., 271
Tyson, P., 58

Uhlenhuth, E. H., 127
Ulanov, A. B., 38
Underwood, E. D., 271
Underwood, M. M., 271
Unger, R. K., 87, 88, 169, 171, 280, 300
Urbelis, D. P., 237

Vaillant, G. E., 114
Van Buskirk, S., 271
Van Herck, J., 33, 300
VanArkel, W. G., 209
VanBuskirk, S. S., 202
Vance, C. S., 217
VandenBos, G. R., 238, 251
Vandenberg, J., 286
Vandiver, S., 271
Vaughter, R. M., 303
Veeder, N. W., 237
Verbrugge, L., 88, 225
Vernon, L. J., 202
Veroff, J., 98
Veronen, L. J., 199
Vesell, E. S., 115
Vessey, E. S., 233
Vida, G., 160
Vierra, A., 188
Vigersky, R. H., 124
Vigilanti, M. A., 202
Villanova, P., 108
Visher, E. B., 163
Visher, J. S., 163
Viveros-Long, A., 117
Voda, A. M., 148
Vogel, S., 248
Von Franz, M., 38

Wade, M. J., 285

Waites, E. A., 178, 240

Waitzkin, H., 240

Wakefield, J., 264

Waldron, I., 225

Waldroop, J. A., 253

Walker, A., 102

Walker, G., 269

Walker, L. E., 143, 144, 238, 240, 266, 271

Walker, L. S., 271

Wallen, J., 240

Waller, J. V., 124

Wallis, L. A., 240, 271

Wallston, B. S., 87, 169, 281

Walsh, T., 123

Walstedt, J. J., 303

Walton, J. B., 303

Wardle, J., 131

Warner, C. G., 202

Warner, G. M., 246

Warren, M. P., 78

Warrior, B., 144

Washington, M. N., 113

Wasmuth, M., 192, 303

Wasser, S. K., 290

Wasserman, C., 301

Waterman, C. K., 217

Watson, J. S., 49

Watts, D. L., 196

Waxler, C., 233

Webb, A. P., 79

Weber, D. P., 79

Webster, P., 83

Weick, A., 271

Weinberg, G., 160

Weinberg, M., 154

Weingarten, K., 182

Weinman, M. L., 108

Weintraub, M. I., 153

Weisberg, M., 217

Weisheit, R. A., 144

Weiss, S., 116, 240

Weiss, S. D., 67

Weisskopf, S., 217

Weisskopf, W. C., 187

Weissman, M. M., 108, 110, 111, 272

Weisstein, N., 300

Wellens, W., 120

Weller, G. M., 49

Welton, N. R., 239

Wenzel, H. W., 36

Wermuth, B. M., 131

West-Eberhard, M. J., 285

Westmoreland, G., 294

Wheeler, A., 225

Wheelock, A. E., 228

White, P. N., 169, 202

White, R., 122

White, W. C., 130, 131, 132

Whitehead, M., 282

Whiting, B. B., 89

Whitley, B. E., 272

Whitman, J. R., 272

Whitney, S., 147

Wickert, G., 22

Widom, C. S., 240

Wiesmeier, E., 272

Wiggins, A., 95

Wilkinson, D. Y., 272

Willack, S. C., 116

Willard, D. E., 285

Williams, E. F., 272

Williams, F., 51

Williams, G. C., 285, 286

Williams, J. B., 258, 272

Williams, J. H., 79, 89, 217

Williams, P., 128

Wilson, C. P., 131, 137

Wilson, E. O., 284, 285, 287

Wilson, M., 287

Wimpfheimer, M., 33

Winges, L. D., 186

Wingrove, C. R., 170

Winickoff, S. A., 205

Winokur, A., 126

Winokur, G., 126

Winston, T., 196

Wirtenberg, J., 169, 280, 300

Wise, S., 280, 299

Witkin-Lanoil, G., 89

Wittig, M. A., 74, 92

Wolfe, B. E., 264

Wolfe, J., 37

Wolff, D. G., 160

Wolfman, B., 272

Wolowitz, H., 153

Wood, M. M., 221

Wood, V., 187

Wood, W., 165

Woodman, M., 39

Woodman, N. J., 156, 160, 272

Woodruff, R. A., 126, 153

Woods, N. F., 226

Wooley, M. J., 202

Wooley, O. W., 137

Wooley, S. C., 137

Worell, J., 281

Wortis, R. P., 188

Wortman, R., 294

Woskow, P. R., 264

Wright, C. T., 273

Wright, J., 299, 302

Wright, R. W., 273

Wycoff, H., 273

Wyrick, L., 120

Yalom, M., 270

Yamauchi, J. S., 294

Yang, H. Y., 233

Yasinki, L., 30

Yasinski, L., 257

Yllo, K., 140

Yogev, S., 118, 188

Young, D., 209

Yurgelun-Todd, D., 131

Zackson, H., 199

Zaslaw, M. J., 209

Zeiss, A. M., 163

Zeiss, R. A., 163

Zelen, S., 249

Zelis, R., 115, 233

Zelkowitz, P., 185, 188, 228

Zell, F., 244

Zellman, G. L., 82

Zigler, E. F., 103

Zigler-Shani, Z., 207

Zilbergeld, B., 273

Zillman, D., 101

Zimmerman, I. L., 188

Zuckerman, E., 240, 273

Zuger, B., 49